The First Stone

The First Stone

Homosexuality and the United Church

Michael Riordon

Canadian Cataloguing in Publication Data

Riordon, Michael, 1944-
The first stone : homosexuality and the
United Church

ISBN 0-7710-7522-7

1. Homosexuality - Religious aspects - United
Church of Canada. 2. Ordination - United Church
of Canada. 3. United Church of Canada - Clergy -
Sexual behavior. I. Title.

BX9881.R56 1990 262'.14792 C90-093320-8

Printed and bound in Canada

McClelland & Stewart Inc.
The Canadian Publishers
481 University Avenue
Toronto, Ontario
M5G 2E9

To my mother, Mollie,
always a searcher in the dangerous realm of the spirit

CONTENTS

FOREWORD

I am not one of those people who is overwhelmed with dismay whenever a branch of the Christian Church finds itself embattled by controversy. Jesus Christ was nothing if not controversial. The early Christians found themselves attacked constantly from every side. What's more, the notion that the Church of the Apostolic Age was somehow free from internal dissension and strife simply doesn't stand scrutiny. Total order and absence of conflict belong to cemetaries rather than to a community called to live out a Gospel that turned the world upside down. The denomination that never makes news is the one that is conformist, self-satisfied, and not just irrelevant but moribund as well.

That the United Church of Canada, the nation's largest Protestant body, has been constantly in the news ever since the early 1980s and that the issue has been its attempt to come to grips with a modern understanding of human sexuality is, in my view, an exhilarating sign that this Church is very much alive. There is no dimension of human life that has been more warped and clouded by negativity and downright fear in the name of religion than sex. But, in study after study – with much prayer and pain – the United Church has had the courage to grasp this nettle and to refuse to let it go.

Small wonder, then, as they have gone on to wrestle with the thorniest issue of all, that of the place of gays and lesbians in the Church's membership and ministry, they have not only made news; they have attracted the attention and eager observation of major Churches all over the world.

Homosexuality is not a United Church issue. It is one for every denomination and faith in our society. The issue has been divisive and will likely continue to be so for the forseeable future. So, too, of course, is the issue of Apartheid among the Christians of South Africa or that of Liberation Theology in the churches of Central and South America!

Michael Riordon has given us an eminently readable, detailed account of the homosexuality debate in the United Church. But, he has done much more. He has given the controversy its true perspective by setting it in the context of the much larger issues at stake – the nature of the authority of the Bible for contemporary morality and the question of whether one's vision for the Church is static or open to fresh winds of the Spirit. Above all, he has given the often bitter controversy a human face. This book is not about dusty meetings and resolutions of committees. It's about ordinary Canadians from all walks of life struggling deeply to discern God's will for them and their Church. We meet gays and lesbians, including those already ordained. We meet the parents of some of these people. And we hear the distress – sometimes the rigid prejudice and the hostility – of those who are opposed.

I warmly commend *The First Stone* to all who seek a fuller knowledge and understanding of what the United Church is about and why it is currently in turmoil. I particularly commend it to the members of that great Church no matter where they stand on the question of officially admitting homosexuals to the pulpit. Spiritual growth is, among other things, a matter of self-knowledge. *The First Stone* offers that to United Church members in full measure.

Tom Harpur

PREFACE

This is not a history book. The story it tells is far from finished. Nor is it an authorized portrait of the United Church of Canada. It's a book of impressions, of fragmentary glimpses into an astonishing, complex Canadian institution fighting for its life somewhere between God and humanity. I'm not a member of this church, nor of any other. That's said without pride or shame.

Early in my research I decided not to pursue people who had left the church for one reason or another. No doubt they have important and moving stories to tell, but already the scope of this book is vast. It concerns United Church people – who they are, what they believe, why, and how these beliefs when acted out affect the life of their church and the world around them.

Members of this church, as many as I was able to reach, shared their thoughts, feelings, and impressions with me. Many of them welcomed me into their real and their spiritual homes. I believe that some of them bared their souls to me, always a risk even with friends. To all who did this for a stranger, I'm deeply grateful. Some who didn't feel they could speak out themselves led me to others who could. Some shared their thoughts and feelings quite generously but asked that their names be withheld. In their own time they'll be known.

My heartfelt thanks to Dinah Forbes, my editor, without whom this book would surely not have come to pass.

CHAPTER 1

The Fiery Furnace

Ten past five. The clock in the grey stone tower got stuck there a few years back. Some say it looks bad, the United Church being the biggest in town and right out there on Main Street. But with the way things are, what can you do?

In a large wood-panelled room, twenty-six women talk husbands and family over lukewarm coffee and tiny white sandwiches. Cartons are stacked along the back wall for the Thanksgiving rummage sale a week Saturday. Jesus looks down from a needlepoint, the sky florid pink behind him. The women form and reform in grouplets, like eddies in a pond. A few stay behind the coffee table – as good a defence as any. They're here to talk about The Issue. Again.

A few here can remember the awful fuss back in 1936, when the first woman got into a pulpit. Practically everybody ended up fighting, the church lost some good givers, and some of the women here parted ways with dear friends. That's hard in a small town. But this time it's worse, much worse, what with The Issue. Again.

A few blocks along Main Street at the coffee shop, no matter how cold it gets they have to leave the door open. If they don't, the smokers set off the alarm. For some reason, today no one is talking about the United Church. Thank God, says Henry to himself. He's an elder at the Church. Maybe for once he can finish his coffee and the paper without some jackass who's got nothing better to do ribbing him about how are things over at the gay God-shop. There's nothing new they can say, but that's never stopped them before. If only TJ doesn't come in. . . .

An earlier meeting of the women's group nearly turned into a riot. They were supposed to do this exercise where each one told of the first time she heard about sex. A few refused right off. No way, it was none of anyone's business what they did in the privacy of their own bedrooms. Not the first time you *did* it, Grace said, the first time you *heard* about it. So they started. Or rather Grace did. She loves to tell what she calls her off-colour stories, just so she can see the others squirm. She told how she and this friend of hers went to a Saturday night dance when they were sixteen – she didn't think she ought to name this other person, it wouldn't be right with her not here to defend herself. Oh Lord, thought several of the women, here she goes. . . .

TJ aims his red Bronco into the parking lot and honks twice in case anyone didn't notice. Henry jumps up, rummages in his pocket for change. Some of the men already have their dumb grins on. TJ walks in, all cocky. He checks out the audience. Henry loses his wallet under a stool. "Guess what I just heard?" says TJ. "I don't know, TJ," Henry says, fishing for his wallet. "And to tell you the truth I don't much care." "Well maybe some of these other boys do." The audience nods like crazy. Henry fumbles in his wallet, comes up with a ten. TJ sets himself on a stool and starts in, "Okay. Well, there was this minister who didn't know his ass from. . . . " They were laughing already, honking like a flock of geese heading south.

Then there was the meeting of the women's group where one of *them* actually showed up. She had been invited, but no one really expected. . . . Anyway, there she was, large as life. A lesbian – Barbara – from the city. A few of the women wouldn't even say hello to her, they just walked out. To some others that didn't seem exactly Christian, after all the woman had been invited, and whatever else she was, she *was* a human being. Not that everyone wanted to invite her in the first place. At the time Patsy had said she knew she was speaking for a great many others when she stated, "We don't need someone from the city to tell us what's right or wrong, especially when it's one of them." Still, there she was, smiling at them. Arla – wouldn't you know it – walked right up to her and shook hands with her, just like that. Really it wasn't Arla's place to do that, not being chair any more. But if they had had to wait for Marjorie to make a move – she was the current chair – they could have waited till Christmas.

TJ's off into his homo act, flapping his hands and lisping so much you can hardly make out what he's saying. This is what they've been waiting for. Brenda behind the counter waves the ten. "Haven't you got anything smaller?" Henry turns on TJ. "You're pretty good at that, TJ. Where'd you pick it up?" TJ stops, his mouth wide open. Then he shuts it. Brenda bangs the counter. "Hah!" she says. Henry knows he's made a direct hit. Why the hell didn't he think of it sooner? "It looks like you really know what you're doing. Comes natural after a while, eh?" The audience looks from one man to the other, goggle-eyed. "Are you kidding, me?" TJ's on the run. "It's your damn church that's up to its neck in – " Henry cuts him off. "Takes one to know one, eh? That's what they say."

Sometimes things come out at meetings that shouldn't. Barbara, the lesbian from the city, was talking about her parents. Suddenly Catherine started to cry. She didn't make a lot of noise, Catherine never did, but you couldn't help noticing. Barbara, who had made herself right at home, asked if there was something Catherine wanted to share with the group. (Besides being a lesbian she was also a social worker, and talked like one.)

Catherine began to talk about her son Matthew. Everyone except Barbara already knew about Matthew. He had been killed three years ago in a car accident up north. Ernie and Catherine had both been active in the church; Ernie in the men's association and Catherine in the Sunday school. Then Matthew died and they both pulled away. This was the first meeting in years that Catherine had come to. Now she got so quiet the women at the back could hardly hear her. "It wasn't an accident." Someone called from the back, "Could you talk a little louder please?" Catherine did. She talked louder than she had in years. "We've never told this to anyone before. We were always too ashamed. Matthew was a homosexual. He died. . . of AIDS."

"Your coffee's on the house, Henry," says Brenda. "Oh yah?" says TJ. "And what about the Bible?" He gets off his stool. "What about it?" says Henry, half out the door. Idiot, he says to himself, why did you stop? "When's the last time you read it?" says TJ. "This morning," says Henry. "How about you?" TJ pushes on. "Did you read the part where it says if a man does it with another man he's gonna go straight to hell? Did you read that part, Henry? Did you?" TJ is practically dancing. Henry sighs. "Have you read the part, TJ, where it says a dumb ass spoke with a human voice?" Henry turns and walks out of the coffee shop.

This is not his battle, it never has been. But it is his church. Damn, he says to himself. Goddamn United Church.

The women have studied The Issue, they've tried to get the men to study The Issue, they've reported on The Issue, they've voted on The Issue, they've petitioned on The Issue. They have done everything that Toronto asked them to do on The Issue, and now here they are talking about it again. They can't ever get through a meeting on any subject without somebody or other detouring into The Issue. People have quit over it, and someone is always threatening to quit over it, or to boycott the collection plate over it. Will things ever get back to normal?

And another thing – the clock's still stuck at ten past five.

CHAPTER 2

In the Beginning

Perhaps the troubles began in the Garden of Eden. According to the Christian Bible, God created the earth in seven days and everything in it was good. Then a serpent recommended the forbidden fruit to Eve, and she to Adam. As smoothly as night follows day, sin followed free will. Original sin, church authorities called it. According to them, the human race would struggle with it for the rest of time.

Or the troubles might have started when the Bible was written. For millions of Christians, it's the one record of the one true God. But which Bible, which version? By which authors were its contents recorded, edited, and translated? What were their sources and their agendas? These questions have provided centuries of work for scholars the world over.

Modern versions of what came to be called the Old Testament originated from Hebrew manuscripts and Aramaic records of oral traditions handed from one generation to the next in hundreds of local dialects. What came to be called the New Testament is believed to be a collection of writings by people who were close to Jesus of Nazareth, who followed him during and after his life. These writings tell the story and teachings of the Christian messiah, believed to be the Son of God, who died on a Roman cross for the sins of the world.

Early in the 1500s, William Tyndale prepared the first English translation direct from Hebrew and Greek sources. Church authorities accused him of wilfully perverting the meaning of the Scriptures, and his New Testaments were destroyed. Tyndale himself was burned at the stake before an enthusiastic crowd.

Several versions later, King James I of England put forty-seven scholars to work for seven years, using all the previously known Judaic and Christian texts. In 1611 they produced the Authorized or King James Version, which became *the* Bible wherever English was spoken and Protestants held sway. Its language became the language of public institutions, its vision the vision of the British Empire.

By the mid-nineteenth century, the development of biblical studies had revealed a great number of errors in the Authorized Version. A series of revisions in England and the United States led to the Revised Standard Version of 1951, produced by thirty-two American and Canadian scholars. As with others before and since, its publication was met with howls of indignation. Though burning at the stake has gone out of fashion, truth and untruth in the Holy Bible has lost none of its power to set the faithful on each other's throats.

Some say the United Church troubles began at its birth. Certainly the creators of the new church were fighting history. Not long after the execution of their messiah, Christians began to bicker and break up into splinter churches, each of them claiming that it alone held the absolute, eternal truth. Then, finally, in the first quarter of the twentieth century, Canadian believers in three of these absolute truths – Presbyterian, Methodist, and Congregationalist – agreed they'd be better off together than apart. Federal and provincial legislation made it legal.

Sunday, June 10, 1925, in a Toronto skating rink, members of the new church celebrated their first worship service together. Never before had Christians of different denominations merged on such a grand scale. Together they would form the United Church of Canada, claiming 600,000 members. It would be, in its own visionary term, "the united and uniting church."

But its birth could hardly be called an easy one. It took twenty-six years of intricate, on-again-off-again negotiations. When congregations in each of the three denominations voted to join or reject the union, families split, townsfolk who had been neighbours for generations stopped talking to each other, congregations divided and the entire Presbyterian church broke into two parts, with two-thirds joining and one-third staying out. For more than a decade after union, court battles raged over who would get the property. In some Atlantic towns United and Presbyterian churches still glower at each other from opposite sides of the street, and the feuds are not forgotten. A retired United Church minister still warns young colleagues that they'd better know what denomination their congregations were before union. The disunited past has faded, but its ghosts still sit there in the pews, looking for a fight.

Even so it is an amazing church. Of all the mainstream denominations, this is the only one that is one hundred per cent made in Canada, with no ties to any parent body elsewhere. Early in 1989 more than 850,000 people belonged to it in 4,000 congregations in every part of the land. It operates hospitals, social service agencies, seniors' homes, and four universities.

From birth, the United Church has been a ground-breaker, some would say a trouble-maker. Over the years its public stands on every issue in the public arena have made it a thorn in the side of one powerful institution after another. More than a few business and government leaders – some of them members of the church – would like to see it back off, settle down, leave to Caesar that which is Caesar's.

Some say the church started to go wrong when it let women into the pulpit. No less than Saint Paul himself had written: "The women should keep silence in the churches," and "If there is anything they desire to know, let them ask their husbands at home." For two decades this issue bedevilled the founding churches and then the United Church. Again and again the ordination of women was proposed; again and again it was defeated. People complained they weren't being heard, there was wild talk of congregations splitting, ministers predicted chaos and ruination. Even when a majority of church representatives finally gave their assent, fully one-quarter still said no. Nevertheless in 1936 Lydia Gruchy became the first female United Church minister, the first in any major Canadian church.

Some say the trouble started in the sixties. At the dawn of that riotous decade, the nineteenth General Council set itself firmly in line with prevailing social attitudes, at least on sexuality. It denounced homosexual conduct as "a moral problem in four ways: it violates the will of God as an offence against the proper expression of sexuality in monogamous marriage; by misuse of natural functions, homosexual activity is a sin against the self; since it involves at least one other person of the same sex, with or without his consent, homosexual activity is unedifying and destructive of 'neighbour love'; it tends to undermine the foundations of stable society based on heterosexual marriage and family responsibility."

The next two General Councils made clear the place of women. In 1962 the Commission on Ordination recommended that "ordination for women is to be open only to those women who are unmarried or widows, or at that time of life when they are no longer required in the home as mothers." A 1948 policy was reaffirmed, that "a married woman minister settled in pastoral charge, when with child, shall request leave to absence or resign her pastoral charge to the Presbytery." It took more than ten years to change "shall request" to "may request."

Then in the middle of the decade, when the era called the sixties really began, the New Curriculum was published. It laid out an entirely new way of teaching Sunday school. From now on the wisdom and truth contained in the Bible could be interpreted and adapted in ways that would be meaningful to daily life out there in the real world. Hundreds of Sunday school teachers and thousands of parents were delighted. For them, and for some of their young charges, the dusty old Bible was suddenly born again. But other United Church people felt the New Curriculum had been foisted on them by a bunch of radicals at head office. As far as they were concerned, it broke with centuries of Christian tradition, and it replaced a clear set of God-given rules with a call to question all kinds of givens. In short, along with many other dangerous trends in the sixties, it threatened the very foundations of family, church, and nation.

At the same time, inspired by initiatives in the Vatican, Roman Catholic priests in Latin America were igniting the most powerful explosion in the Christian church since Martin Luther and his Protestant followers broke with the same Church of Rome. Christ's church had been a church of the powerless, it was radical enough to get its first leaders executed. But as more and more of Europe's rulers converted to this new religion, it became more and more the church of power. The Holy Roman Empire fused religion and state into an unholy alliance, which has both driven and plagued the Christian world ever since.

Now the Latin Americans priests were saying that to be true to their faith they would have to move away from complicity with the few, the powerful landowners and industrialists, into an active alliance with the meek of this earth, the countless peasants and workers. They found new truth in the Old Testament's account of the exodus from slavery, and Christ's good news in the New Testament: Why should the meek have to wait until they died to inherit the earth?

Liberation theology reinterprets most of what Christians have been taught, including the nature of sin. Acts of charity and salvation from personal sin no longer guarantee a place in Heaven. The sins of groups – classes, societies, nations, and even churches – can only be overcome by working for human justice, by rooting out and eliminating inequities in every sphere of life, in other words by working for the kingdom of God on earth. It wasn't long before this message rang through Christian churches on every continent. Not surprisingly, it was more welcome in some than in others.

In the United Church the good news translated into increasingly assertive policies and initiatives in every aspect of the public arena: drugs, gambling and lotteries, unemployment, disarmament, native land claims, abortion, foreign policy and human rights, bilingualism and multiculturalism, loss of family farms, smoking, economic justice, energy and the environment, genetic engineering, labour relations, Sunday shopping, pornography, tax reform, capital punishment, free trade, and, of course, The Issue. None of these struggles was taken on lightly. Every one of them was initiated at the grass-roots level, by individuals in congregations demanding action by the wider church. The result was a church not only to be seen in the pulpit, at the baptismal font, and at the graveside, but also on the picket line and at the United Nations, at peace vigils and before parliamentary subcommittees, in the prisons and at annual meetings of large corporations, raising hell in the name of God.

More often than not the United Church has been a leader among Canadian churches. It moves cautiously, in a very Canadian way, with much study, appointing of task forces, publishing of lengthy documents, and endless debate. It uses up staggering amounts of paper – the record of proceedings from the 1980 General Council runs more than a thousand pages. Nevertheless, the church does move. And the powers that be have tended to listen, partly because it's the second-largest church in Canada, with a great many members who are also voters, and partly because its interventions have been carefully researched and well presented. But more recently as turmoil has escalated in the church, the powers that be have begun to ask, often with ill-disguised malice, on whose behalf church leaders presume to speak.

In the early seventies everything seemed to be in motion. The blue hymn book with all the old favourites was going out of print, and the red hymn book (with most of the old favourites but also many unfamiliar new hymns) was taking its place. Impossible questions turned up everywhere. Women, especially, were questioning their place in the order of things, and by so doing how could they avoid questioning the order of things itself? They were more than 50 per cent of the world's population, and more than 60 per cent of the United Church membership. Why then were so few of them in a position to shape important decisions? Why in countries that claimed to be free did they have so few real choices? Why did the structures and even the language of the church – the hymns, the lessons, and the scriptures – so effectively exclude them? Surely God hadn't willed these things to be so. Men had. In which case surely these things must be subject to change.

Just as the liberation theologians were doing, feminist Christian theologians had begun to question and challenge some very long-standing assumptions about God, Christ, the Bible, and humanity. They were particularly interested in tracing how religious structures and biblical authority had been used throughout history to keep women in their place, as quasi-property, as servants, and as the eternal dependents of men. Those archaic moulds had never been part of God's plan, said the feminist theologians, and they contradicted the teachings of Jesus Christ.

During those same turbulent years, other forms of theology threw open other windows in the Christian church. Rather than holding God's creation to be over and done with, fixed for all eternity, process and creation theologies regard it as ongoing. God doesn't sit idle on a throne, but lives and acts in the world today. Because of their creation by and relationship to God, human nature and culture cannot be treated as frozen entities. They are subject to continuous evolution, as are human attempts to come to terms with God. These are not theologies of final answers and absolute rules. Instead they constitute a humble search for fragments of meaning in the infinite mystery of an unfathomable universe.

Since 1977 it has been United Church policy to promote inclusive language: the use of both male and female images, metaphors, and pronouns for God. Instead of mankind, why not say humankind or humanity? In hymns that said God the Father, why not say God the Creator? Or why not say Father in one line, Mother in the next? From most of the pews a great silence greeted this and other initiatives. Until recently it seemed that most church members simply didn't care.

Even the role of minister has been held up to question. One General Council after another passed resolutions calling for a ministry of the whole people of God, a priesthood of all believers. The fact that Martin Luther himself had originated this idea four-and-a-half centuries before didn't make it any less threatening. So what in God's name were the ministers supposed to do? "Hatch them, match them, and dispatch them," says one. "That's about all that's left."

And as if all these wrenching challenges weren't enough, suddenly in the middle seventies the church started to talk about sex. Actually it had talked about sex all along, but always discreetly and usually only to remind the faithful that it wasn't there to be enjoyed. Now even that was changing. One middle-aged woman recalls she nearly fainted the first time her minister used the word genitals in a sermon.

United Church study groups began to wonder about the role of sex in Christian life: could there be more to it than the act of procreation? True to form, in 1972 the twenty-fifth General Council called for a comprehensive study of human sexuality, to investigate how this "beautiful gift of God" could end up in such mayhem – adultery and divorce, abortion and venereal disease – and what the church ought to be doing about it.

After sixteen months' work, a ten-member task force (five of each gender, no self-declared homosexuals) presented its report, *In God's Image. . .Male and Female*, to the 1980 General Council in Halifax. Dorothy MacNeill was a commissioner there, as she would be eight years later in Victoria. In an interview she called the new report "a lot of hullabaloo over nothing." People would not, she predicted, want to talk about sex in church. "If you've grown up with all kinds of repression about sex, how can you suddenly open up just like that?"

A grandmother, Dorothy MacNeill calls herself a product of the United Church. She grew up in it. Her faith and her vision of the world were formed by Sunday school, then in church youth and women's groups. She had to choose between being a minister and marrying one – in those days only one minister per couple was allowed, and the man was it. When her youngest child went off to school Dorothy MacNeill did paid work for a while, but found unpaid church work more rewarding. Leading youth and women's groups, she would encourage others to think for themselves, to understand their church's decision-making structures, and to explore actively their own faith. Eventually she served as president of the United Church Women of Maritime Conference, then moved into a variety of roles on the regional and national executives of the church.

Dorothy MacNeill doesn't consider herself particularly pious. For her, serving the church is an act of thanksgiving. "I've been pretty lucky in my life – a few rough spots – but having received much I want to give something back. If you're serving the church, you feel you're offering something to God. Of course you can't pinpoint if God appreciates it, but you can see that the people around you do. At least that was the case until The Issue came along."

Most church people didn't read the report that went to Halifax. They skipped the first ninety-seven pages – theology, testimonies, questions – and went straight to the last page. Now it seems like an afterthought. First the task force sets out some common prejudices and facts about homosexual persons, then it touches on civil rights. The use of "persons" instead of "people" is United Church talk. It attempts to distinguish individuals from a faceless mass. The report concludes: "On the basis of this report there is no reason in principle why mature, self-accepting homosexuals, any more than mature, self-accepting heterosexuals, should not be ordained or commissioned."

There it was in black and white. Out of a richly detailed, provocative report, 90 per cent of which deals exclusively with aspects of heterosexuality, this would be the only item to hit the headlines: United Church Okays Gay Ministers.

At the 1980 General Council, debate on this report set the tone for others to follow. No self-declared homosexuals spoke. Rev Morley Clarke of London, Ontario, warned, "This is the most dangerous and misleading document ever to come before the church in my lifetime. It will split our denomination wide open if it is ever approved and used as a basis for further church policy." His statement made instant headlines.

Morley Clarke was ordained in 1948, worked in several parishes, then for twenty years was on staff in London Conference, assigned to such areas as Christian education, marriage, family life, and evangelism. What danger did he see in the report? "It was saying that sexual orientation was just a preference, not a moral concern. That was a radical departure from the clear moral teaching of the church down through the ages. I could see a modernistic, humanistic element creeping in, and a dangerous element of relativism – no longer were there to be any absolutes, no longer were the Scriptures to be the only authority in terms of lifestyle." To the press he concluded, "We're like a ship going out to sea with no stars to guide us."

Another commissioner told the assembly that she'd been raped when she was nine by someone in her own family. For years she felt condemned by God and rejected by everyone else. Repressive church attitudes on sex had kept her silent, she couldn't tell anyone until she was twenty-one. As far as this commissioner was concerned, the new study guide on human sexuality was long overdue.

After three hours and more than thirty speakers, General Council voted to distribute the report throughout the church, as an initial study document. The published preamble stresses, "It is not a policy statement of the United Church of Canada," and "It is not an attempt to tell people what to believe or do." But many would react as if it had been written in stone. The church needed the help of all its people, the preamble went on bravely, to study and discuss the report, then to suggest ways it could be improved. "Out of this process the church hopes to have a comprehensive statement on human sexuality for discussion at General Council no later than its thirtieth Session," to be held four years later.

At about the same time, a young woman presented herself for ordination at Hamilton Conference in southern Ontario. She had fulfilled all the conditions and studies for ordained ministry. But at this point she felt it only fair to tell the interview board that her marriage was in the process of dissolving. Well this was the late seventies, the interviewers said, even ministers got divorces these days – what was the problem? There was no problem, she said, not any more. She was ending the marriage because, after a long struggle with herself and with the help of God, she had come to accept that she was a lesbian.

CHAPTER 3

The Small Voice

Hamilton Conference refused to ordain their first "self-declared" homosexual candidate, and she didn't fight the decision. Instead she became a minister in the Metropolitan Community Church, a growing network of urban congregations that minister primarily to lesbians and gay men. But the alarm had been sounded, and Hamilton Conference slammed the door. They wrote into policy that they would not ordain or commission to ministry any self-declared practising homosexual. (The United Church has two official categories of minister, ordained and commissioned. Ordained ministers have to study longer, get paid more, are addressed as "the reverend," and can administer the sacraments: baptism and communion. Otherwise the work is similar.)

Hamilton Conference asked the national church to enact a similar policy of exclusion. As it happened, British Columbia Conference was asking for guidelines as well. Up to now a policy hadn't been required. In practice a conspiracy of silence had prevailed – ask me no questions and I'll tell you no lies. As long as candidates and ministers kept their sexual orientation to themselves, they would be allowed the benefit of the doubt. Even when ministers were driven out of their congregations and communities, sometimes on no more substantial grounds than the suspicion of a few, still the conspiracy of silence usually held. Now it had been shattered. Something had to be done.

There were already in place two organizations that had been warning of impending disaster for some time, the United Church Renewal Fellowship and Church Alive. Until now they had both been voices crying from a rather chilly wilderness.

In March 1966 a few United Church people created the United Church Renewal Fellowship, "for an evangelical witness within their branch of the Christian Church," wrote founding member Lloyd Cumming. They felt that the church had gone astray in two areas. Its leaders had been neglecting their first priority which was, the UCRF believed, "to proclaim clearly the gospel of salvation made available to every person through the atoning death and resurrection of Jesus Christ." Instead of that church leaders were substituting the second priority of the church "which is to help people who need help – feed the hungry, heal the sick, clothe the naked." The church had also permitted various theologies and "liberal teaching," which departed from "the evangelical doctrines of the founding Churches."

In those days the UCRF saw itself as a small, brave band of faithful Christians whose mission was to bring the whole church back to its proper course. Indeed it was small and it stayed small, its membership over the years never exceeding four thousand. They would find their inspiration not from within the United Church, but from the evangelical and charismatic boom that hit the United States in the late sixties and early seventies. The goal was, and still is, personal salvation by a personal saviour. It also includes a missionary zeal that others should undergo the same experience, often described as being born again.

"These people are desirous of sharing their joyful experience with others in their congregation," wrote UCRF executive director Lloyd Cumming in 1979, "and they are praying that the movement will grow as others come into a similar experience. To the faithful Christians, who have been 'pillars' in the Church for many years, this movement has been somewhat disturbing and, sometimes, almost threatening. The result is a buildup of tension in many congregations and, when allowed to grow, leads to division."

The Renewal Fellowship's course was clear and unalterable from the beginning. The fact that it hasn't changed in over two decades is a source of pride and satisfaction to its members. Rev Ralph Garbe joined in 1980 and served as chairman for several years. He grew up in Germany and the U.S.A., becoming deeply involved in the Presbyterian church there in his teens. He married a Canadian woman, and in the same year the UCRF was formed he moved into his first United Church pulpit.

Why did he join the UCRF? "In my personal life I had experienced a new awakening, a new experience of God's holy spirit. For the first time in my ministry, I experienced people coming to faith in Jesus Christ and growing in that faith. That ministry was a very powerful one." He was born again. When members of the congregation objected to his new evangelical style, he resigned and found a congregation where he would be appreciated.

Ralph Garbe needed the Renewal Fellowship for support, and so he believed did the United Church. What did he feel had to be renewed? "First, a personal relationship with Jesus Christ, so that one's total life is seen in relation to one's service to God. Second, biblical and doctrinal renewal; without that theological definition and framework we have no real way of knowing what's true and what's false, what's Christian and what's not, how I am to be formed as a person and what my mission to the world should be."

The UCRF calls itself "an association of evanglical Christians within the United Church of Canada." What does evangelical mean? "An evangelical is a person who believes in sharing with all people the good news of Jesus Christ," says Garbe. "That is the universal truth, the universal gospel, the universal call to come to God through Jesus Christ." In the last two decades the United Church has moved away from this traditional kind of missionary zeal. It recognizes that there may be more than one path to salvation. But Garbe disagrees. "We're part of God's mission to call mankind out of sin into a new life, to restore the world to what God's intention is for the world, to what it was right from the beginning."

The Renewal Fellowship's magazine, *The Small Voice*, and various policy statements chart that mission. In a 1969 issue, Michael Tymchak takes Moderator Dr Robert McClure to task for celebrating the United Church's theological pluralism. "Is not a church which has forgotten its responsibility to agree on the truths which define its character and purpose, like a ship about to fall apart, dumping its passengers into the midst of the sea?"

In a 1983 issue, columnist Ron Pegg writes, "Dad must run the family. Mother must be supportive. The two must work together. That is a basic that we cannot avoid. You can try, but I guarantee you, your children will suffer in the long run, as well as your relationship with your husband or wife." In the same issue, missionary Dale Whetter writes, "Arriving in South Africa [from Nigeria] was like returning home, with its Western style buildings, highly developed agriculture, and beautiful parks and flower gardens. With all the criticism of the South African government, we were impressed to see blacks working at all levels of the labour force – farming, road maintenance, bus and transport truck driving, banking, as well as street sweeping, etc. . . . Neighbouring countries have benefitted much from the technology and stability of South Africa."

In a 1981 UCRF newsletter, executive director Lloyd Cumming reported that there were now forty-two chapters and a larger office staff, also that the Renewal Fellowship had incorporated, "to give our organization a legal status and to provide a measure of personal protection to our board members." He says it is high time "that those of us who believe the church's priority is to proclaim the gospel of new life in Christ and that our policy decisions should be determined by the Scriptures (as they are spelled out in our Basis of Union) stand up and be counted in our church courts."

For the Renewal Fellowship, signs of "moral decay" are clearest in matters of gender and sexuality. Inclusive language poses a grave threat to the UCRF vision of church and world. According to their sixteen-page tabloid, *The Language Issue*, to call God Mother as well as Father, Creator instead of Lord, is "a contortion of faith" and part of "the feminist subversion." UCRF people always claim their authority direct from God, via the Scriptures. In her reponse to the first report on human sexuality, *In God's Image. . .Male and Female*, Maxine Hancock writes, "Surely every Bible reader is aware that the Scripture continuously expands upon earlier revelations until the great moment when Jesus Christ is revealed to the world. But while later Scriptures revisit themes from more ancient works, expand and refine them, they do not correct them, for the Word is given unalterably."

As for The Issue, UCRF policy on human sexuality has always been fixed and clear. Sex should occur within heterosexual marriage, not before or outside it. The purpose of sex is procreation, and "fulfilment of the husband-wife relationship." Human life is sacred and precious to God, within the mother's womb as much as beyond it. As far as the Renewal Fellowship is concerned, that's the Christian program, and anything that deviates from it is sin.

In 1974 another organization was set up to bring the United Church back on course. Smaller and more obscure than the UCRF, it was the child of six ministers. One of these men was Rev Graham Scott of Noranda, Quebec. Brought up Presbyterian, he formally resigned from the church at age fourteen, and fell into a period of what he now calls apostasy, a total desertion of one's religion or principles. The power of reason became his sole guide, and religion an evil, dangerous force that threatened it. But while he was studying at the University of Toronto, suddenly Graham Scott turned around 180 degrees again and discovered faith. At the same time he discovered his call to ministry.

His conversion took an unusual form. "Aside from the spirit of God, I was converted at the human level by the Mass in B Minor by Bach. It spoke to parts of me that I didn't know existed." Bach's B Minor Mass is a collection of music worthy of the angels, written before the Age of Reason dawned, light years before communism, feminism, liberation theology, or The Issue clouded a clear and radiant horizon.

After theology school, Scott did post-graduate work in Strasbourg, France. His doctoral thesis sits in two bound volumes on a shelf by his desk. On the wall is a plaque from the U.S. Seventh Army in Europe for services rendered in ministry to the troops. He was ordained in 1967, taught religious studies for several years, then moved into a series of pastoral charges. For sixteen years he's been minister at Appleby United, a suburban church in Burlington, Ontario. Dr Scott chose the United Church because more than any other church it symbolized ecumenism, which means Christian unity. It also implies a direct link back to the ancient prophets, the Messiah, and his apostles. But already as a theology student in the sixties Scott was hearing things in his new church that he didn't like.

"The 1966 World Mission report said that God was creatively and redemptively at work in the religions of the world. I don't mind God being creatively at work in these religions," he says, "but redemption is another matter. It impinges on what Jesus did on the cross. He made a once-and-for-all sacrifice, for all the sins of the world, past, present, and future. To suddenly say that redemption is possible through Buddhism, Hinduism, and those other religions, you're giving up the catholic doctrine of the atonement." Scott is clearly a man who feels deeply about the past.

Behind him hangs his personal coat of arms, which he commissioned from the chief herald of Ireland.

He calls the New Creed that came out in 1968 "sub-Christian and implicitly heretical." By referring to "the true man Jesus" it downplayed his divinity as the son of God, he says, and thus took "a unitarian rather than a catholic stance." At the same time, with its ministry of the whole people initiatives, Scott believes "the Church started a concerted attack on the ordained ministry. The question is, did Jesus institute an apostolic ministry? Radicals today say no, but catholic tradition says yes. The ministry is meant to be the conveyor and transmittor of the catholic faith as delivered to the apostles."

If he was so upset, why didn't he join the already established Renewal Fellowship? "The UCRF was inclined to see the Scriptures as infallible. While I believe the Bible to be trustworthy, I cannot accept that it's infallible. Though I admired the UCRF, I couldn't join it because I couldn't buy that particular party line." So in 1974 he and five others formed their own group, Church Alive.

First they became incorporated, through the Ministry of Consumer and Corporate Affairs. This allowed them to obtain charitable, tax-exempt status, which later turned out to be useful. Next they composed a manifesto, Fifteen Affirmations. In the preamble they declared, "In the valid struggle to relate the Gospel to contemporary life, many have uncritically identified novelty with truth and have fallen prey to doctrinal distortion." In response to the threat posed by ministry of the whole people, affirmation nine says, "We believe that every Christian is called to live his faith in all areas of life. But we believe also that some Christians are called to a specialized ministry of preaching, teaching, sacramental ministration and pastoral oversight – in short, of equipping the Church to minister to God and the world."

In response to ominous rumblings about abortion on demand, affirmation thirteen says, "Although we recognize that there may be exceptional circumstances in which human life must be taken to preserve other human life, we affirm the sanctity of human life before birth and afterward." If that sounds as if a lawyer had a hand in it, Rev Gordon Ross, one of the authors of Fifteen Affirmations, was exactly that.

The manifesto was mailed to every minister and congregation in the church, asking for their support. Graham Scott says that two hundred ministers and three hundred lay people signed. But the group didn't grow. "We remained a small group of people who knew each other. We were small potatoes, too egg-headish to be popular." From time to time they would put out an issue of *Theological Digest*, in which they would analyze the latest heresies of head office.

For the time being Church Alive would remain small, eggheadish, and largely unheeded. But, along with the United Church Renewal Fellowship, their time would come.

CHAPTER 4

Under a Bushel

Long before the Bible was written there was homosexuality, apparently in most cultures. If the Bible is to be believed, there were homosexual acts, and if anthropology is to be believed, there were homosexual people. In some cultures they had special status as seers and healers, in others they were reviled and cast out. Cultures that embraced Judeo-Christianity have tended to do the latter.

In our century the rulers and the ruled have come more widely and more violently into conflict than ever before. The meek are demanding their inheritance here on earth – more rights, more freedom, more power, more life. At the same time advances in understanding of human psychology and sexuality caused homosexual people in the so-called developed world to start acknowledging themselves as other than degenerates and perverts. Inspired particularly by the women's and civil rights' movements, gay and lesbian people began to press the structures around them – family, employers, governments, science, and the church – for equality and human rights.

Sinful, sick, and criminal – these were the labels they faced. But little by little the structures began to yield, grinding slowly as these weighty structures do. Families began to acknowledge and then embrace their self-declared homosexual daughters and sons. In 1968 the Canadian government decriminalized sexual acts between two consenting adults in private. In 1973 the American Psychiatric Association dropped homosexuality from its list of neurotic disorders, declaring that when the person was well adjusted a homosexual orientation was not a disorder. In 1980 the government of Quebec became the first in Canada to include sexual orientation as a protected category in its human rights code. That left the church, and sin.

For most of its existence Christianity has been ruled by the apostle Paul's image of a divided self, with a lot of help from Plato, Aristotle, and Augustine. The good part is the spirit, the bad part the flesh. The church said the only way to tame the dark forces of the flesh was either to marry or be celibate. Anything else would lead to the breakdown of marriage and to moral anarchy. But now even this central pillar of church doctrine was being questioned, particularly in an influential 1978 book called *Embodiment,* by James B Nelson, Professor of Christian Ethics at United Theological Seminary of the Twin Cities, in Minnesota. He argues compellingly for the full reintegration of sexuality into Christian life.

"Christian faith ought to take embodiment seriously," he writes. "'And the word became flesh and dwelt among us, full of grace and truth. . . ' (John 1:14). The embodiment of God in Jesus Christ is, in faith's perception, God's decisive and crucial self-disclosure. But for those who believe in God's continuing manifestation and presence, the incarnation is not simply a past event. The Word still becomes flesh. We as body-selves – as sexual body-selves – are affirmed because of that. Our human sexuality is a language, and we are both called and given permission to become body-words of love. Indeed, our sexuality – in its fullest and richest sense – is both the physiological and psychological grounding of our capacity to love." Forces that would deny this capacity to love could only be evil, even demonic, argues Professor Nelson.

As for homosexuality and the church, he writes: "It is finally a theological matter, an issue of faith. If we must find an important part of our personal security in a status which depends upon the negative definition of those who differ from us – and if we must find the security of our social order through rigid demarcations of behaviours regardless of their causation, their motivations, their moral intent, or their actual consequences – then we are living by something other that the grace of God."

James Nelson turned upside down the whole notion of sexual sin. Some church people, both heterosexual and homosexual, welcomed these ideas like a cleansing rain. For others they were much more sinister, the kind of "novelty" and "doctrinal distortion" that Church Alive attacked in their Fifteen Affirmations.

In the early eighties small groups of gay and lesbian United Church people began to meet for mutual support, in the safety of their own homes – first in Montreal, then in Vancouver and Toronto. Parallel groups were forming in other denominations and religions. Most of the Montreal pioneers were clergy and theology students. They compared notes on the stresses and strains of being invisible members of a church where practically everyone assumed that everyone else was heterosexual.

The 1980 report on human sexuality included a small paragraph on homosexuality, and the General Council called for further study. For some United Church lesbians and gay men it seemed only fair that if they were to be studied, they ought to have some say in the process. In 1982 the Montreal group contacted the other groups and several individuals in smaller communities across the country. A meeting was called, and Affirm was born.

It describes itself as "a worshipping community celebrating the Biblical and theological liberation which recognizes gay and lesbian people as members of the whole people of God. It is the purpose of this group to affirm gay and lesbian people within the United Church of Canada, provide a network of support among regional groups, act as a point of contact for individuals and speak to the church in a united fashion encouraging it to act prophetically and pastorally both within and beyond the church structure." They were ambitious.

Rev "Glen" was one of the founding members of the Montreal group. They had to be very discreet back then. Even now he can't afford to publish his real name. Glen had a parish and lived with his partner. Amazingly, no one questioned him about his "friend"; the conspiracy of silence held. Glen chaired the first meeting of Affirm. It wasn't easy. "Affirm is like the church," he says. "We've never been able to come up with a consensus statement on Christian lifestyle. Some members of Affirm believe they're called to a celibate lifestyle, whether in a relationship or not, and others believe that our sexuality is one of God's gifts to us, so who are we to restrict the sharing of that capacity to love other people?" His partner, "Jim," nods in vigorous assent.

Together with a gay male friend in Saskatoon, Sally Boyle called a meeting in 1983 to launch an Affirm group in that city. Fifteen people showed up. Some of them, including Sally Boyle, were ordained ministers. She grew up on a Saskatchewan farm and in the United Church. By age three she knew she was different, less inclined than her peers to the preoccupations that little girls are supposed to have. By age sixteen she knew she wanted to be a minister. "I still don't have the words to describe the intensity of that call. It was an overwhelming sense that this was something I had to do." Since she didn't know and no one told her that women could be ordained, she planned to become a deaconess, now called a diaconal or commissioned minister. But by the time she was eighteen Sally Boyle had acknowledged to herself that she was a lesbian. She wondered how on earth she could ever be acceptable as a person, let alone as a minister, in the eyes of God.

People she trusted, including an ordained United Church minister, challenged Sally Boyle to venture beyond that question and to grapple with a larger one: What would she make of her life as a Christian? She went to theology school and was ordained in 1976. Why ordained, why not commissioned? "I wish that we didn't have ordained ministers at all, that we could dump that whole hierarchy. But for now it's an unavoidable reality that there are things I can say – and be heard – and there are things I can do simply because I have a Rev in front of my name."

The things she could say were tightly circumscribed by her own fear of exposure. Working with young people in a small-town congregation, she buried herself deep in the closet. "You pay a terrible price for hiding like that. I suffered in both my emotional and my physical life. A chiropractor I was seeing told me that if I went on this way I'd end up in a wheelchair within five years." Instead she ended up in Affirm.

One of her first challenges was to work side by side with gay men. By and large men still run the church, as they do the business of the nation, and they outnumber women in every Affirm group. "In a way we lesbian women are the original feminists," she says. "We're fighting the same fight as feminists in the straight world, for women to be recognized as people – sexual people, thinking people, people with the right to make their own life decisions and choices. I'm saddened when we must also carry on that fight with some of our gay brothers, but carry it on we do. We struggle over it, argue over it, fight over it, and we move. I must say we do move ahead." One of Sally Boyle's dreams is a gift to heterosexual women. "As lesbian women become more vocal and obvious to the world, so too must our sexuality. Maybe then straight women will come to be seen in a different light as well. Maybe we can provide some freedom for them, too."

After a decade of uphill struggle, Rev Glen is convinced that Affirm has made progress. "Back then people could actually say there are no lesbians and gay men in the church, so this isn't an issue for the church. Now they can't say that any more. We're here to stay, we're the sons and daughters of United Church people, and we're United Church people ourselves, actively involved in all aspects of church life. In fact I think we've become a sign or a symbol for a new way of being and relating as a Christian sexual person."

To say nothing of a red flag.

CHAPTER 5

The Word and the Flesh

The machinery had been started and now, whether anyone liked it or not, it couldn't be stopped. The 1980 General Council had asked church people to study, discuss, and respond to the human sexuality study, *In God's Image. . .Male and Female*. Their responses would help in shaping a new document, a sort of White Paper with policy recommendations.

Five people undertook the thankless task of writing this second document. Each of them believed that Christian life was incomplete without full and frank discussion of sexual issues. They were all married, with children. They would work for four years, unpaid and anonymous.

The 1980 report was made available to all congregations, accompanied by a 1975 statement called *The Permanence of Christian Marriage*. People nominated by the conferences led workshops wherever churchgoers indicated they would participate. A few took part in the study, some discussed it, and in the end about a thousand of the United Church's nearly nine hundred thousand members responded in writing, along these lines:

"This [study] brought about a great feeling of release and openness. Sex was no longer a no-no topic. It was as if the church now encircled it within its arms as every aspect of life."

"We disagree! There is only one way to listen to Scripture; that is through the guidance of the Holy Spirit! Other 'voices,' i.e., sciences, philosophy, art may have value but certainly no real 'authority' when placed next to God's Word."

"I would like to commend the United Church for at last taking a stand. The permanence of marriage is of great concern in modern society and I feel convinced that a great contributing factor in its downfall is lack of Christian understanding of each other's sexuality, with too much emphasis on the physical aspects of sex."

"I feel saddened, shocked, angry, and deeply concerned about the Study's conclusions and by the way it could so affect the thinking of those who read it into accepting those conclusions and positions as being right for Christians."

At that point the authors of the new report began to wrestle with a question that has haunted church debates ever since: Who runs the United Church of Canada?

Out of their three traditions, its founders had created a system of councils by which the decisions of the whole church would be made. Without a doubt this is the most democratic structure of any mainstream Christian denomination, and the most cumbersome. Each congregation elects from its members a board or session. These representatives elect area councils called presbyteries, and these in turn elect regional councils called conferences. From the presbyteries and the conferences, commissioners are elected to the General Council, the highest court of the church. A new General Council meets every second year. The powers and responsibilities of each court are clearly set out in the Basis of Union and the

Manual, which together form the constitution of the church.

Now comes the grey area. In their decision-making process, the representatives of each court must take into account not only the views of the people they represent, but also their own conscience and experience, the collective wisdom of their fellow councillors, the traditions of their faith, and above all they must seek the guidance of God. It was clearly understood by the founders, nearly all of them with academic backgrounds, that no decisions would be made in the United Church of Canada without consultation, prayer, and much careful, disciplined study.

With all this in mind, the authors of the new report waded in. They identified in the responses five recurring concerns: the authority of the Bible, sexual orientation, sexual morality, sexual identity, and sexism. Over the next four years they would attempt to explore each of these vast territories.

One of the authors was Rev Don Gillies, now a minister at Bloor Street United in Toronto. He grew up in a devout but liberal Baptist family. Ministers were less priestly to them than to other Christians. "I remember older lay people who could lead in prayer so beautifully, they'd do as good a job as any minister. So it never occured to me that ministers were a special category, only that they have special functions." At his ordination service Don Gillies refused to wear the standard white clerical collar, the symbol of that specialness. The ceremony came to a halt. Officials consulted the church manual. To their surprise, they found no dress code for ordination. Don Gillies became a minister.

What else did he bring to the task? To begin with, his Baptist mother was a skeptic. "When she'd read anything, before she'd accept it she'd always want to know who wrote it and why. I inherited that. I find it much easier to get along with people who are struggling with their doubts than with the most devout and pious believers." For him the only absolute is God, and all the other absolutes that human society holds up for worship are false gods, idols. That includes ministers, the church as an institution, even the family as an object of worship. His own family background – lots of bickering, this one not talking to that one – led him to seek a church that was wide enough to embrace everyone. And the God he believes in isn't a vengeful god, but one who identifies with all forms of suffering and its victims.

Don Gillies knew homosexual people whose lives as Christians, even as United Church ministers, seemed cramped and incomplete from living in the closet. As a heterosexual he enjoys being a sexual person, so why shouldn't they? In a church where many still consider it a sin even to name sex in more than embarassed or technical euphemisms, Don Gillies uses pungent words such as juice and fire. "One of the problems we're dealing with all the time," he says, "is that some people are absolutely terrified of anything to do with sex and sexuality." With a mischievous grin, he calls The Issue "a fight between the wets and the dries."

After setting out the issues, the authors of the new report looked at how and why people feel the way they do about sexuality in Christian life. They included insights from the Scriptures, stories from people's lives, and questions for study and discussion. Each chapter ends with a series of affirmations, offered as general guidelines for use in the church. The whole report, *Gift, Dilemma and Promise*, would be submitted to the next General Council for its consideration and possible action.

The authors knew they were venturing onto thin ice for the average churchgoer. Affirmation C of Chapter 2 reads: "We affirm that the giving and receiving of affection, whether physical or emotional or both, is a basic need. The forms which this may take are many and varied. Because the hunger for intimacy is ultimately a hunger for God, this is a profoundly spiritual experience. It may lead to a more profound humanness or to manipulation, distortion, control."

Affirmation B of Chapter 3: "We affirm that in Christian marriage a man and a woman give themselves to each other in the full intention of a lifelong commitment. Nothing less can measure its totality, even though they may fail in their best intentions and efforts."

Affirmation D of Chapter 4: "We affirm singleness as a state in which people may find intimacy and fulfillment. We acknowledge that the church has too readily accepted marriage as the norm for society and so has not valued single persons for themselves or given them the place that is rightfully theirs, nor allowed them the opportunity of sexual fulfillment. Each person needs to struggle faithfully with these decisions."

Affirmation B of Chapter 5: "We affirm that the essence of equality is the acceptance and appreciation of the gifts of all persons female and male. We acknowledge that all sexism in language, in social and economic structures, in the conventions of our society, and in the attitudes of individuals, is destructive to human dignity and opposed to the will of God."

Affirmation B of Chapter 6: "We affirm salvation for all people is by grace through faith and that all believers in Christ are accepted as full members of the Christian church regardless of their sexual orientation. We acknowledge that the church has encouraged, condoned and tolerated the rejection and persecution of homosexual persons in society and in the church, and call it to repent."

Heavy reading and hard enough for many to swallow, but there's nothing here about homosexual ministers. What happened to those conference requests for national church rules on sexual orientation and ministry?

In 1982 another division of the church had set up another task group to work on it. (By then "task forces" had become "task groups" in the United Church, it was a less militaristic term.) It would study the issue and make recommendations for the church to consider at its next General Council. Five people – some elected, some selected – met seven times for two- or three-day periods over the next two years. For the sake of economy and because research had already begun there, all of them lived in the three most western conferences: Saskatchewan, Alberta and Northwest, and British Columbia.

Rev Bob Stobie co-chaired the task group. Grandchild of Presbyterian missionaries in China and son of a United Church minister, he fought long and hard against his own call to ministry. When he finally gave in, "the social gospel, and the need for the church to be inclusive were already established as important parts of my inheritance." For several years he's worked at the Naramata Centre, among the fruit groves in British Columbia's Okanagan Valley. It's a Christian lay training facility that his father helped build, to put into practice Martin Luther's priesthood of all believers.

The task group used its first few sessions to lay out feelings and perspectives about sexuality in general. "This stuff isn't easy to talk about, it takes time and a lot of trust," says Bob Stobie. Seated in his pleasant office with sun-splashed apricot trees outside the open window, he looks incapable of discomfort. "We had to ask each other questions that are rarely asked in church settings: How do we define ourselves as sexual and Christian beings? What does it mean to be sexually responsible? How do those of us who define ourselves as heterosexual relate to people who define themselves as lesbian or gay?"

Next the task group compared current attitudes and information about homosexuality, Christianity, and the church. They sought guidance from church members, theologians and ethicists, the church's Judicial Committee, the human rights commissions of all ten provinces, and other major Christian denominations in Canada and the States. Also, for the first time ever, an official church body openly sought input from the new gay and lesbian group, Affirm. To be balanced, they invited the United Church Renewal Fellowship to contribute as well.

Many have asked why the church devoted so much attention and resources to sexuality. Partly because it was asked by conferences that were seeking guidelines, but also because "Christianity is about the wholeness of being," says Bob Stobie. "Since sexuality is an essential part of who we are, we can't just ignore it. In our sexual experience, at the very point where we're most open and vulnerable to human loving, we may also be most open to God's grace." He smiles as he utters this large and rather frightening thought. "Maybe that's why we put so much energy into denying the connections between our sexual and spiritual lives. Sexuality's such an intimate, fragile part of us, when we're challenged on it we tend to respond defensively, even violently."

Bob Stobie didn't drop his own defences in one easy move. "As a basically heterosexual person raised in this culture, you don't shed your discomfort or your prejudices that easily," he says. "What tipped the balance for me was getting to know real live lesbian and gay people, and discovering that other people I already knew were actually gay as well. All of them are as loving, as committed and responsible as I could ever hope to be."

One of the people who tipped the balance for him was "Kim." Now she's Rev Kim, a United Church minister, and too much is at stake for her to use her real name. Raised United Church – "Saturday night bath, Sunday morning church" – like many North Americans, in her teens she abandoned it as irrelevant. Later, when she was coming to terms with both her gender and her sexuality, she learned that so was the United Church. She began to believe this is what church should be about, "struggle, opening up, finding the places where the Holy Spirit and human life interact." She even began to wonder about the ministry. But childhood memories prevailed. "Being a minister always looked like ninety per cent public relations and having no say in your own life." Hard to imagine for someone who was just finding her own way.

Kim first encountered Affirm in an upstairs room at Bloor Street United, in Toronto. The group had just started meeting, and she recalls that people were very cautious with each other. In 1983 she moved to Vancouver and joined the Affirm group there. That was the year the United Church task group on sexual orientation and ministry sought input for the first time from homosexuals. Still resisting the ministry for herself, Kim volunteered to work with the task group. After the first meeting, she recalls, "I thought the whole thing was going to be a total waste of time. They seemed so stuck, your typical United Church group, with the usual prejudices and the usual rationalizations for those prejudices."

Apparently they became unstuck, and so did she. "It was amazing to see how those people opened up! By about the third meeting, they were shedding all kinds of stereotypes about us. I started to think if this group can do it, then why not the whole church? I actually believed that ordination would go through at the 1984 General Council, I thought it would be a landslide!" She laughs, and then shrugs. "That belief played a large part in my decision to accept the church as my vocation."

For Bob Stobie, this kind of journey is both a privilege and a problem. "People who get elected to the various courts and committees of our church have much more opportunity to study and explore than most, and often their views are changed by it." The shelves behind him are spilling over with books on theology, sexuality, feminism, and a dozen other matters of the spirit and the world. "So when these courts and committees bring out their study documents or policy decisions, the people in the congregations wonder where on earth they came from."

Late in the winter of 1984, sixty members of the church division that initiated the report met to debate its recommendations. They approved its principle conclusion and recommended that the thirtieth General Council – only six months away – do the same. The full text of the report, *Sexual Orientation and Eligibility for the Order of Ministry*, would be published in the April issue of the *Observer*, the United Church magazine. It would reach more than a quarter million Canadian households. But first someone leaked it to the Toronto press, which had been clamouring to see it.

The hungry reporters skipped Section A on how the task group had reached its conclusions and Section B covering the six main attitudes it had encountered on the ordination of homosexuals: don't know, no never, no, yes but celibate, yes but not yet, and yes. They ignored the biblical and theological reflections in Section C, including the discussion on whether or not homosexuals could be "cured" through the intervention of the Holy Spirit. They found the plum they were looking for in Section E, recommendation 7.1.2: "That in and of itself, sexual orientation should not be a factor determining membership in the Order of Ministry of the United Church of Canada."

United Church Approves Gay Ministers. That's how the best of the headlines transmitted that subtle, ambivalent recommendation. These headlines preceded the report into the nation's households. And followed it. And more or less eclipsed it. And all hell broke loose.

Over the next six months the United Church magazine received more than two thousand letters on The Issue. Only 10 to 15 per cent were positive, says Hugh McCullum, *Observer* editor at the time. The rest were negative, most of them vehemently so. The magazine published representative excerpts: "The United Church is in danger of being overthrown." "Those who uphold this suggestion should be removed from leadership and disciplined for the evil they are doing." "The breadth of the examination, the honest scrutiny of irrational fears, the deep respect for all human life and strong commitment to universal ideas displayed, from the beginning of the report to the end, moved me greatly." "Here we are faced with tons of print, published at our expense, telling us how to perform in bed." "I abhor the publicity that homosexuality is receiving the world over. I can't think of one percent of them being Christians. I don't want to see them as Sunday school teachers, Scout leaders, and I learn that the RCMP will not accept them. I want Canadians of virile blood and intelligent children."

The more abusive and obscene letters generally came unsigned. Since the authors of the report were never publicly identified, people looked for available targets. Some told the editor of the *Observer* they hoped he'd get AIDS as his just reward for forcing the hated report on them. A surprising number boasted that they had not and would not read it, they already knew the difference between right and wrong.

Dr Anne Squire, then general secretary of the church division that sponsored the report, had just undergone surgery for cancer. Somehow this became public knowledge. When she returned to work she received letters and calls telling her she deserved it, it was God's punishment for her wickedness.

Anne Squire was born five years before the United Church. One of her earliest memories in Amherstburg, Ontario, is the changing of the sign on the local church from Wesley Methodist to Wesley United. A grandmother now, she taught Sunday school for forty years, and regular school for almost as many. At the same time she studied for her D.D., doctor of divinity, and worked on various church committees, including in 1980 the Education and Students Committee of Ottawa Presbytery.

That year there was a question about one candidate for ministry: Might he be homosexual and shouldn't he therefore be dropped as a candidate? The chair wanted a vote then and there, to get it over with. But in her calm school-teacher voice, Anne Squire asked, wouldn't it be better to give the question some thought before they voted? Members of the committee went on a retreat, a weekend of study, prayer, and dialogue, to work it out.

For Anne Squire the weekend was a turning point. She had already encountered ministers she knew to be homosexual. "My head told me all along there was no reason why gays shouldn't be ordained. But I still had some negative gut reactions." Seated in her Ottawa living room, grey-haired and spectacled, she looks like someone who might be expected to have a few negative gut reactions about homosexuality. "One of the things we saw that weekend was a filmstrip in which a young man was interviewed about his call to ministry, and his doubts about it due to his sexual orientation. At the end of it I realized not only would that man make a wonderful minister, but I'd be happy to have him as *my* minister. That's where my conversion started."

The committee could find no valid reason for rejecting the candidate. But they concluded that the church wasn't ready to accept homosexual ministers. Anne Squire laughs. "Of the ministers our conference ordained that year, three turned out to be gay. Of course none of us knew it at the time. Most of the people who were on that committee still don't!"

One organization that capitalized on the uproar over The Issue was the United Church Renewal Fellowship. But instead of simply attacking homosexuals, which could be called callous or even unchristian, the UCRF offered a solution – a Christian conversion to heterosexuality. In their tabloid, *Healing for the Homosexual, Healing for the Church*, UCRF ministers interview several people who describe miserable, guilt-ridden lives and then a conversion to Christianity and heterosexuality, marriage and kids. The idea originated with American fundamentalists. Former Florida orange juice queen Anita Bryant had planned to open a string of Christian re-education camps for homosexuals, prostitutes, and drug addicts. But a messy divorce and the collapse of her career scotched the ambitious scheme. The possibility of conversion excites the missionary in Christian conservatives. Also, if homosexuals can be converted to heterosexuality, then there's no reason to accept them as they are.

Former chairman of the Renewal Fellowship, Ralph Garbe, helped prepare *Healing for the Homosexual, Healing for the Church*. "God's creation of humankind is male and female, that's consistently upheld in Scripture," he says. "And the proper sexual expression of our creation is through the opposite sex. We see homosexuality as a sin, we see it as brokenness and alienation between male and female at the deepest symbolic level, which is the sexual." His voice is calm, measured, and absolutely certain. "In the past, homosexuals have been misunderstood and persecuted. But now we're able to help these people, to find healing and hope for them, to lead them back to wholeness, back to God's original intention for us all."

Shortly before the 1984 General Council, the church published a four-page tabloid, *Homosexuals and the Church in Dialogue*. As part of their contribution to it, the UCRF included an article by psychologist Peter Grant. He states: "Normal development is heterosexual development. Homosexuality is one product of failed heterosexual development." One of his sources for this theory is Andrew Salter, "a pioneer in conditioned reflex therapy," who undertakes to "help homosexuals to become heterosexual." Grant neglects to mention that conditioned reflex therapy, pioneered by Pavlov and his dogs, often employs electric shocks or drugs that induce nausea and the sensation of drowning.

In the late spring and early summer, United Church conferences across the country held their annual meetings. Two issues dominated the agenda at every one: apartheid in South Africa and The Issue. It seemed that the closer to home an issue struck, the more fear and resistance it generated. Faraway apartheid was attacked as demonic, anti-Christ, and heretical. As for The Issue, after prolonged and intense debate in every conference, final resolutions ranged from outright rejection of the report on sexual orientation and ministry to several requests for further study. One conference called for a remit – a church-wide referendum. Two conferences affirmed current United Church policy and practice in dealing with ordination and commissioning. In every conference, delegates opposing change predicted it would be the end of the church if the report passed.

Nineteen eighty-four would be the hottest summer in years.

CHAPTER 6

The National Sport

The thirtieth General Council met in the hockey arena of Morden, a small town in Manitoba. It was August, and one of the hottest summers on record. The arena wasn't air-conditioned.

As usual the commissioners dealt with many issues. Apartheid and U.S. intervention in Nicaragua were denounced. The commissioners gave unanimous support to a resolution calling for a world-wide nuclear weapons freeze. Two reports dealt with matters of sexuality and gender – *Gift, Dilemma and Promise*, and *The Changing Roles of Women and Men in Church and Society.* Both were debated, and most of their recommendations passed with few amendments.

Whether delegates liked it or not, attention was riveted on The Issue. That's why the press was there, in much larger numbers than ever before. They were looking for a fight, and seized on people like UCRF field secretary Rev Bailey Snow for provocative quotes. Despite several unanimous votes by the 374 commissioners, for example on the nuclear weapons freeze, he attacked the last two moderators for personally turning the church into "a parapolitical organization. The political stance they've taken is way left of centre." It made good headlines, but obscured the democratic complexities of a General Council and of the United Church.

Rev John Moses went to Morden as a commissioner. Born in Nova Scotia, he was baptized in the United Church. When it closed a year later, a neighbour took him to Sunday school at the Reformed Baptist church, which he recalls as "conservative, evangelical, and fundamentalist." He withdrew in his teens, no longer able to swallow the message that "to be a Christian you have to put your mind in neutral." But he recalls that it was there he learned to read the Bible.

A few years later he was drawn back to the United Church by a minister with a strong social conscience. "The major appeal to me then and now was its lack of an intellectual straitjacket." As a minister himself, he left Silver Falls United Church in Saint John, New Brunswick, after his peace activities put him at odds with some of the military enthusiasts in the congregation. Now he's at St Paul's, a predominately working-class church in a Halifax suburb.

The weekend before General Council, commissioners were invited to participate in a "Manitoba Experience," encountering people who put faces on the various issues before Council. Along with a dozen other commissioners, John Moses chose to spend the weekend with church people who were homosexual – "invisible Christians," they called themselves. Fewer commissioners chose that option than any other. Why did John Moses? "I had no direct experience of gay or lesbian people, only the usual stereotypes and college jokes. The people I met obviously had a strong commitment to their faith. Most people who have the difficulty they do finding a place in the church would long since have given up. We have people leave because they don't like the colour of the minister's robe!" His hangs on a coatrack in his office. It's black.

At communion that Sunday, the presiding minister told a story about his uncle, storm-stayed in a Prairie village. He made a pass at a travelling salesman, who responded by beating him to death. The minister called his uncle's death a martyrdom, and compared it to the murder of Jesus by the Romans. John Moses was offended. "What happened to this man was a tragedy and inexcusable, but I'm not sure that it's the same sort of thing. I came away with as many questions as answers."

Rev Duncan White from Port Hope, on Lake Ontario, served on a committee at Morden that dealt with the controversial sexual orientation and ministry report. To prepare himself, he also chose to stay the weekend with "invisible Christians," two Roman Catholic gay men. "I felt as if I'd parachuted behind the enemy lines into a little pocket of Christianity. Not only were they cut off from the body of their church, but they were also looked on with suspicion by the homosexual community because of the way they were wrestling with sexual morality."

Duncan White grew up Presbyterian and evangelical in Scotland. One day he was reading Jesus' parable of the sower and the seed. "I got up, went downstairs and told my mother I was going to offer myself to be a minister." In 1954 he was married and ordained in the Church of Scotland. Returning to Canada where he had been born, he became a United Church minister. "I guess in many ways I'm a Presbyterian at heart, and some of my concerns about the United Church come from its lack of faithfulness to good Presbyterian doctrine."

His weekend with the invisible Christians didn't change his mind. "I still couldn't say that homosexuality was a gift of God. What I can say is that it's an expression of our fallen humanity. That's the clear message of the Scriptures." He also bases his position on "medical grounds. The natural home for the penis is the vagina, it was created for it. The only unique thing about sex, the thing that sets it apart, is its procreative capacity. We can misuse our physical gifts – you can use a knife as a screwdriver, but a knife wasn't meant to be used as a screwdriver – and the primary use of sex is procreation."

The press at Morden paid close attention to three unofficial guests, two men and a woman. Sponsored by the Renewal Fellowship, they called themselves "ex-gays." By now enough people had been found whose guilt outweighed their desire that a movement of such people could be formed under Christian auspices. The three of them offered living proof of the UCRF solution, healing through repentance.

As debate on The Issue heated up the Morden hockey arena, commissioner Genevieve Carder felt that something vital was missing. While their fate in the church was being considered on the floor, a contingent of lesbians and gay men sat in the bleachers, immobilized, without voice. "There were obviously anti-gay commissioners speaking, and the ex-gays were there, but no actual gay United Church people could take part in the debate." She presented a motion that two spokespeople from Affirm be made corresponding members of General Council. That would give them a voice but not a vote.

As a child in a United Church mission band, Genevieve Carder sensed that she was part of a church that embraced the whole world. At the same time she was an incurable questioner, to the chagrin of her Sunday school teachers. She decided to be a minister, but married one and thus became ineligible. Choosing to finish theology school anyway, she's worked ever since in one way or another for the church, sometimes paid, sometimes not. One of her jobs included five years of ministry with handicapped people. "I learned from them what an inclusive church really means, not just on paper but in practical ways. You have to be prepared to put your money where your mouth is." The United Church did exactly that, making building grants contingent on wheelchair accessibility.

On the floor of General Council, Genevieve Carder's motion was narrowly defeated. "I couldn't believe it. We'd never dream of excluding black people or women or native people when we were debating some vital aspect of their lives in the church – never! At that moment it became a justice issue for me." Since it's a guiding principle in her life that "the most faithless thing a Christian can do is to do nothing," she and a few others – among them commissioner Don Gillies – called a meeting of people who'd been upset by the exclusion. People who recall it estimate that between sixty and one hundred supporters showed up. Don Gillies chaired. Out of that tense and tearful meeting emerged a new association called Friends of Affirm.

Genevieve Carder recalls her initial motive: "Since a whole group of people in our church were being denied a voice, some of us felt we had a responsibility to do something more than just vote. We were in a safe position to speak out on behalf of these people who couldn't speak out for themselves, not without risking a great deal. I have children, I'm a grandmother. That means I have credentials." But nowadays even these credentials aren't enough. "Some people dismiss me now, they say, oh well, she's just pro-gay. As if that were a crime!" Her voice rises indignantly.

Rev Eilert Frerichs was one of the Affirm spokespeople who were denied access to the floor at Morden. A few months before General Council he'd come out, or self-declared, in the Toronto media. Few could afford to do so, but he felt secure enough in his life and in his job as a university chaplain to take the leap. He comes from a continuous stream of ministers, on his mother's side, "since well before the Reformation." As postwar immigrants from Germany, the Frerichs family settled in a small eastern Ontario town. Of the three churches there, the United welcomed the newcomers most warmly.

For Eilert Frerichs in his late teens, the path to ministry was blocked by a serious obstacle, his attraction to other men. Given this flaw, he wondered, how could God want him as a minister? "When I was twenty-two I experienced what I can only call a profound religious healing. It's not terribly clear to me how it happened, but I began to feel that God accepted me as I was." Working in the Student Christian Movement and then studying theology, he found communities of people who also accepted him as he was. "That helped me to accept myself. It helped me to change from questioning all the time what God had given me, and instead to ask what should I be doing with these gifts – my life, my sexuality, and my other capacities."

Now at Morden Frerichs was on the firing line, trying to speak to the press both for himself and on behalf of Affirm. "It means you have to be on display, you're expected to talk about aspects of your private life in public – and which of us is comfortable doing that?" He chooses his words carefully. "Also Affirm represents a great variety of people, women and men, lay people and clergy, people who are out and people who aren't, and despite our common goals, those people have many different needs and agendas. It's enormously challenging to say things in public that try to incorporate all of that." Sometimes he didn't succeed. He's been criticized in Affirm for the same thing the reporters love, his quick and sometimes abrasive tongue. When one asked him if he was a practising homosexual, he replied that he didn't need practice, he was an expert.

As the air in the closed arena turned to soup, the General Council elected its new moderator, the person who would be spiritual leader of the church for the next two years. A moderator has very little actual power, but the potential for a fair amount of influence. When the Very Reverend Clarke MacDonald stepped down, The Issue was under debate. Freed from the restrictions of chairing, he decided to intervene.

Clarke MacDonald can't remember a time when he didn't want to be a minister. From his mother he inherited a simple Methodist fervour and piety. Growing up on a Nova Scotia farm during the Depression and never lacking for the basics, still he learned about haves and have-nots. "We lived near a mining town. Every day you'd hear the mine whistle: one blast meant the men would work that day, two blasts meant they wouldn't, three meant they wouldn't work the next day either. So even though we always had enough to eat, I learned very early about poverty in the community sense, and some of the forces that cause it."

The former moderator calls himself "an unashamed evangelical, a liberal in theology, and an unrepentant social activist." By evangelical he means someone who feels compelled to share with others the commitment to Jesus Christ that gives meaning and purpose to his own life. By liberal he means someone who is "open but responsible – open to the movement of the Holy Spirit, and to the wisdom in people led by the Holy Spirit, but also responsible to the Scriptures and traditions of the faith." As a social activist he's inspired by a brief command in the Letter of James: "Be doers of the word, and not hearers only."

For Clarke MacDonald, doing means putting his body where his faith is – walking on a peace vigil, working on an anti-poverty task group, presenting to Parliament a United Church brief on human rights for lesbians and gay men. It does not necessarily mean ordaining homosexual ministers. At Morden he argued that "ordination is not a human right. It's a spiritual and ecclesiastical rite." His Bible tells him that God created male and female, "that's virtually written into the constitution of the universe." And as far as he's concerned the jury is still out on whether homosexuality is inherited, and therefore conceivably part of God's plan, or derived from social contacts and desires, and therefore subject to change. At this point he was certainly not prepared to open the door, he told the assembly.

The newly elected moderator, the Right Reverend Robert Smith, is the son and grandson of United Church ministers. (When ordained ministers become moderators they're called the Right Reverend. When they step down they're called the Very Reverend.) Bob Smith's faith journey gave him a series of bumps "that propelled me into new worlds where I was forced to see with new eyes." First he discovered feminism, but certainly not by choice. "My wife wasn't satisfied to be the minister's wife and assistant any more, so she decided to change the rules of the marriage." She took up her own career as a teacher. Suddenly the husband was responsible not only for a large urban ministry and a partly finished doctoral thesis, but for five kids and the house as well. "I nearly went out of my gourd," Bob Smith recalls. But everyone survived, and he got a crash course in "the ideological assumptions that determine the roles and limitations of gender."

The next stage in his uncharted journey followed the massive 1980 police raids on several gay steam baths in Toronto. At the time he was a minister in Toronto. As a favour to another minister he agreed to preach at the Metropolitan Community Church, a congregation of lesbians and gay men. "The first person my wife and I met there was the seventeen-year-old son of two of our closest friends. You can imagine the shock. Then after the service there was this incredible release of feeling. People told me, you can't imagine how much your being here means to me, I'm an elder in such-and-such a United Church, the pastor of such-and-such a church is gay. Suddenly I started having to replace all the stereotypes I'd had with real people."

Now Bob Smith is senior minister at Shaughnessy Heights United in one of Vancouver's wealthiest neighbourhoods. The year before General Council, the elected board of the church let the local Affirm group use their chapel for Sunday evening services. Furious, some members of the congregation organized a meeting to overturn the decision. "That was the worst church meeting I've ever attended," Bob Smith says. He stops a moment, gazes out the window, and clasps his hands together on his large desk. "It was packed. We'd never seen a lot of those people in church before. For me it was horrifying to see so much ugliness and hatred in supposedly educated people." Among other things he was called a homosexual. "My wife and kids had a good laugh over that."

The decision was overturned. But the elected board fought back, and won.

With his stance on The Issue so widely publicized, Bob Smith was quite surprised when the Morden General Council elected him moderator. His first duty was to chair the sexual orientation debate, a turbulent meeting of close to four hundred determined people. He remembers it as a nightmare. "There were all these wrangles over parliamentary procedure. I was getting incompetent advice from my parliamentary adviser, and it kept being contradicted from the floor." A commissioner moved an amendment that in effect would have declared homosexuals unwelcome, even as members of the church, unless they repented. The moderator ruled the motion out of order – incorrectly, he believes now – and the General Council voted to sustain his ruling. "I think if they had not sustained my ruling at that point, the motion might have passed, it was that close." His voice drops. "I believe our church was in great danger of taking a stand that would have been very hard for many of us to live with."

But it didn't. The motion that finally passed took a United Church middle road. Instead of saying yes or no, it postponed the decision. It affirmed ordination procedures already in place, and called for a process of study and dialogue to take place among all members of the church, heterosexual and homosexual. The divisions of the church responsible for this process would report back no later than the thirty-second General Council, to be held four years later in Victoria. The report would be "a comprehensive statement concerning sexual lifestyles of all members of the Church (heterosexual and homosexual), and concerning fitness for ordination/commissioning based on findings which come following consultations with sessions, congregations, presbyteries and conferences." Back to the drawing board.

Morley Clarke voted against this compromise resolution. By now he was a minister at Metropolitan United in London, Ontario, the largest and one of the wealthiest congregations in the United Church. "There is going to be a lot of anger about this," he told the press. "The church at the grass roots has spoken unequivocally on this issue. They have done everything in their power to say no." As he recalls it, an unprecedented 150 petitions had addressed The Issue. "The church leaders who initiated that report capitulated completely to the gay liberation movement. But now they had to pull in their horns and back off."

John Moses from Halifax voted with the majority to put things on hold for a while, as he puts it. "But I really did think that when it came around again, if I were a commissioner I would probably have to vote for the ordination and commissioning of homosexual people."

Some commissioners feared that in the repressive climate that seemed to be developing, homosexual people already in ministry would now become targets of a witch-hunt. To block it they moved to affirm the ministry of people in the church of different sexual orientations. Once again debate was fierce. "Affirmed" was finally amended to the more neutral "acknowledge," and the motion passed.

To Don Gillies this was a sell-out. "They wouldn't even allow that one small gesture. At the end of it the moderator asked everyone in the hall to join hands. I just stood up, thumbed my nose at the chair and walked out. I've never done that before, and Bob Smith is one of my best friends. But I couldn't go with him at that point."

Its business done, the thirtieth General Council closed. The commissioners went home, and the ice-machine got to work cooling off the steamy-hot arena for the new season.

CHAPTER 7

Forgive Us Our Sins

By putting The Issue on hold the Morden General Council meant to give the church some breathing room. It didn't last.

At General Council's request, a task group had been appointed to examine the church's incredibly cumbersome decision-making structures and to recommend some practical improvements. When this group produced a report, which did a good job of analyzing the problem, but then casually proposed an entirely new structure for the whole church, the executive shelved it. The executive of General Council, some seventy representatives from across the church, carries on decision-making between General Councils.

"Shelving that report was a mistake," admits former moderator Bob Smith. "We should have published it and let people see for themselves how impossible it was. Instead it was used by some people to sow seeds of paranoia, they put the idea about that there was a conspiracy in the leadership at 85 St Clair." A nine-storey, yellow-brick office building in Toronto, 85 St Clair is the United Church national headquarters. In fact the seeds of paranoia were probably sown long before, as far back as 1925 when the office of the new church was located for convenience in Central Canada.

As far as The Issue was concerned, the moderator asked both his Advisory Committee and the United Church Judicial Committee whether it was his duty to lead or to follow the membership. To lead, said both, that was his job. Until the church declared its mind at the next General Council – all it had done so far was call for more discussion – his responsibility was to lead, to be in advance of the church. This would take him into increasingly hot water. "It was difficult. I'm one of those people who likes to be liked." At the same time he was about to experience another of the bumps that moved him along in his faith journey.

In the spring of 1985 Smith made the first of several clandestine trips into the war zones of Guatemala and Nicaragua. "One day in Guatemala City I happened to see a copy of *The Globe and Mail*. There was something in it about the strike at Eaton's, about the United Church being in trouble with business people for supporting the union. I sat down on the curb and just started to laugh, I couldn't help it. Suddenly it hit me how amazingly comfortable my own situation was. Up there in Canada of course there'd be hell to pay, but here in Central America I was meeting people every day whose Christian convictions could easily cost them their *lives!* It certainly put things in perspective for me, to see what people were willing to endure for what they believe."

Back home the heat was endurable, for the time being.

In 1986 the thirty-first General Council met at Sudbury, Ontario. Important and contentious decisions were made there, as they are at every general council: inclusive language would be promoted, the church's investments in South Africa would be dismantled, free trade would be challenged. But the event for which the Sudbury General Council would be remembered wasn't another debate on The Issue, it was the historic public apology to native congregations.

For some time the church had been advocating aboriginal people's needs and rights in Canadian society, including self-government. To be consistent it had also been moving to increase native self-determination within its own structures, by hiring a native coordinator, initiating a National Native Council and Consultation, as well as adapting native-based training methods for clergy and lay people. As the next step in this process, and in the tradition of Christian confession, the outgoing moderator presented an official apology to native elders. They were gathered in a traditional tipi, built for the occasion in a Sudbury parking lot.

Long before my people journeyed to this land
your people were here,
and you received from your elders
an understanding of creation, and of the Mystery
that surrounds us all
that was deep, and rich and to be treasured.
We did not hear you when you shared your vision.
In our zeal to tell you of the good news of Jesus Christ
we were closed to the value of your spirituality.
We confused western ways and culture with
the depth and breadth and length and height of the gospel of Christ.
We imposed our civilization as a condition of accepting the Gospel.
We tried to make you be like us
and in so doing
we helped to destroy the vision
that made you what you were.
As a result you, and we, are poorer
And the image of the Creator in us
is twisted, blurred and we are not
what we are meant by God to be.
We ask you to forgive us and to walk together with us
in the spirit of Christ

so that our peoples may be blessed and
God's creation healed.

An astonishing moment in Christian history, the apology typifies the United Church at work. Confession is at least as old as Christianity. Without it repentence is impossible. Without repentance – the acknowledgement of wrong-doing – no change can occur. In this case the Christian church had labelled a group of people as unchristian and therefore sinful, and with that label attached, it did everything it could to wipe out their sin. If it meant wiping them out in the process, it was sad, but it was all done in the name of Jesus.

Not everyone celebrated that an apology had at last been made. Over the years native people had seen enough paper promises torn to shreds that now they would wait to see what happened in real life. Most other churchgoers simply ignored the apology and went about their business. But some actively resented it. Wasn't it dismissing centuries of Christian outreach by brave missionaries, some of whom had been martyrs to the cause? And why was the United Church always pandering to every minority group that made a fuss?

One of the nominees for moderator at Sudbury was Dr Anne Squire. Despite the storms that had swirled about her as general secretary of the division that sponsored the 1984 report, she had been nominated by three separate conferences, each for its own reasons. A woman hadn't been elected since Rev Lois Wilson in 1980 (she was the first), a lay moderator hadn't been elected since mission-doctor Robert McClure in 1968, and this particular lay woman had proved she could survive the intense fire of The Issue, which everyone knew would soon be erupting again. To her amazement Anne Squire was elected.

Something else happened at Sudbury. The National Coordinating Group for the Programme of Study and Dialogue on Sexual Orientations, Lifestyles and Ministry checked in. The executive had launched it right after Morden General Council, as requested by that body, to carry out the onerous task that its ponderous name described. The National Coordinating Group reported its progress to the Sudbury General Council. The commissioners at General Council told the NCG to carry on, but with more emphasis on human sexuality in general.

The NCG carried on, like a ship to God knows where.

CHAPTER 8

Sex and the Spirit

Between March 1985 and January 1986 six women and seven men from different parts of Canada met thirteen times. They had been nominated to the National Coordinating Group by their conferences and chosen on the basis of several criteria: gender, clergy/lay and geographic balance, a range of theological perspectives, a variety of expertise, and presumably a certain amount of nerve. An ordained staff person worked half-time with them, and Betty-Jean Klassen chaired. Called BJ since childhood, she teaches at Emmanuel College, a United Church theology school in Toronto.

In 1945 her brother was a British Army photographer, one of the first to enter the Nazi concentration camp at Belsen. By accident she saw some of his photos. And then the world's first atomic bombs were dropped on two Japanese cities. In the horror of that summer her faith was tested. "I couldn't answer why there was all this evil, but somewhere in the midst of it all I knew there must be a God who could show us a way out of it, through Christ." BJ Klassen wanted to share this tempered faith with others, but like other women of her generation she had to choose between being a minister and marrying one. She married one, and went to work in adult education, which she understands as "helping people find their own power through a sense of belonging to a community."

Despite her experience in various courts of the church, she had grave misgivings about chairing the NCG. From the beginning it looked like a no-win situation to ask the whole church to examine all at once its faith, its sense of God and the Scriptures, ministry and the church, sexuality in general and homosexuality in particular, and at the same time to ask a group of very diverse strangers to come up with a report on all these thorny matters that would somehow be faithful to a deeply divided church. She consulted a number of people, all of whom believed she could do it, so she did. "But I never saw it as *our* work or *our* report. We were stewards doing this work on behalf of the church, and when it was done that's who it would belong to, the whole church."

The group undertook to reach its decisions by consensus, a challenge even for a homogeneous group used to working together. That this group went on to produce the volume of work it did in the time it had may be something of a miracle.

In the beginning there were twelve people on the NCG including, as General Council had suggested, openly gay and lesbian people. But at the first meeting in March 1985 it seemed to the chairperson that an important voice was missing, the kind of voice that could be heard in the United Church Renewal Fellowship. She requested that a thirteenth member be added by the second meeting.

John Howard was a minister at Collier Street United Church in Barrie, Ontario. He describes himself as married with three children, a theological conservative, a member of the UCRF, and a former homosexual. "For about twenty years I had a homosexual orientation. I struggled greatly over this because, as I read the Bible I saw it to be consistent in its condemnation of homosexual behaviour, and believed that this still held true for today." He struggled to deny, repress, and control his feelings until 1983, then finally in desperation he confided in Rev Bill Fritz, the senior minister of his own congregation. They talked and prayed together regularly, while he undertook "the process of understanding, redirecting, and healing of my emotions."

In their initial meetings, these thirteen strangers from very different places would tell each other of their journeys, where they had come from spiritually, sexually, and in other deeply personal ways. They told of their different visions and hopes for the NCG. As they struggled to find common ground, one of their first joint acts was to write a prayer. Its first verse shows they had no doubts about how difficult the journey would be: "Break in upon our church, O God, with your Spirit. You are able to bring order out of chaos, and community from division. Work out your will and purpose among us."

Dr Pam Brown believed she could make her best contribution as a scientist, gathering for the NCG the best available information on human sexuality in general and homosexuality in particular. A doctor in Halifax, she specializes in pregnancy, birth control, fertility and other sexuality counselling. She also teaches a human sexuality course to medical students.

In the mid-seventies her work brought her into contact for the first time with openly lesbian and gay people. "It became clear to me that these were ordinary people who might have made some different choices than I had, but they were being royally screwed for them." Then she read *In God's Image,* the 1980 human sexuality report. Along with later church studies it confirmed some connections she was making for herself between sex, the human spirit, and the Holy Spirit.

She appreciated that her church was wrestling with some of the variations in human sexuality. "As a sex counsellor I see so many dysfunctions and difficulties that people have, all based in the obsession that sex can only mean intercourse." Pam Brown talks in a faded English accent, seated in the large, comfortably rumpled Halifax house she shares with her daughters and her husband. "If only we could broaden that vision of sex and sexuality, we could not only eliminate a lot of dysfunction, but we'd also make the whole thing so much more honest and true to life for so many more people."

Rev Duncan White came to the NCG with an entirely different perspective. At Morden he had voted against the ordination of homosexual ministers, and both the Scriptures and the human sexual apparatus still told him that homosexuality was a sign of humanity's fall from grace, that it's a sin. From the beginning he was at odds with the rest of the group. "The NCG should have been composed of entirely different people. I was the only one who said from the beginning that I was opposed to ordaining lesbian and gay clergy. Nearly all the others were in favour or at least they were inclined that way. That wasn't a cross-section of the United Church of Canada. The makeup of the group predetermined the kind of report we'd eventually get – it could have been written after our first meeting."

At each of its meetings the NCG dug deeper into the issues that faced it, exploring the enormous implications for their church. One afternoon two of them, John Howard and another ordained minister, spent three hours comparing how each of them read the first three chapters of Genesis – the story of creation and original sin. The others listened intently. Pam Brown recalls it as a moment of truth, the first time the NCG saw clearly revealed the heart of the whole debate. "The two of them went deeper and deeper into what they believed, and what was at stake for them in what they believed. In the end the whole thing came down to a question of interpreting the Scriptures. Are the Scriptures permanently set as written – this was the fundamental issue – or do they offer continuing revelation for our times and our situations?"

Morden General Council had asked for study and dialogue thoughout the whole church. In its first year the NCG produced two resource kits to facilitate this process. "There wasn't any question of our legislating that every congregation would do this study," says chairperson BJ Klassen. "It was all done on an invitational basis. We put the resource kits together and publicized them, we encouraged people to participate, but that's as far as we felt we could go."

The first kit was a bundle of paper held together with an elastic band. Adapted from kits already used in the Saskatchewan and the Montreal and Ottawa Conferences, it included a range of materials on biblical interpretation, sexuality (including the perspective of a self-declared ex-gay), and justice, as well as a response form. The second kit included a variety of theological reflections, exercises in ethical decision-making and coping with feelings that might arise in difficult discussions, a short play about a man coming to terms with his homosexuality, and a new video made by the United Church Renewal Fellowship. It offered homosexuals and the church the UCRF solution – a Christian conversion to heterosexuality.

Past UCRF chairman Ralph Garbe explains how this video came to pass. "We in the Renewal Fellowship knew that there was a lack of resouces stressing healing for the homosexual person, not only in the United Church, but anywhere." They moved to fill the gap by producing *Homosexuality: A New Direction.* Says Ralph Garbe, "It was thrilling to witness the guiding and providing hand of God putting this production together." Two conservative Christian psychiatrists from the U.S.A. contributed their thoughts on homosexuality and ex-gay ministries. By way of proof that sexual conversion can be done, the video features several ex-gays, including the United Church's own John Howard.

Long before congregations received any of these resources from the NCG, letters flooded in. Most of them railed against homosexuality. There was nothing to be studied or discussed, the Bible said it was a sin, and that was that. Homosexuals had no morals, they were child molestors, and how could anyone in their right mind consider them as

Christians, much less as ministers. AIDS was God's punishment on them for their sins. These letters saddened Dr Brown. "They made the church seem like such a dinosaur compared to other sources of wisdom and knowledge. What these people seemed to be saying was 'don't confuse me with the facts.'"

Each conference and some presbyteries appointed their own coordinating teams to facilitate study and dialogue within congregations. Workshops and study groups were set up across the church, and by the end of 1987 more than five hundred of them had met – out of more than four thousand congregations.

Barb Marchinko chairs the Alberta and Northwest Conference Sexual Orientation and Justice Task Group, responsible for facilitating study and dialogue in its area. (Later it would add pastoral care to its title and its work.) For as long as she can remember the United Church has been central to Barb Marchinko's life. At times she finds its multi-level structure frustratingly slow in confronting urgent issues, sexual and otherwise. "But once you've worked through something and the whole church finally arrives at a position, then you've really got some weight behind you. You can deal much more effectively with other large structures – governments, the welfare system, international agencies, and so on." One of her jobs in Calgary is caretaker of a downtown church.

Another member of the task group, former nurse Kathleen Hatfield attends church in a gymnasium. Calgary's Woodcliff United built its Christian education building first, then other priorities intervened. Her four daughters were all married in its gym, their sanctuary. Her own sense of spirituality rests on "a feeling of connectedness to the whole created order. In such an awesome universe, how can anyone limit God to such a petty level as to get upset about something like sexual orientation?"

Rev George Millard also works with the task group. In 1988 he decided he could no longer serve his Calgary congregation after it reacted with great hostility to the NCG's final report. Now he works part time as chaplain in an extended care hospital and part time as a travel agent. His definition of minister is "anyone who searches for a deeper understanding of God and who wants to share that search with others, so that people can learn to take better care of each other. During this debate we've seen some ministers get awfully caught up with their own status, as if somehow they were closer to God than the rest of us."

These three, and others on the task group, organized workshops and provided resources as requested by congregations. One of the first emotions to surface in many of these workshops was anger. "We were breaking the silence," says Barb Marchinko. "When people assume that everyone agrees on these things – marriage is good, homosexuality is bad, if you're single it's only because you can't find a partner – they can easily see it as some kind of betrayal when you question these assumptions." Often people would reveal deeper feelings in one-on-one encounters after the workshop had ended. "You find out how much violence and abuse people have experienced. Men who suffered incest as kids are especially bitter. In fact women experience it a lot more than men do, but unfortunately we've learned to internalize it in a different way."

One elderly woman told George Millard quietly after a meeting, "In such a lonely world as this, if any two people can find love with each other, I don't care who they are." Another person wrote to Kathleen Hatfield that, since her divorce, the church had been the only place where she felt welcome and included. But now with the homosexuals taking over, she didn't know if she'd be able to stay.

As the General Council had requested, whenever possible the task group tried to include homosexual people in workshops, to put a face on the issue. It wasn't easy to find volunteers willing to face the heat, especially in smaller communities. For balance, the facilitators invited participation by the Renewal Fellowship, and by "ex-gays" from Homosexuals Anonymous or Homosexual Christians. After a

Calgary workshop that featured both gays and ex-gays, one of the ex-gays was so impressed by his counterparts that he decided being healed as a Christian could only mean coming to terms with being gay. The ex-gay was converted to an ex-ex-gay.

The General Council had asked for responses from across the church. By mid-1987 the National Coordinating Group had received so few, relative to the whole church membership, that it extended the deadline from June to November. As time ran out, the rate of response began to increase and the tone began to change. It seemed that righteous indignation was exhausted for the time being. Instead people were saying that this was an extremely complex issue with such profound implications that it needed more time, more study, and more dialogue.

BJ Klassen interprets this change as revealing three distinct United Churches, which have coexisted since its birth: the activist church, the conservor church, and the middle church. "This last group is the largest by far. It's made up of people who belong to the church for a great variety of reasons, they're slower than the others to express themselves, and more resistant to getting involved." In her corner office at Emmanuel College, overlooking the spinning traffic of Queen's Park Crescent, she considers the implications. "I believe it was voices from this middle ground that we were beginning to hear toward the end. And I wonder what difference they might have made if we hadn't run out of time."

In the last half of 1987, after two years of meeting, praying, analyzing responses and grappling for consensus, the NCG began to compose its final report – with responses still arriving. Representatives from all conferences and the two divisions of the church that were sponsoring the report met to give their final comments on which issues ought to be addressed and how. Final revisions were made at the last meeting of the National Coordinating Group, January 2-4, 1988.

It's clear from reading their report that they didn't set out to please everyone. All but two members believed they had done what they had been asked to do, "to engage the church in an intensive study-dialogue process, and to produce a comprehensive statement concerning the sexual lifestyles of all members of the Church and fitness for ordination and commissioning." The report set out a range of perspectives on Bible interpretation, Christian tradition, human sexuality, homosexuality, sexual ethics, and ministry. It found its way through these various minefields to a vision which eleven of the thirteen members of the NCG believed was true to the traditions and current reality of the United Church.

The long list of recommendations includes "that the United Church warmly and openly welcome morally responsible sexually active single adults, lesbian, gay and bisexual people into all aspects of the life and ministry of the Church," that it consider these categories of people for commissioning and ordination "on the same merits and standards as any other candidate," and "in dialogue with its gay and lesbian members develop liturgies celebrating their covenantal relationships" – in other words, if it believed they were better off in committed relationships, it ought to marry them.

In interviewing candidates for the order of ministry, "questions regarding sexual orientation are inappropriate." This was already the established practice. On the contentious subject of role models the NCG says, "Our understanding of ministry is that it is Christ's ministry to which the whole people of God are called. All Christians are to strive to be role models according to a single standard for all: lay members, commissioned and ordained."

Each of these recommendations builds on statements already passed at previous General Councils. Even so the authors of the report recognized that they were bound to get very mixed reactions. They recommended that the Church provide pastoral care and education "in order to help us all adjust." The chapter on Biblical interpretation and sexual ethics includes this prophetic statement: "The fact that our church contains irreconcilable differences will create tensions and make clear and unambiguous decisions and actions difficult, if not impossible."

Those differences were evident in the report in two dissenting statements by John Howard and Duncan White. The latter writes: "I cannot say with spiritual sincerity and intellectual conviction that our sexual orientation is fixed and irreversible, or that the gay/lesbian sexual lifestyle is an expression of the Perfect Will of God. . . . I do not believe there is an easy solution to this dilemma. In the meantime we will have to live with it. If we seek hasty resolution of this tension, we are in danger of surrendering the vision of one-ness that Christ offers us."

White believes the NCG failed to carry out its mission. "We were supposed to be preparing a report on where the church was at. The feedback we got said that ninety per cent of the church was still in a very traditional position. We should have produced a report that reflected that; it should have said this is where we are now, and this is what's appropriate for a church at this position. It was a chance to see exactly what the church's functioning grass-roots theology was at the time – not what some of us would like it to be, but what it actually was."

John Howard wrote of his own conversion and his ministry with those who want to be free of homosexuality. "I believe that God has created us all to be heterosexual, and that homosexuality, bisexuality, and wrong expressions of heterosexuality (such as promiscuity or extra-marital sex) all reflect the 'Fall' and sinfulness of humankind." He called his differences with the majority of the NCG "irreconcilable," and since he believed the approach to Bible interpretation presented in the report was at odds with the majority view of United Church members, he recommended that "we therefore seek to provide ways for amicable parting." In other words, the United and uniting Church would have to figure out how to break up.

The differences between the two dissenters and the rest of the group weren't new, and they didn't originate with The

Issue. One side was saying here's how things are in the United Church, and that's exactly how they should be. The other side was saying here's how things are in the United Church, but that's not the way they should be, we can do better. Both sides spoke as Christians.

At a special February joint meeting of the two divisions responsible for the process, ninety-five representatives from across the church met in a Toronto church to consider the NCG's recommendations. First they gave its authors a standing ovation – the only one they would ever get. Then they debated through the day and late into the night.

Pearl Griffin recalls it as a very long, hard day. Then president of the national network of United Church Women, she had encountered a huge range of opinion, feeling, and experience on The Issue. Some women believed it was wrong for the church to deal with it at all. Others had met in discussion groups. In many congregations women were the only ones to do so, to tackle the delicate, explosive matter of sex. And as if that weren't enough, it was that other kind of sex. Pearl Griffin says, "In the absence of a human face, quite a few found the physical aspect of male homosexuality – almost always that's what was mentioned – repugnant. Where they were able to meet with an actual homosexual person it often made a great difference."

Like many others, Pearl Griffin was caught between her own beliefs and her sense of responsibility as a leader. From a background that includes a Salvation Army mother, an Anglican mother, and a Baptist sister, she joined the United Church at age twelve. "I believed then and I still believe that Christ makes a difference in the world, and so can Christians." To her way of thinking, the lifelong task of understanding what Christ taught evolves from her own background and experience, her sense of the world around her past and present, prayer and Bible study, alone and in concert with others. For her, as for many others in the church, to worship in community is essential.

When asked where she stands, she makes it clear she's not speaking for the UCW but for herself. "I'd find it hard to be in a church that said Christ's teachings mean this and only this, and anything else is a deviation. Look at how the church has evolved over the years on the question of divorce. We know now that it's sometimes better for two people to separate than to stay together no matter what – better for them and for their children."

After fourteen hours of intense debate the two divisions had approved some recommendations, dropped others, and added a few of their own. They knew what was at stake. In place of the two about welcoming "morally responsible sexually active single adults, lesbian, gay and bisexual people" into ministry, they substituted a more ambiguous recommendation: "that sexual orientation in and of itself is not a barrier to participation in all aspects of the life and ministry of the Church, including the order of ministry." But they also affirmed "that heterosexual, gay and lesbian adults can engage in sexual behaviour within a committed relationship with the intention of permanence that is morally responsible." The joint meeting defined morally responsible as "faithful to God's call to be just, loving, health-giving, healing, and sustaining of community."

Toward a Christian Understanding of Sexual Orientations, Lifestyles and Ministry was released to the public at a 9 a.m. press conference on March 4, 1988.

It was open season on the United Church of Canada.

CHAPTER 9

The Whirlwind

REPORT OPENS DOORS TO GAYS. HOMOSEXUALS COULD WIN BUT CHURCH COULD LOSE. STAND ON GAYS WILL DESTROY CHURCH. UNITED CHURCH SHOWDOWN LOOMS.

Some of the articles that followed these headlines were informative, but many weren't. Most commentators distilled the report's 104 intricately reasoned pages into three hot items: homosexuality was like being left-handed, it was a gift of God, and the United Church had thrown open its pulpits to homosexual ministers.

Given the fate of the report, *Toward a Christian Understanding of Sexual Orientations, Lifestyles and Ministry*, it's worth a last quick look before it disappears. On the origins of sexual orientation it lists several conflicting "understandings, all of which are held within our society and within the United Church of Canada": All people are created and called by God to be heterosexual. Homosexual orientation is a delusion, a mistake, a self-deception. Sexual orientation is no more significant than being left- or right-handed. Being homosexual is like being an alcoholic, and the only solution is to abstain. Some people choose a particular orientation for particular reasons or in particular circumstances – a radical feminist to make a statement, a homosexual to live in the safety of a heterosexual marriage, or a heterosexual to survive in prison. Homosexual or bisexual orientation is like a birth defect, and people with this condition are to be accepted and encouraged to make the best of their situation, perhaps even allowed to form stable sexual relationships. Compulsory heterosexuality is a human construct, and if it weren't for social taboos and pressures we might all be bisexual.

Without a trace of irony, the report points out that not all of these understandings can coexist in the same church. Based on its research it reaches "a provisional understanding" that the second of them comes closest to the truth, sexual orientation is like being left- or right-handed. "We are sexually conceived females and males who yearn to relate with other human beings. . . . It is this relational aspect of life that gives us identity as sexual persons. And this relational identity is enhanced by Christian values."

As for the recommendation on fitness for ministry, the report traces its reasoning back to 1962 when the United Church began to re-examine the role of minister. The 1986 General Council in Sudbury most clearly placed the minister on the same level as everyone else: "All church members are called to become full participants in the body of Christ and to be the church in mission." The report takes these precedents to mean that instead of ministers being role models to look up to in the old hierarchical sense, "we become role models for each other" in an exercise of mutual trust and accountability. And in the end "All disciples are accountable to God for their life commitment and actions."

The report derives its qualifications for ministry directly from the *Manual* of the United Church: call from God, gifts for the office, appropriate training and experience, good character, and a commitment of faith. There appear to be no grounds, the report says, to exclude homosexual persons from the order of ministry.

Its final statement sounds like a visionary plea. "To be the embodied representation of Christ makes demands. It entails offering the ministry of Jesus among the outcast and facing rejection by those in positions of power. It also means a willingness for all disciples to step away from cultural and other constraints to focus directly on the work of the Spirit, alive in many forms in the life of the church and the world."

An explosion was inevitable. Long-standing, deep-seated differences within the church provided the powder, and the report provided the fuse. But who lit the match?

In most places where the bang was loudest, ministers made the first moves. In Halifax fifteen of them called for various pressure tactics, including economic boycott of the national church. In Ottawa eighteen ministers, and in London, Ontario, more than forty ministers, did the same. On Vancouver Island a dozen ministers placed advertisements in local newspapers attacking the report and threatening, "We are exploring various alternatives including the possibility of establishing a new association of congregations."

From the pews, reaction to media reports and angry sermons was swift and thunderous. Once again *The United Church Observer* became a lightning rod. The staff there kept two files of letters, The Issue and Other. While Other hardly filled a single manila folder, The Issue overflowed one drawer after another. Themes were similar to the deluge of 1984.

"If you [the editor] and the Executive of General Council are deliberately setting out to destroy the church, you have started out well. Satan must be rubbing his hands with glee!"

"The possibility of the manse being inhabited by a gay/lesbian minister and his/her partner or by a single heterosexual minister living with his/her friend in a 'committed' relationship with the intention of permanence will drive our family out of the United Church."

"I do not understand what is behind the homosexual preference. What I do understand is that they are people to be loved and respected. I endorse the report going to the General Council."

"The church should condemn homosexuality, not condone it. Do we as a church support clubs for drunks, wife beaters, rapists, et cetera? No, only an exclusive club called Affirm for degenerates. Let's wake up and treat homosexuality as it is, a dreadful sin."

"When a child wants to play with matches, wise caring love says 'No!' Wise love does not acquiesce to a weakened and weakening moral position such as this report advocates."

"If we believe that ministry is a call from God, then who are we to deny a person the opportunity to fulfill God's plan? If on the other hand we believe ministry is a job, then what right do we have to deny a person employment on the basis of their sexual orientation?"

"It is good to see that the United Church can still get excited about something."

At the centre of the storm, Moderator Anne Squire got so much mail that an extra person had to be hired to sort it. Some writers attacked the moderator for not giving any leadership, but then what could you expect, they said, she was a woman. Others attacked her for leading the church to hell. How dare she call herself a Christian, she was nothing but an agent of Satan! "Having lived through this kind of thing in Ministry Personnel and Education, I'd already developed a fairly thick skin. You have to keep telling yourself it's not directed at you personally, it's the role they're attacking." Still, some of the letters stung.

One writer described herself as a lifelong member of the United Church Women. She listed a string of biblical references against homosexuality, then a string of stereotypes. She closed by telling the moderator, "My prayer is that you will be stricken with AIDS." She signed "Yours in Christ," and her name.

After the *Observer* printed some of these letters, suddenly there was a flood of support. Many said they hadn't seen any need to comment until then. Since the volume of mail made individual responses impossible, the moderator and her co-workers developed a system of seven formal responses. Obscene letters that were signed got a note acknowledging receipt of the letter but making no response to it. "Obscenity doesn't deserve a response," said the note. The moderator, a former school teacher, checked and signed all the replies herself. "As long as they addressed the issue and didn't resort to personal attacks, I appreciated even the negative letters. It meant a lot to me that people were agonizing over this."

In many congregations meetings were called. Most often the minister initiated the process, and most often the meetings were ferocious: this whole thing had come out of the blue, and church leaders were shoving it down the throats of the people. Aside from being a sin, homosexuality undermined Christian values, the family, and heterosexuality. Homosexuals couldn't tell right from wrong, they molested children, and either they caused AIDS or they were being punished by it. Sex was for procreation, the Bible said so. And the church had no business saying anything else.

Dr Pam Brown of the now-retired National Coordinating Group was invited to address some of these meetings in the Atlantic provinces. "In some situations where people actually had the chance to read the report, and where the minister or someone else had set up a process for the meeting, or at least an agenda, then sometimes people would listen, and we could actually share experiences and feelings. In some of those meetings we ended up having really good discussions. But in others it was just awful. It was a case of ready, aim, fire! Sometimes I thought I was going to be run out of town on a rail. Especially when I had a lesbian or a gay man with me – they'd be crucified."

In one meeting, a minister recounted how his congregation had hired him when he was married, in fact partly *because* he was married. It was part of the job description. When his marriage started to collapse he fought desperately to keep it alive. A primary motive, he said, was the fear that he'd lose his job. But he didn't. The congregation lived with his new status and so did he. Could there be a parallel, he wondered.

In another meeting the minister used her own divorce to illustrate the evolution of church values. After the session an older woman scolded her bitterly: How dare she suggest that divorce was anything but a sin? As a Christian and a minister of God she should have stuck with the marriage come hell or high water. "I myself have been living for thirty-six years," the woman finished, "with a man I can't stand."

Facing their opponents has always been a test of faith for Bill Siksay and Brian Burke. They're lovers, or partners as some United Church people say of relationships in either sexual orientation. Both of them believe that when people encounter a human face instead of an abstract issue, it can make a difference. On occasion in those stormy days it may have. At one meeting the minister in a small British Columbia town grilled them aggressively for nearly an hour. After the meeting he told them privately that they'd shaken him. He could no longer be certain that homosexuality was a sin.

The two of them have their darker memories, too. In one meeting the congregation was tearing homosexuals to shreds. God would never call people like them into ministry and in any case what could they possibly have to offer? Through all of this the minister didn't say a word. He sat at the back of the hall, paralyzed. Brian Burke and Bill Siksay knew why. Through the elaborate informal network that's grown up among lesbian and gay people and their supporters within the church, they happened to know that this particular minister was one of them.

During her two-year term the former moderator logged 235,000 kilometres and attended more than five hundred meetings, coast to coast. When she describes how she got through some of these sessions, echoes of the school teacher come through. It was Anne Squire's practice not to argue, but to meet arguments with questions. "When someone would throw the famous Leviticus 18:22 at me – it's an abomination for a man to lie with a man – I'd ask them what Leviticus says about menstruating women being unclean, or wearing a garment made of two fabrics, or planting two crops in the same field. That's different, they'd say. How is it different? I'd ask."

When people accused her of ignoring the Bible, she replied with unnerving calm, "I take the Bible quite seriously, seriously enough to read it every day. Do you?" And when they'd remind her that Paul says homosexuality's a mortal sin, she'd remind them that the same Paul said women were not to speak in the church. Did they believe that? In almost every meeting at least one man would shout yes! Then the meeting would break into laughter, which Anne Squire took as an opening of sorts.

Often from the podium she saw people – usually women – raise their hands to speak, then the hands would withdraw. Some of these women would only speak to her in private, after the meeting was over. "I was afraid to say anything," one elderly woman told her. "In a town like this everyone knows everyone. But to tell you the truth, I'm not so sure what all the fuss is about."

The fuss was just beginning.

CHAPTER 10

Heavenly Weapons

Because of its public image as a gadfly, the United Church has often been called the NDP at worship. In fact the majority of its people tend to be reasonably comfortable, middle-of-the-road, small-c conservatives, and most of them want to continue that way. To many, "church" means the local church. Of course the national church is always on about something or other, but it seems so far away it could be in another world.

The seventies and eighties have been good to conservative Christians. One of them even won the White House. The war over public opinion that started in the sixties is clearly going their way. Many men are threatened by real and imaginary loss of power on all sides; many women by what they perceive as attacks by feminists on the status of wife and mother. The yearning for communal solutions to social problems has largely succumbed to the marketing of personal solutions – for those who can afford them. Forget about organizing to clean up the public waters, get a home filter. Farewell VIA Rail, the minister of transport has declared the personal car environment-friendly. And in North American churches the relatively new concepts of corporate sin and community salvation haven't taken hold to nearly the same degree as much more deeply-ingrained beliefs about sexual sin and personal salvation.

By the end of the eighties *The Small Voice* had become bigger and glossier. Now it's called the *Renewal Fellowship Magazine for Concerned United Church People.* But the group's original image, a plucky band of faithful Christians, hasn't changed. Rev Peter Hartgerink wrote in the March-April 1989 issue, "We in the Renewal Fellowship lament the slide of our beloved United Church into theological confusion, moral decay and spiritual emptiness. . . . We are up against Satan and his host. This is not merely a human struggle. Only heavenly weapons can win this battle."

Why had the Renewal Fellowship membership got stuck around three thousand? Former chairman Ralph Garbe says people were afraid to join. "Once you join the UCRF you're labelled, you're perceived as narrow-minded, militant, and exclusive. That perception has hurt us a lot. But all we've tried to do is witness to an orthodox Christian faith that we've seen slowly disappearing in the United Church. We see the United Church losing its Christian identity. It's rapidly becoming a unitarian church, concerned only with making good people. We in the UCRF don't believe that we're saved by our good works. We're saved by Jesus Christ and what he did for us on the cross."

When it came to The Issue, the Renewal Fellowship didn't restrict itself to the church arena. In 1986 it lobbied against Bill 7, while the United Church supported it. The Ontario government proposed to include sexual orientation along with several other categories to be protected in the provincial Human Rights Code. Not only would this protect "a particular minority group in society," the UCRF argued, but the government was also "in danger of legislating morality, thus violating the moral conscience of the majority of people both in our society and in our province."

While the UCRF hadn't grown in size, in the current climate it was making gains with the General Council executive. Throughout 1988 the executive initiated a series of meetings with the UCRF leadership, in an attempt to find common ground. None was found. In the January-February issue of the *Renewal Fellowship Magazine*, former pro-football player and police chaplain Rev Robert Rumball writes, "Just as the evil of communism doesn't change its goals, neither do those who promote a 'different lifestyle.'"

The other opposition group, Church Alive, remained small and obscure. The handful of ministers who kept it alive would occasionally publish an issue of their *Theological Digest*, but by and large they were ignored by the Church.

Then came the report.

An article in the February *Observer* had already indicated which way the soon-to-be-released document would go. If ever there was a time to strike, this was it. Bill Fritz of Barrie, Ontario, suggested to his colleagues in the Renewal Fellowship and Church Alive that they launch a protest. Raised a Roman Catholic, Bill Fritz underwent "a religious crisis" in his first year of university. "Until then I guess you could say I was a nominal Catholic. Church wasn't very important to me. But after a period of wondering about the meaning of my life, I decided to follow the Christian way of life, including ministry." He joined the United Church and was ordained in 1959. Excited by the impact of Christianity on world history, "I wanted very much to be on that side, which would make the same kind of impact for God in our lifetime." In 1972 he settled in at Collier Street United in Barrie.

Until 1980 Bill Fritz had felt comfortably at home in his adopted church. Then *In God's Image*, the human sexuality report, loomed on the horizon. "Some things that I consider non-negotiables were suddenly being called into question, particularly the sanctity of marriage and family life. Instead of strengthening that area of our ministry, the church was becoming nothing more than a pale imitation of what was happening in society." In Canadian society 40 per cent of marriages end in divorce, and less than one quarter of families actually fit the traditional image of wage-earning husband, full-time housewife, and kids. The more these institutions decay, the harder their defenders have to fight for their preservation.

At about the same time, another minister at Collier Street confessed to Bill Fritz that, although he was married, he had homosexual tendencies. "He and I both knew that we had a problem," says Fritz. "While as a Christian church we can accept the homosexual person, as we do an alcoholic, we cannot make the quantum leap to approving that lifestyle." So he helped his associate, John Howard, convert to functioning as a heterosexual. This would be Bill Fritz's first success in "a homosexual healing ministry."

To him, healing means that "the homosexual, although perhaps never being free of the orientation, nevertheless through prayer, through therapy, and through support groups abstains from the lifestyle and the practice, abstains from finding pleasure in sodomy and all other unnatural forms of sexual behaviour." But through the eighties one report after another, one General Council after another, seemed to be softening on this question, reinterpreting Scripture to allow doubt "where until then we'd had a whole scheme of things for society that seemed to me very straightforward." Bill Fritz became increasingly alarmed. For him the March report was the last straw.

He and several other ministers, all men, met in Toronto two weeks after *Sexual Orientations, Lifestyles and Ministry* hit the press. They prepared a draft statement, and from their list of potential supporters they organized a public meeting. Two hundred and fifty people showed up. In high excitement ten of them expanded the draft statement into a ten-point petition, the Declaration of Dissent, and the meeting appointed a steering committee of thirteen: eleven men, two women. (Two more women were added later.) The thirteen were all ordained ministers. The new group called itself the Community of Concern, and its chairman was Bill Fritz.

The Declaration of Dissent rejected "the essential thrusts, directions and conclusions of the report, because they are a drastic departure from historic Christian faith and obedience," and it declared "we are convinced that the Biblical intention for sexual behaviour is loving fidelity for life within marriage and loving celibacy outside marriage. This has been and continues to be the standard upheld by the vast majority of Christian Churches."

On the last point they were correct. Among the mainstream denominations the United Church is clearly in the forefront. Evangelical churches all maintain that homosexuality is a sin, so ordination is out of the question. Most of them believe the solution is repentance, and conversion to heterosexuality. For Roman Catholics everywhere, priests must be male and they must be celibate. The Presbyterian Church of Canada is currently studying the issue, and its General Assembly will likely take a stand within the next year. But in 1985 its doctrine committee distinguished between orientation and practice. The Anglican Church of Canada requires that homosexual candidates for ordination be celibate. In 1989 the Evangelical Lutheran Church in Canada decreed that no openly practising homosexual person could be admitted to ministry or called to a congregation.

But the United Church is not alone. Both the United Church of Christ in the U.S.A and the Christian Church (Disciples of Christ) there and in Canada have accepted openly homosexual ministers in some of their regions. So has the Reform Church in Holland. At its General Conference in 1988, United Methodists in the U.S.A. voted to maintain their ban on ordaining "self-declared practising homosexuals." But within the same church, a reconciling congregation program was launched in 1984, for "the intentional inclusion of lesbians and gay men in the life and ministry of the congregation." By spring 1989 thirty-nine United Methodist churches had declared themselves to be reconciling congregations.

Bill Fritz and a team of volunteers mailed the Declaration of Dissent to every minister and congregational governing board in the United Church. By mid-July more than a thousand ministers and missionaries had signed, and some thirty-two thousand lay people. Across the country individuals and groups, some with discontents that long predated The Issue, formed themselves into Community of Concern chapters. The group had no official status in the United Church, and neither did its petition. But virtually overnight the Community of Concern became a force to be reckoned with.

Many people at Eastminster United in Belleville, Ontario, were outraged by the March report, or at least by what they'd heard about it from the local media. Their minister, Ed Bentley, ascribes their reaction partly to a kind of culture shock. "People see everything around them changing at a frightening rate and in ways that don't make sense to them. They see their kids doing things they could never have imagined doing themselves. We have people in this congregation whose kids aren't married but they're getting into all kinds of relationships. Some of them are even homosexual. These people see their church as the last safe place on earth, a bulwark against all these alarming changes in society. When the church appears to be letting the kids do whatever they like, and even approving of it, then the church has failed."

From his temporary office in a small bungalow, Ed Bentley looks out on the foundations of his congregation's new sanctuary, delayed while they sorted out their priorities. By 1988 Eastminster United, in a growing city of thirty-seven thousand, had outgrown its old building. But the congregation had split over whether or not to build a new one, to cost more than $2 million. It wasn't the money, says Ed Bentley. The split had more to do with what a new building would mean in the life of the congregation. A congregation that works, works like a family. What would happen if this particular family were suddenly opened to new members? Exactly the same prospects that appealed to some members threatened others: the potential for new growth, new openings to the community, all the possibilities of the unknown. Now suddenly on top of all this confusion came the report. People wondered whether their whole church was about to explode. Givings plummeted. Plans for the new building were put on hold.

In this loaded climate, Ed Bentley didn't take a strong stand when the congregation met to discuss the report. Since he was to be a commissioner at the upcoming General Council, he felt it was his duty to listen. In the meeting he heard a variety of opinions and feelings, with many people opposing and some supporting the report. Some of the opponents criticized him for not telling the supporters how misguided they were.

In fact he was deeply offended by the report. He calls it a third-rate document, and signed the Community of Concern's Declaration of Dissent to let the national church know it had gone too far. "We don't know God's intention for us. I believe that most homosexual activity is practised by people who are basically heterosexual. Is anyone actually born homosexual? We can't answer that. In the meantime we're certainly not in a position to say that it's a gift of God, and even less to build a case for ordination on that basis."

In Calgary, Stephen and Jacqueline Istvanffy heartily agreed with their minister, Martin Lynas, that "homosexuality is unnatural, unethical, and unbiblical." Along with most of their congregation, Southminster United, they signed up with the Community of Concern. Martin Lynas is the image of an Irish pastor, white hair, ruddy complexion, and a fine brogue. He trained as a Presbyterian in Northern Ireland, was ordained a Methodist, then twenty-one years ago came to the United Church in Canada. "For nineteen of those years I've been quite happy," he says.

Since the United Church near where Stephen Istvanffy lived didn't have one, he attended Sunday school in an evangelical church. He's been an elder for thirty years now in the United Church, and led a subgroup in the men's association which studied The Issue. "I believe it's the church's job to guide the morals of society. Over the past few years, the inability of the courts of our church to say what's moral and what isn't has come as a shock to me." Now he chairs the Community of Concern in Alberta.

Jacqueline Istvanffy grew up in the Church. "I was taught to believe in the authority of Scripture, as the most clear message that we have on how we should live. Now when people say they're interpreting the Scripture, what they're saying to me is that they're going to rewrite it until it says what they want to hear."

The three of them together paint a grim picture of homosexuality. Jacqueline Istvanffy, a retired Victorian Order of Nurses practitioner, believes that it can't be part of God's plan, because "homosexual men so often do damage to each other in their sexual activities. The delicate tissues of the anus aren't made for that kind of abuse," she says. Stephen Istvanffy believes that most male homosexual relationships involve violence. For evidence he cites prison studies. Jacqueline Istvanffy adds that she's less sure about lesbians, since they don't seem to be so violent with each other. One of her nieces is a lesbian.

Martin Lynas believes that "God loves us but he judges us too. The Bible shows that if we go too far we get into trouble – 'And he sent a plague into their midst.'" Is AIDS the plague? He laughs a little. "I'm not saying it is, and I'm not saying it isn't." Martin Lynas also believes that homosexuals make terrible role models, and therefore must not be allowed into positions of leadership. "The duty of a pastor is to take care of his flock. How could we expect a homosexual to do that?" Says Stephen Istvanffy, "If they're already in ministry they shouldn't wait to be fired. They should resign."

Jacqueline Istvanffy is convinced that homosexuals can change. "They can be healed, we know they can. Or they can abstain." She knows a United Church minister who chose celibacy because the Scriptures told him to. "Instead of condoning this kind of behaviour, the church should be offering hope that they can be healed. We certainly don't want others to be influenced to this way of life." Stephen Istvanffy believes that young people can be converted to homosexuality. "Teens experiment, especially when everyone else is doing it. The social pressure is enormous, it's very difficult to say no."

In Toronto former moderator Clarke MacDonald has been struggling for years with The Issue, in what he calls his "spiritual pilgrimage." The report pushed him into the Community of Concern. Aside from the position it took on sexual orientation and ministry, "It denigrated marriage, family life, and the minister as a role model. We say athletes should be role models. We want our politicians to be role models, so why not ministers?" This seems one of the sorest points for MacDonald. In his youth several ministers had been powerful role models for him. "And in my own life and ministry many people have told me that I've done the same for them."

One of thirteen people who formed the Community of Concern's national steering committee is Rev Allen Churchill, senior minister at Dominion-Chalmers United in Ottawa. "It's the closest United Church to Parliament Hill," he says, "with the finest organ in Ottawa. The CBC uses it for their recordings." He's a tall, imposing man with a good pulpit voice, a former RCMP officer with a PhD from Oxford in New Testament literature, history, and theology. Allen Churchill is convinced that the Scriptures declare homosexuality unnatural "because it doesn't fit with God's plan for populating the earth and building families. Perhaps to the person who has it this desire may seem natural, but that in itself – being comfortable with something which is so clearly unnatural – is a problem, even a sin."

On the other hand he's ambivalent about the minister as role model. "We can't have a double standard, with Jesus up there, the minister in the middle, and the rest of us down here." He concludes that practising homosexuals should be ineligible not only for ordination, but also for membership in the church. On this he parts ways with Community of Concern members who say membership yes, ministry no. As far as Churchill is concerned, right from the beginning it's been too easy to join the United Church. In his United Church, members would have to meet several conditions, including heterosexual marriage or celibacy.

George Morrison was ordained in the Presbyterian Church in Northern Ireland, but in Canada he switched to the United Church. "While it included what was most important in Presbyterianism, at the same time it seemed to be so much broader." Perhaps a little too broad, he says in his Queens Avenue United office, high above the Fraser River in New Westminster, British Columbia. "When the Presbyterians split at the time of union, most of the conservatives stayed with the Presbyterian Church and most of the liberals went to the United. Unfortunately both sides ended up with an imbalance." At the inaugural meeting of the Community of Concern's British Columbia branch, George Morrison was elected president. Since he'd never been a member of the United Church Renewal Fellowship, but he had been president of the Church's B.C. Conference, the COC considered him to be a moderate voice.

To his mind, the Scriptures make it clear that heterosexual relationships in marriage are the only acceptable norm. As for homosexuality, "we're simply not built for sodomy, so it can only lead to serious health problems." He's also an outspoken opponent of the United Church stand on abortion. As set out by the 1980 General Council, it declares abortion morally wrong when it's used as a method of birth control, presses for its avoidance by improved sex education, family planning, and birth control services, but also urges that abortion within the first twenty weeks be removed from the Criminal Code. (In 1988 the Supreme Court of Canada struck down the abortion law from the Criminal Code, and in 1989 a church task group undertook a new study on the question.) For Morrison, the current church stand isn't good enough. "As Christians we must treat life with sacredness from the moment of conception. While I'm sympathetic to the arguments being pushed that women have rights, at the same time it seems to me that once a woman allows herself to become pregnant she has to assume responsibility for the results."

At the end of the 1984 General Council, Rev John Moses had wondered what he'd do next time The Issue came up, as he knew it must. When the National Coordinating Group's first study kit arrived at his Halifax church in 1986, he found it disturbing. It seemed to be reaching much too far. The majority at a St Paul's congregation meeting decided that homosexual ministers would be unacceptable to them unless they were celibate. Two years later the report was released. John Moses was appalled. "It wasn't what the 1984 General Council had asked for, which was a range of theological views. And they seemed to have ignored completely what the congregations wanted."

He preached a fiery sermon attacking the report. His congregation gave him a standing ovation, an unusual gesture in a church service. Along with two other ministers he circulated a letter of protest to every congregation in Maritime Conference, covering Nova Scotia, New Brunswick, and Prince Edward Island. Among other methods of pressuring the national church, they recommended withholding money from the Mission and Service Fund, which provides most of the United Church budget. And John Moses helped establish the Maritime branch of the Community of Concern.

Given his uncertainty about ordaining homosexual ministers, why was he so upset? "I was torn between the reality of discrimination against lesbian and gay people inside and outside the church, and a report which to my way of thinking dismissed the church's traditional moral teachings in a rather cavalier way." Despite the fact that the premier of Nova Scotia is a member, St Paul's ministers primarily to a disadvantaged neighbourhood. "In this community we see the results of the sexual revolution in very concrete ways – over twice the national average of live births to single mothers, venereal disease, abused children, young men fathering children without the slightest sense of their responsibility, young women dropping out of school at fifteen to live on welfare and their children following the same pattern."

A window high above John Moses's desk is covered in wire mesh, and on his desk a scrap of paper prominently displays the phone number of the police. "For well-educated and reasonably well-off people, of course we can talk about choices," he says. "The report speaks to people like that. But here we see the real victims of the sexual revolution, and what did that report have to offer them? As far as I could see, not a thing."

CHAPTER 11

Some Kind of Fatal Disease

Throughout the spring and summer of 1988, The Issue dominated the life of the entire United Church. It came up at every meeting in every corner of the church. There were calls for resignations in the national leadership and for a church-wide referendum. Since referendums can be called only by General Council, that option would have to wait. People threatened to withhold their donations, in fact to boycott the national church, to punish it financially the same way it had taught them to boycott Nestlé's over infant formula, and South Africa over apartheid. Ministers threatened to quit. That was nothing new, people had always threatened to quit the United Church over this or that – an annoying sermon, a bad choir, the colour of the new rug. But now the threats included taking congregations out, too.

As early as the fall 1986 meeting of General Council executive, Margaret McPherson and a colleague had proposed that debate on The Issue be delayed until the thirty-fourth General Council in 1992. This would give the church time to develop two major projects that might help it to meet the current crisis. One is a church-wide study on the authority and interpretation of Scripture, the other a plan to make theological training more readily available to lay people. But if The Issue continued to preoccupy everyone's attention, energy, and resources, the motion argued, then the church might never again get around to doing anything else.

Margaret McPherson calls her own faith practical and down-to-earth. "I believe that every child is a child of God, and therefore that every person has a personal relationship with God – not should have, but does have – no matter who we are. Because of that I believe that every person has worth, and all of us should strive to the best of our ability to be worthy of that relationship." This is what she tried to teach her own children, and over the years the chidren who came her way in Winnipeg Sunday schools. She found it got better results than telling them they were bad.

She also takes very seriously the ministry of the whole people. "Over the years I've discovered that I don't need an intermediary between myself and God." To her a good minister is one who sees the gifts in others and enables them to do things in the name of God that they don't believe they're able to do on their own. That includes ministers who are homosexual. Margaret McPherson knows more than one, "and very fine pastors they are." How does she know they're lesbian or gay? "Rumour. They haven't said anything. And I wouldn't ask, it's none of my business."

She didn't find it hard to propose putting off debate on The Issue for a few years. It had taken her family a whole decade just to talk about a cousin who is gay. As a visitor at the 1984 General Council she'd seen how contentious The Issue was going to be. And as a math teacher, now retired, she had learned how painfully slow the process of learning can be. "You don't rush in and teach people algebra when they can't do additions and subtractions. That's just asking for failure." It was clear to her and to her executive colleague Rev Terry Shillington that more work, much more work would have to be done before The Issue could be resolved without splitting their church.

Some executive members agreed. Others argued that it couldn't be put off, nothing else could be accomplished until it was settled. In the end the executive neither accepted nor rejected the motion, it was tabled. Now in the tense summer of 1988 several senior staff people revived the idea. They urged individual executive members to put petitions to that effect before their conferences, and from there to General Council. But somehow the initiative got lost. Margaret McPherson still thinks it was the right idea.

A flood of petitions poured into presbytery and conference offices across Canada. Petitions are one of the vehicles by which United Church members convey their concerns and suggestions to the various councils that determine church policy. The concerns are set out, then actions are proposed. While most issues generate a handful of petitions, in extreme cases a bundle or two, The Issue produced bag-loads. The few people who knew the petition process coached the many who didn't.

According to church policy, delegates to each court have to determine whether they concur with petitions sent to them by the lower courts. The elected session or board of a congregation votes concurrence or nonconcurrence on petitions from individuals or groups within the congregation, presbytery delegates vote on petitions from congregations, and conference delegates do the same with all the petitions they receive from the lower courts. To concur doesn't necessarily mean to agree; it may suffice to recognize enough significance in a petition that the next court ought to include it in its deliberations.

Presumably by this filtering process the founders of the church hoped to avoid swamping the regional and national courts with irrelevant or repetitive requests. They believed that each council, in response to the Holy Spirit, would reach its own decisions, ones that would be right for the part of the church it stood for. Thus the board of a congregation would consider the needs of that particular community of worshippers, a presbytery the larger community formed by several congregations, a conference the needs of a whole region, and General Council the entire church.

Normally congregations and presbyteries are required to send on to the next court all the petitions they receive, whether they concur with them or not. Conferences on the other hand are only required to send on to General Council petitions with which they concur. Uniquely for The Issue, the national church suggested that any petition sent to any court of the church be allowed to continue on unhindered all the way to General Council, whether with presbytery and conference concurrence or not. For beseiged officials the problem of overloading General Council seemed less dangerous at this point than appearing to censor the process in any way. This decision would have grave consequences.

Across the country, ministers turned the March report into material for Sunday sermons. In Shoal Lake, a small farming community in Manitoba, Rev Glenna Beauchamp considered the document both biblically shaky and tactically risky. "It asked people to go from A to Z without adequately exploring all the steps in between." As a commissioner to the upcoming General Council, she hoped to see it defeated. "But I hoped we wouldn't just drop it and forget it. That wouldn't be the faithful thing to do. For many people, including myself, there was a clear issue of justice involved."

Glenna Beauchamp grew up Anglican. In her teens, when she decided she wasn't ready to be confirmed, she was told she couldn't join the youth group. The United Church had no such restrictions, so she joined the youth group there, then the choir and the Bible study group. Over the years her faith deepened to the point where she considered going into ministry. She knew that thirty years after the first one had been ordained in the United Church, women in ministry were still pioneers, still encountering more obstacles than support. But the intensity of her call overcame her doubts.

She calls her faith at the time conservative, "based on an individual relationship with Jesus Christ and not deeply concerned with anything else."

As Glenna Beauchamp got more involved in the various courts of the church, she began to explore another relationship, between faith and justice. "Christians visiting here from Third World countries transformed my faith," she says. "They opened my eyes to a new vision of God's kingdom. It wasn't to exist only in heaven, but here on earth as well. I also learned from them that as a group, as a nation or a church, we could commit corporate as well as individual sins. If you believe that, then it follows naturally that seeking justice is a way to seek redemption."

The first Sunday morning after the report came out, Beauchamp told her Shoal Lake congregation a story. In her last year at university she had become close friends with a man. After they had gone out a few times, "I began to feel that Craig and I would become more than friends." He was a committed Christian who worked in a hospital while he studied for the ministry. He was also "a great looking guy with a delightful sense of humour; a strong, sensitive man who enjoyed skiing as much as reading and discussing a good book." About six months after they met, "Craig told me that if he could ever get married it would be to someone like me. But he knew it wouldn't work. Craig was a homosexual."

Glenna Beauchamp told the congregation she was horrified. "My knowledge of homosexuality was limited to a brief talk from my parents when I was thirteen. A homosexual was a creature from another planet, he was effeminate and acted strangely and talked with a high-pitched voice. And as a woman I felt insulted and angry when I realized that the man I'd been going out with found other men more attractive than he did me. I felt like I'd found out someone I'd hoped to share my life with had some kind of fatal disease." Somehow their friendship survived, and she learned more of his story.

Craig had gone to his minister for help. The minister told Craig to pray. For months he'd prayed, but he didn't change.

Next he tried a psychiatrist. The psychiatrist administered conditioned reflex therapy, with electric shocks. Craig was still gay. "Finally he decided that no one really knew what made a person gay, and nobody could fix it. This was simply the way he was and would always be. God knew he was gay, and still loved him." Now whenever she thought about The Issue, she told her congregation, "Craig is always at the back of my mind."

"Christ's church was never called to play it safe," her sermon concluded. "We are not called to be popular, but faithful. We are not called to reflect and reinforce the values and opinions of society, but to proclaim and live God's will on earth."

The annual meetings of conferences in late spring were dress rehearsals for the main event in Victoria. Tensions ran extremely high. At Maritime Conference the election of commissioners to General Council took a new and unusual turn. When lists of nominees were circulated on the floor, some had checks after the names of well-known conservatives. One of these names was Rev Leander Mills of Silver Falls United, in Saint John, New Brunswick. He explains, "We had to make sure we got the right people to General Council." The right people? "The ones who'd made it clear they were going to defeat the report," he says in his small office on the outskirts of Saint John. Next door a noisy gang of Cub Scouts prepare to meet.

A former military chaplain and private-school teacher, Leander Mills joined the Community of Concern "to get the United Church back on the right track." As far as he's concerned, the Bible is the word of God, the ground rules for every human activity. He was a little ambivalent, though, about the role of a General Council commissioner. "We don't need to listen to people on all issues, but when a large vocal group says no we have to be tuned in to that. Never before in the history of the church have there been so many petitions against a policy."

Leander Mills ministers in a city that has a history of religious strife, Catholic versus Protestant, and that now offers eight separate pentecostal churches – serious competition. The Saint John city council banned the controversial Hollywood film, *The Last Temptation of Christ.* Lean and sharp-featured, Leander Mills has no doubts about homosexuality. "God's order of creation is clear: faithfulness in heterosexual marriage or chastity in singleness. Society is built on the family – that is, on heterosexual marriage – that's where children learn their morals." And that makes sexual relationships under any circumstance with a person of the same gender a sin. But there's hope, says Leander Mills. "I've worked with homosexuals, with alcoholics and drug addicts. I don't condemn these people, but I do have to tell them they've got to acknowledge that their lifestyle is unacceptable. They've got to get back on the right track."

Barb Rumscheidt of Halifax was one of the "wrong people" who weren't on the safe list, but she was elected a commissioner anyway. She was raised in a comfortable white middle-class United Church family. But her own faith journey has been a series of revelations. Working with kids in Montreal slums, with Latin American refugees, and with battered women, she encountered "human beings acting out the reality of the Gospel in real life, struggling in all kinds of ways to transform their lives." This was a Gospel she could understand. And in the United Church, at least some Christians were saying that the way things are surely is not the way they're meant to be. "Oppression was never meant to be part of the divine plan."

Once Barb Rumscheidt encountered "real live lesbians and gay men, The Issue couldn't be an intellectual one for me any more. I could see how the structures work against them, and I could see the devastating effects that has in their lives." Off to a church picnic on a drizzly summer morning in Halifax, she pins a pink triangle on her sweatshirt. The symbol derives from World War II, when homosexual prisoners were forced to wear it in Nazi concentration camps. Barb Rumscheidt's gesture is borrowed from Denmark. When the Nazis occupied that country they ordered Danish Jews to wear the Star of David, so they'd make easier targets. The Danish king immediately put on a Star of David, as did many other Christian Danes.

The gesture is consistent with her activist faith. "I had to deal with my own privilege as a heterosexual. Obviously it's terribly risky for most lesbians and gay men to speak out on their own behalf. That's one of the things someone like me can do, someone who's married with kids, who has all the right credentials." And do it she does, wherever and whenever she can.

In congregation meetings leading up to General Council, Barb Rumscheidt recalls, "I overheard a very proper churchwoman refer to another as 'that bitch,' just because she'd dared to say something positive on The Issue." She raises her eyebrows. Behind her sailboats bob at anchor in a Halifax inlet. She rents a house here, at the Atlantic School of Theology, with her children and her husband, theologian Martin Rumscheidt.

She was elected a commissioner and went to General Council a well-known quantity. For her own theology studies she's writing a thesis on heterosexism in the church. She defines heterosexism as the system of thought and action by which heterosexual men manage to maintain their power. Prior to General Council Barb Rumscheidt attended dozens of meetings, all of them on The Issue. "Of course it was hard to listen to all the hatred and bigotry that came out in those meetings. On the other hand no one could say that as a commissioner I didn't have a clear sense of the so-called grassroots church, and what was at stake."

At every conference annual meeting, debate swirled around morality and biblical authority, inclusiveness and tolerance. Many speakers stressed that their church was in grave danger, but in quite different ways. Some saw it flying apart and losing its members, some saw it closing in on itself and losing its soul. As always the final resolutions were complex, each with a number of recommendations to General Council. On the ordination question they ranged from Newfoundland and Labrador's barring of homosexual persons from the ministry whether sexually active or not, to Toronto's "sexual orientation in and of itself should be no barrier," without reference to practice. That was as far as any conference would go. Echoing earlier calls, one asked for a church-wide referendum. Three called for further study, not only on the ordination issue but also on the authority and interpretation of Scripture.

Throughout the early summer, the pace picked up. Friends of Affirm organized a campaign in which 450 ordained and lay people paid twenty dollars each to purchase two pages in the May issue of the *Observer.* Their statement called for "a church that is open to all who are drawn by God, and to God, through faith in Jesus the Christ." It concluded that "we must ensure that there are no barriers to ministry based on race, colour, age, disability, economic status, gender or sexual orientation."

The Community of Concern countered with a full-page ad in the June issue of the *Observer*. It would be the first of a series. "We are convinced," it said, "that the Biblical intention for sexual behaviour is loving fidelity within marriage and loving celibacy outside marriage." Would-be supporters were directed to Collier Street United Church in Barrie, Ontario.

Earlier that spring the *Observer* had decided it was time to take the ailing church's pulse. It commissioned national pollster Decima Research Ltd to collect and analyze data from 500 phone interviews with randomly selected *Observer*-subscribing households, coast to coast. The results from seventy detailed questions were published in July. It's clear the Church is getting old, six in ten of its members are over fifty-five. (Among Canadian adults as a whole, the ratio is three in ten.)

The membership is heavily rural and small town. Only fourteen per cent live in cities of over one million people, while thirty per cent of Canadians do. Sixty per cent care a lot more about local concerns than they do about national church issues. Seventy-two per cent agree somewhat or mostly with what they know of national church policies. Twenty-five per cent disagree.

Two out of three oppose practising homosexuals in ordered ministry, but fifty per cent would allow practising homosexuals already in ministry to continue. Two out of three oppose sex outside marriage. The twenty-eight per cent who say yes to practising homosexuals in ordered ministry are likely to be under forty, with higher incomes and more formal education, living in the cities.

Seventy-six per cent of United Church members believe in heaven, and forty-nine per cent in hell.

Commissioners preparing for General Council received their workbooks in advance, containing documentation on the various reports and issues they would have to consider. They also got mail telling them how to vote on The Issue. In Ottawa Rev Sharon Moon had said in public that she believed lesbian and gay candidates for ministry should be considered in the same way as everyone else. For this she got a storm of calls and letters telling her that as a minister she had no right even to hold, much less to voice, such an opinion. Obviously she wasn't reading her Bible, writers said, she was destroying the church, and she would surely burn in hell. Many of the letter writers identified themselves as belonging to other denominations. One concluded, "May Christ judge you." Says Sharon Moon, "Better Christ than you!"

Last-minute attempts at peace-making produced some unlikely partners. Rev Eilert Frerichs is a spokesperson for Affirm, the association of lesbians and gay men in the United Church. In the spring the Very Rev Clarke MacDonald had joined the Community of Concern, the group set up to organize opposition against the March report. The two of them were about as far apart as two people could be in the same church.

But they had worked together for several years, as chaplains at the University of Toronto. They respected each other as serious thinkers and doers of the Word. In conversation over the years they'd covered The Issue, inside and out. Clarke MacDonald had presented to the federal government a United Church brief on human rights that Eilert Frerichs had helped to write. And now despite the fact that both of them had rejected the March report as inadequate and unsatisfactory, more clearly than ever they seemed to represent opposite poles. If the two of them could arrive at a position of mutual trust as Christians, could their church do the same?

The short statement they published says that "sexual orientation in and of itself is not a barrier to participation in the life and ministry of the church, including the order of ministry." "In and of itself" is the phrase to watch here. It comes up again and again. Unlike the Roman Catholic church, the United Church was not born on a rock, but on a verbal tightrope. Its engineers wove three quite diverse, sometimes contradictory philosophies into one constitution, by using language that could be understood in a variety of ways.

For example, the Basis of Union empowers the General Council "to enact such legislation and adopt such measures as may tend to promote true godliness, repress immorality, preserve the unity and well-being of the Church, and advance the kingdom of Christ throughout the world." Each of those phrases sounds sensible and agreeable. But on closer examination they can be understood in quite different ways. Take "repress immorality." To some church members that means barring unrepentant sexually active homosexuals, while to others it means challenging unrepentant business people who get rich by exploiting others. By this kind of elegant verbal balancing act the United Church had managed to stay in one piece – until now.

While Clarke MacDonald doesn't believe that "practising," or sexually active homosexual people should be eligible for the ministry, Eilert Frerichs believes they should be eligible on the same basis as everyone else. By saying "sexual orientation in and of itself," without defining whether sexual orientation included or excluded actual sex, the two of them could agree. And so, they hoped, could their deeply divided church.

In the last few weeks before General Council – her last few weeks as moderator – Anne Squire talked with people whenever and wherever she could about the system of councils by which decisions are made in the United Church. "It's amazing and frightening how little people seem to know about these very important structures in their own church. Of course that makes it much easier for misinformation and paranoia to take hold."

By August all hopes and fears centred on the capital of British Columbia, Victoria. On the shoulders of the General Council commissioners rested the future of the United Church. Until now, like birthdays, these biennial gatherings had marked its sturdy and measured maturing. While it was hard to predict exactly what would happen at any General Council, it had always been clear that beyond each of them the United Church of Canada would carry on, as far into the future as anyone could imagine.

Now for the first time in its sixty-three years, that was far from clear.

CHAPTER 12

A Gift of God

After lunch on Monday, August 15, two days before other commissioners arrived at the University of Victoria, twenty-four brave souls gathered in a small classroom to start work as Sessional Committee Eight. This was a first. Every commissioner to General Council works on one of these committees, responsible for preparing a particular subject or issue for presentation to the whole decision-making body. Other sessional committees meet only after a General Council begins. But no other sessional committee had ever faced such a critical task. And to the media, there *was* only one sessional committee at Victoria – number eight: Sexual Orientations, Lifestyles and Ministry.

The twenty-four agreed to set their chairs in a circle. Few of them had met before. All of them were nervous, and with good reason. They would be venturing into the strange, uncharted territory between sex and the spirit, every inch of it a minefield. Most sessional committees complete their task in about a day's hard work. In this case the members had already been doing homework for two months before they met.

They had waded through the report again and again, as well as the recommendations of the two sponsoring divisions, and a mountain of petitions – more than eighteen hundred of them – which had been passed on to General Council with presbytery and conference votes of concurrence or nonconcurrence attached. They lugged workbooks almost a foot thick into the classroom they would share for the next eight days.

These two dozen people had been chosen to represent a broad cross-section of their church. Overall this would be a much more conservative group than the one that produced the March report. Bill Fulford comes from Morris, south of Winnipeg, where he and his wife run a garden centre and greenhouse business. He grew up working class, went to a conservative evangelical Sunday school, then moved to the suburbs and the United Church. Church is central to his life; in fact he believes his faith impelled him to change jobs. First he worked for a loan company, then for a credit union, which seemed to do less harm. But still he had to make decisions that could make or break local farmers, his friends. Now he works a little closer to the creation, growing things.

In 1982 Bill Fulford and his wife represented their church board at a meeting in Winnipeg, a workshop on sexual orientation and ministry. They were shocked by the liberal views they heard there. "We felt the church was under attack, and our Christian traditions were seriously threatened." So Bill Fulford joined the oppostion, the United Church Renewal Fellowship. Now at his first General Council, he'd been elected by his presbytery. He expected to be odd man out on a liberal-biased committee. He was surprised to find that he wasn't the most conservative person in that classroom, far from it.

Neither was Rev Vera Sampson from St Stephen, a small town on the New Brunswick-Maine border. Brought up United Church, she wandered away for a while, checked out some other denominations, then returned to a church that seemed willing to wrestle, as she was doing, with the role of spirituality in the real world. As a commissioner she felt many pressures, including that of somehow representing her gender. Maritime Conference had sent twenty-seven men and only twelve women to General Council. Of these women, Vera Sampson was the only ordained minister.

When asked in early June to work on Sessional Committee Eight, she balked. This was clearly a no-win situation. About twenty people in her congregation had studied the report. "I was a little surprised how uninformed people were on the subject of homosexuality." Then as a delegate to Maritime Conference she was closely watched when votes came up on The Issue. Ever since, people had been pressuring her to vote right. She received no such pressures on any other issue.

Vera Sampson felt a fierce tension between two conflicting duties. "In my experience most congregations are very centred right where they exist physically. But I don't operate like that. I don't see myself simply as the minister of this particular congregation. I'm also a minister of this whole church of ours." Back home, she sits cross-legged on an old sofa in her office. At her elbow a candle burns, softly scenting the small room. Outside it's raining, and a dog barks. Otherwise it's quiet. "We're one church, and we're one humanity," she says. "Though it's often a temptation, closing ourselves off from the wider community can't be healthy."

Community of Concern member Rev Don Collett was one of the people Bill Fulford found to be more conservative than himself. Son of a United Church minister, "in my teens I kicked the church out of my life, it seemed so irrelevant." He went for a master's degree in political science, but found the spiritual void too great. Ordained in 1981, now he serves a congregation in Taber, a fast-growing community in southwest Alberta. He was astonished when General Council organizers invited him to join the hottest of all the sessional committees. "I've been known as a gadfly, a rebel within the family who's been pretty critical of the Church." Why?

"We seem to be more concerned with being relevant, with adopting the norms of society, than we do with the Scriptures and Christian tradition."

He'd struggled with The Issue since theology school. There he heard of homosexual ministers who had suffered ridicule and been driven out of their congregations. When they got no support from the church that was supposed to be their community, some of them committed suicide. He knew he had been well served by ministers who were homosexual. Yet the Bible told him it was wrong. "It's not God's intention for us. His image of human life is a complementary relationship between male and female. Anything other than that can only be seen as a warp in creation." When the March report came out, he found it "completely off the wall," and joined the Community of Concern to kill it. Now at Victoria he would be in a position to do just that.

Janice Scrutton came to the sessional committee from Hamilton Conference in southern Ontario. It had been the first official body in the United Church to ban "self-declared practising homosexuals" from the pulpit. She grew up Methodist in England, and married a Methodist minister. After doing missionary work in French West Africa they came to Canada, where he became a United Church minister. She teaches primary school and community college, adult upgrading.

She considered the March report "not faithful to the Scriptures," and homosexuality "not according to the moral standards of the Christian church down through the ages. Neither is heterosexual sex outside marriage." Particularly disturbing was the recommendation that homosexual people should be considered for ordination in the same way as heterosexual people. "My objection to practising homosexuals in the pulpit is that they would be living, and therefore, directly or by implication, teaching and/or condoning behaviour which I believe to be wrong according to Scripture and ecumenical Christian tradition." She also believed "the report went against the beliefs of a big majority of United Church people.

We had to stop it, it was as simple as that." To do so, Janice Scrutton had joined the Community of Concern.

She rejects any charge of prejudice. "It is perfectly possible to love, accept, and respect any person without necessarily agreeing that his or her behaviour is also acceptable. Any parent knows that – I have four grown children and at last count two grandchildren, and I certainly can attest that over the years I have loved them all dearly, while at times disagreeing strongly with certain behaviours!" The parent-child model recurs often in love-the-sinner-but-hate-the-sin arguments, based on the assumption that the parent always knows what's best for the erring child.

Marion Best, who chaired the sessional committee, is also a mother. As a child she had attended Baptist Sunday school, then she taught in it until she couldn't stand the biblical literalism or the rigid lifestyle any more. Later through friends in nursing she discovered the United Church; the birth of her first child, "a mystical experience," drew her deeper into faith. She was teaching Sunday school again when the New Curriculum came out. "Suddenly I felt so relieved to know that there really *was* truth in the Bible," she recalls, "that you could find the deeper truths by working at it. Starting to read the Bible in that way was quite an exciting experience for me." Eventually she and her husband gave up their jobs, moved to Naramata in British Columbia's Okanagan Valley, and worked at the United Church lay training centre. Marion Best specializes in helping small groups work together under difficult conditions.

She had worked on a sessional committee at a previous General Council. "It was easy. We dealt with a handful of petitions, we worked for a few hours and that was that." Now she would chair a committee of twenty-four strangers on whose shoulders rested the future of their church. Was she nervous going into that classroom? "I worked for several years as a nurse in an intensive care facility. No matter what happened there, you absolutely had to keep thinking clearly. That was good training." Her greatest fear was that if the sessional committee arrived at a position she couldn't support, as chair how could she present it to General Council?

At ease in her living room overlooking Okanagan Lake, she recalls her own disagreements with the March report. "I can't say for sure what God's intention is for us. There's so much about sexuality in general that's not clear to us yet. Given that, I would have preferred to see something a little more ambiguous in the report." At the same time she believes there's more to sin than sex. "To me, sin is a denial of the power that God gives to each of us. We need to talk more about all kinds of behaviour that's destructive to community, and to the earth we share. This is a time when we have to be questioning, not just handing down decrees that are written in stone."

The sessional committee questioned. For hours and days they questioned, prayed, laughed, cried, argued theology and sex. They fought for hours over single words. The first decision they had to make was how they would work together, by majority vote or by consensus.

Reaching decisions by consensus is basic to Marion Best's faith and work. She leans forward, speaks with a quiet intensity. "As far as I know consensus is the only way to be faithful to where people really are. With parliamentary procedure you get people who know how to use it and people who don't. And when you vote, some win and some lose. What do you do with the people who lose, do you just ignore them?" In consensus decision-making, a decision is only reached when everyone involved can accept it. If one person can't live with it, the process resumes. Even for people who've built mutual trust by working together over time, reaching consensus can be enormously frustrating and time-consuming. Two things this group didn't have were mutual trust and time. But they decided to give it a try. Only if they became hopelessly blocked would they resort to a vote.

Their second decision was to add three corresponding members to their committee, who would participate equally except that they wouldn't vote or take part in consensus decisions. John Howard was the self-declared ex-gay minister who had written one of two dissenting statements with the March report. He was turning into a kind of ex-gay-in-residence. (Since General Council he has left the United Church to set up his own congregation.) In the late seventies Tim Stevenson had been one of the first self-declared gay man to seek ordination in the United Church. He's still trying. Weary after more than a decade of struggle, he declined to tell his story along with the others here. He'll tell it in his own way, in his own time.

The third corresponding member, Alison Rennie, grew up in a Vancouver family much involved with the United Church. At age eleven, she had a religious crisis when they moved to a small town and a small church where she found the quality of worship deficient. "I submitted a proposal to the official board asking that something be done to include kids in the life of the church. I was amazed, it worked! The church started offering an alternative intergenerational service, where families would lead the worship. It's that kind of possibility that's kept me in the United Church, a place where people of all kinds are welcome and valued, and where you can do things." At the same time, Alison Rennie knew she was different, and in a way that would not be quite so welcome.

At university she began to struggle consciously with her feelings, her attractions to other women, and what these might mean to her life as a Christian. Her church seemed to say one thing – everyone welcome, the signs outside many United Churches say – yet in practice the doors were much harder to open. Then she found other lesbian and gay church people, not many but enough that she didn't feel alone. She got a job at the Naramata Centre. "For the first time I knew what it was like to experience unconditional acceptance. Through that I developed a strong sense of calling to do education within the church, to help people think about questions that affect all our lives and to find their creative power."

Marion Best had asked Alison Rennie to suggest lesbian and gay resource people to work with the sessional committee. None of the people she recommended were available or willing to take the potential risks involved in such public work. "Three days before the sessional committee started meeting, Marion Best asked me if I'd do it," she recalls. "I'd spoken at congregational meetings before, but when anything more public came up I always got such a knot in my stomach that I'd have to say no." What could be more public than a General Council in the eye of the media? "But for some reason this time I had no feeling of tension at all. There was just this strong, clear feeling that I was meant to be there."

In one of their first sessions, the members of the sessional committee asked each other a crucial question: What do you need to stay in the church? Alison Rennie said she needed to hear people acknowledge that sexuality is a gift of God, and as such it deserved to be celebrated. "Some of them couldn't do it," she recalls. "Some could say it, but only if sexuality meant heterosexuality. Some of them just couldn't bring themselves to say that homosexuality is a gift of God. That was the most saddening moment for me in our work together."

The sessional committee would bear the brunt of the decision to short-circuit the church's normal petition procedures. All of them had read all the petitions. In them they found a tangled picture. Some petitions were more detailed than others, but most made a series of recommendations, based on a variety of arguments. In effect the sessional committee had to consider a total of six to eight thousand often-conflicting requests.

On top of that they couldn't ignore the judgements of other church courts. The only conferences that supported nearly all the petitions they sent on were the Maritime, and the Newfoundland and Labrador. Sixty per cent of the petitions from congregations asked General Council to throw out the recommendation that "sexual orientation in and of itself is not a barrier." Of twelve conferences only three concurred with this request, all of them east of Toronto. Many presbyteries had also voted nonconcurrence as well. Eight conferences supported requests that homosexuals be welcomed as members of the Church, the other four made no comment on membership. Seven conferences concurred with petitions asking that the present system of ordination be maintained – no doors were to be opened or closed – but five said nothing about these procedures. Six per cent of the petitions asked for acceptance of all the division recommendations on the report, while no conferences concurred with these requests.

If the sessional committee was to remain faithful to the church's conciliar decision-making methods, it would have to take all these impossibly conflicting voices into account.

God help them.

CHAPTER 13

With Faith to Burn

Wednesday, August 17, 1988. Three hundred and eighty-eight commissioners occupied the University of Victoria. The auditorium where they conducted their business sits on a pleasant hill, ringed about by the retirement capital's voluptuous flowers, lawns, and shade trees. For the next eight days in this setting, the commissioners would determine policy for the next two years in the turbulent life of their church. They would eat, sleep when they could, pray, sing, reflect together and alone. They would debate until they were ready to drop and vote on many vital, complex matters. But from the beginning everyone there knew that the unity, perhaps even the survival of their United Church hung on one, only one, of those issues. The Issue.

Looking back on those days is like flipping through a series of snapshots, taken from various angles by people who were there. All these memories are small-frame glimpses into the making of history by ordinary people thrust into extraordinary circumstances. Now we can shuffle through them, and wonder.

Before the actual work began, a commissioner from Halifax toured Victoria. Dorothy MacNeill is a grandmother, born and raised United Church. She wore her thirty-second General Council T-shirt, with arcs of many-coloured rainbow on white. As she walked she kept hearing, usually after she'd passed, "Oh, she must be one of them!" and "You'd think she'd be ashamed to wear that in public, wouldn't you." The arcs of the rainbow are almost circles. From a distance they could be mistaken for a target.

Of the 388 commissioners here, only one was a self-declared homosexual, Tim Stevenson. But there was more than a handful of undeclared lesbian and gay commissioners, some of them ordained ministers with congregations back home. And quite a number of commissioners were self-declared opponents of self-declared homosexuals. Some had announced in public that they would quit the church and take their congregations with them unless the doors were firmly closed.

Commissioner Jean Gibson lives in Victoria with her husband Walter, in a townhouse not far from the university. But she decided she would get more out of General Council if she stayed in residence with the other commissioners. One morning in the washroom a fellow commissioner confessed to Jean that her son, a homosexual, had committed suicide a few years back. Just before she left for Victoria, this woman's husband had told her that if she didn't vote right, she could forget about coming home. What did he mean by right? No homosexuals in the pulpit. Not now, not ever.

Six a.m., Wednesday, August 17. The thirty-second General Council held its first event, in an atmosphere of excitement and hope. Everyone knew it wouldn't last, but why not make the best of it while they could? The journey of reconciliation that began many years ago between the church and its native members would now take a bold step forward. To celebrate its official birth, members of the All Native Circle Conference – the first autonomous union of native congregations in any major Christian church – conducted a sunrise service and ceremonial dance. From a university parking lot sweetgrass smoke curled up into the pale blue sky, an offering.

Elder Edith Memnook acknowledged but didn't accept the 1986 Church apology to native people. The distinction becomes clear in her last statement: "The Native People of the All Native Circle Conference hope and pray that the Apology is not symbolic but that these are the words of action and sincerity. . . . In the new spirit this Apology has created, let us unite our hearts and minds in the wholeness of life that the Great Spirit has given us."

Rev Alf Dumont was received as the first Speaker. In any other conference he'd be called executive secretary, but in this conference things would be done differently, the native way. Alf Dumont and his brother grew up between three worlds. "My mother came out of the native community, and taught us how to think in an open way, the native way. But my father, whose background was Métis, thought in a much more structured way. For us these two blended into our way of looking at the world, and talking about it." All around them was the white world of Christianity.

The two brothers took up Bible study on their own, without curriculum or guidance. "We came to our own natural way of looking at how the universe functioned, and why." Both of them took native studies at university, and both entered United Church theology school. Then one brother chose to explore his native spirituality, but Alf went on to be ordained. Gradually through his years of soul-searching, and then as intermediary in consultations between the church and its native members, he learned how to merge the different streams within himself. "At first I walked around outside the circle, as a kind of convenor. But the circle is very open, so now I consider myself to be fully within it." He learned that growth for the individual is closely tied to growth for the whole community.

Now Alf Dumont faced his first General Council as Speaker of the All Native Circle Conference. Having finally won its autonomy, the new Conference – some forty congregations, about five thousand members – would have to prove to its own members and the rest of the church that it could stand on its own. At the same time it stood within the wider church. Native commissioners faced the same thorny issues as everyone else.

On The Issue, Alf Dumont sees in the Native church as broad a spectrum of experience and attitudes as anywhere else. "People whose way of thinking is shaped by traditional native teachings tend to see both the family and the community as circles in which everyone is welcome. But for others more influenced by the pentecostals it's harder to accept this kind of freedom. They tend to draw more lines." Native congregations had struggled with this dichotomy in forming their own conference; some didn't want to join the circle, instead choosing to remain less autonomous but more secure within their established conferences. Now they would have to go through it again, on The Issue.

The General Council did most of its work in a large, windowless auditorium, with long rows of seats and no aisles. The commissioners sat in groups by sessional committee. To caucus as a region or interest group they had to meet outside between sessions. Visitors sat in the gallery. When The Issue was on, it filled up. Among the invited guests were Muslims, Buddhists, Jews, Catholics, Baptists, Moravians, Anglicans, Unitarians, Presbyterians, and Lutherans, from Canada, Nicaragua, the Philippines, West Germany, Cameroon, and Uruguay. Some had been invited to share their theological impressions of General Council with commissioners caught up in the turmoil. Others were there specifically to observe debate on The Issue. As it had been so often, once again the United Church was a pioneer.

The press had their own room, but hovered everywhere, buzzing. Some commissioners felt the whole world must be watching. In fact a larger portion of it than usual actually was. It was a fight, and it was about sex, forbidden sex at that. Also for United Church people back home, the stakes were high. For others, churchgoers or not, something important was happening here, something about the meaning of God and sex, and the place of church in human life. Did it still have a place? Statistics vary on the religious habits of Canadians. Alberta sociologist Reginald Bibby reported in 1982 that while 90 per cent of people he's surveyed claim affiliation with one of the Christian churches, less than one-third attend regularly. As to the future, three in ten people believe religion will gain in influence, nine in ten believe science will gain. In any case many were watching Victoria, and come hell or high water this church would play out its agony in full public view.

On the afternoon of the second day, Thursday, August 18, the nominees for moderator were questioned, with queries submitted earlier from the floor. All seven were men, all but one clergy. Naturally one of the questions pertained to The Issue. Only one candidate, Rev Morley Clarke of London, clearly opposed homosexual ordination. By now he had retired from the pulpit at Metropolitan United. But he and his wife still lead the marriage preparation courses, and he still does elder training. "The church hierarchy just keeps pushing this thing at us," he says. "They won't take no for an answer. Someone once said that a general who gets too far out in front of his troops is liable to be taken for the enemy. I'd add that it's even more likely if he isn't just out front but way off in left field."

Rev Sang Chul Lee of Toronto told General Council that he was unfamiliar with The Issue and had no opinion either way. He had been convinced that homosexuality was a problem that occured only among white people. But a few days before he left for Victoria, a member of the Korean United Church phoned him, in tears. Her husband, the father of several children, had just told her that he was gay.

The same afternoon, a motion was introduced to make two Affirm spokespeople corresponding members of General Council. At Morden four years earlier, an identical motion had been defeated. This time it carried; Erin Shoemaker and Eilert Frerichs became corresponding members. The following Monday, just as debate on The Issue was getting underway, a Community of Concern motion passed which made Duncan White a corresponding member, as well. A member of the group that created the March report, he had written a dissenting statement against it.

Erin Shoemaker had been waiting a long time for this moment. She grew up in Manitoba, in a United Church family. She went through Sunday school, the youth group, and Canadian Girls in Training – an ecumenical church version of Girl Guides – then led the last two groups, sang in the choir, and played piano for the Sunday school. She married at seventeen, had three children and moved to London, Ontario.

Two years later she and her husband separated. She also abandoned her church, or vice versa. "The church did nothing for me, it made no attempt to reach out to me as a woman leaving her marriage, and leaving my kids with my ex-husband because I couldn't see any other viable solution at the time." Returning west in 1971, she found a welcome in the Saskatoon feminist, peace, and gay movements, and a home with her new lover, a woman. Then in 1983 Sally Boyle invited the two of them to the first meeting of a new group in the United Church, called Affirm. Over the next decade, Erin Shoemaker discovered another kind of United Church, more like the one she remembered from her youth, and once again she became deeply involved in its life.

The year before General Council, Affirm elected Erin Shoemaker and Eilert Frerichs as their designated speakers, to deal with the press and to speak at General Council if they could. It was nerve-racking front-line work, with a particular added frustration for her. Reporters kept asking her if she was a minister. Yes, she tried to tell them at first, the work she did constitutes what church people call lay ministry – so she had been told by others. With degrees in sociology and psychology, she's Executive Director of AIDS Saskatoon. It's the latest of several community-based jobs that she's done. But the reporters weren't interested. Since she wasn't ordained, could she please get them someone to talk to who was?

Finally Erin Shoemaker would have her day in court. Now for the first time in United Church history, lesbian and gay people would be allowed to speak out openly, on their own behalf, in the highest court of their church.

On the third day of General Council, someone asked the Chair to have styrofoam cups removed from the cafeteria. If the church was to take seriously its commitment to the Creation, then how could its representatives continue to use cups that would contribute to the breakdown of the ozone layer? Words were spoken and messages passed. The weary local arrangements commmittee would see what they could do. This was the United Church at work.

Also on the third day, while changes to the *Manual* were being debated, ballots were cast to elect the new moderator. It took five. After the third ballot Rev Morley Clarke, Rev Walter Farquharson from a Prairie congregation, and Rev Sang Chul Lee remained. After the fourth ballot two moderates, Farquharson and Lee, remained. Both had presented themselves as healers. After the fifth and final ballot was counted, the new moderator was named: the Reverend Sang Chul Lee, sixty-four, Korean-Canadian United Church minister and human-rights activist. He confessed to the assembled commissioners, "I'm excited, but at the same time I'm scared!" Outgoing moderator Anne Squire called from her seat, "You should be!"

Commissioner Dorothy MacNeill recalls the moment, "I'm usually proud of my church, but at that moment I was thrilled." She'd voted for Lee, but didn't believe enough of her fellow commissioners would do the same to get him elected. Youth Forum delegate David Moors had scribbled notes on the candidates when they were presented the day before. Of Sang Chul Lee he wrote, "The most human of all."

The new moderator was not scared because of The Issue, he says, but because he was now the spiritual leader of "such a large, very active church that is willing to take heavy responsibilities in society." What kind of responsibilities? "People are easily tempted by greed or power. If we are selfish we can create all kinds of hurt. The church has to remind people how Christ asks us to be, and of the part we should play in the divine order."

A man of slight build with a halo of white hair and beard, Sang Chul Lee is not easily scared. He documents an amazing life journey in his autobiography, co-written with Erich Weingartner. He grew up a Korean refugee, first in Siberia then in China, under brutal Japanese occupation. There he became a Christian, "very pentecostal, trying to forget what the Japanese were doing to my people, trying to think only of heaven. I was so devout I almost became a saint!" But all around him people were being imprisoned, tortured, and executed. "How can you say in the name of God that you don't care?" He feared that he couldn't be a Christian and still care. But then how could he not be a Christian, surely without that foundation his whole life would collapse. "*That* was a very frightening experience," he acknowledges. Later he would find another, broader vision of Christianity, in which there was no separation between the world and the sacred. "The whole world is in His hands." He demonstrates with his own hands, holding them out in a generous cup.

Ordained a Presbyterian in 1954, Sang Chul Lee experienced first-hand the bitter theological struggles that tore the Korean Presbyterian church apart. "Theology has lots to do with history, culture, and even personal experience. Sometimes a theology that works for one kind of person – let's say Calvinism for a Swiss or Presbyterianism for a Scot – might not work for another kind of person in another situation." He joined the United Church in 1964, and believes its unique blend of theologies is worth fighting for. "We have here all kinds of people who are willing to work together, love God together, and seek our way in the world."

As the target of missionaries in Asia, he had also felt the arrogance of Christianity. "The missionaries told us that our culture and our religion were pagan, we had to drop all that if we wanted to be saved." He laughs. "Even the Korean card games we played – they told us if we were going to play cards it had to be western style!" It would take him many years to rediscover the treasures of his background. "Third World theologians have been telling us that long before the missionaries came, God was with us. He doesn't abandon people because the missionaries say so. The Holy Spirit doesn't sit still in this church or that one. She's active and alive. She runs around everywhere." She? When he thinks of the Holy Spirit, he says, that's how he thinks.

Imprisoned and tortured, an exile for most of his life, Sang Chul Lee faced his new challenge as moderator with humility and hope. "My prayer is that my becoming moderator of the United Church of Canada may be seen as a symbol, however insignificant, of God's all-inclusive purpose, a small glimmer of hope that our church, our country, and our world can succeed in living in unity, in peace and with justice for all according to God's will and wisdom."

Throughout that same long day the General Council considered proposed changes to the church *Manual.* While the Basis of Union can be changed only by referendum, the rest of the *Manual* is under constant review, subject to approval by General Council. Commissioner Jean Gibson of Victoria worked on the *Manual* sessional committee, about as far as anyone could get from the drama of The Issue. But in its own way this, too, was a test of faith. The committee had to plough through hundreds of densely printed church bylaws, for example to eliminate all references to "deaconesses and certified churchmen," titles which had been replaced by the gender-free "diaconal minister."

"As I sat there listening to debates on The Issue," she recalls, "I followed along in the *Manual,* especially when we were looking at questions on membership, ordination, and remits [referendums]. I actually started to understand what all that stuff was about!" Jean Gibson has a particular stake in the debate. One of her daughters is a lesbian. She lives with her lover in central British Columbia. Though the daughter isn't a church member herself, her mother can't imagine belonging to a church in which someone like her daughter couldn't belong.

Both she and her husband, Walter, were born and raised in the Salvation Army, that's how they met. But by the mid-sixties they found it suffocatingly dogmatic. "By then our kids were established in their own faith, so we felt it was okay for us to choose ours," says Jean. They tried an evangelical church, then in a kind of quantum leap they tried the United Church, and there they've stayed. It would take Walter Gibson many years to get over the blind acceptance of Scripture that he learned as a child in the Salvation Army. "On the other hand, one of the valuable things we inherited from them is the idea that action is a vital ingredient in faith," he says. "If someone is starving, you deal with that before you start talk about a loving God."

When the March report came out, the session of their own congregation wouldn't touch it, so Jean and Walter Gibson went to a study group at another church. They liked much of what the report said, but by omission it seemed to downgrade marriage. "We've been married over forty years, and our marriage has been a very important experience in our lives." The two of them sit together in the living room of their Victoria townhouse, their retirement home. "We would have liked to see that experience affirmed a little more."

On the other hand, neither of them can see any reason why a sexually active gay man or lesbian shouldn't do as good work in ministry as anyone else. Jean Gibson says, "Our marriage is made of many building blocks. The mortar that holds them all together is a strong, vital sexual experience that we don't share with anyone else. As far as I'm concerned my daughter's relationship with her lover is no different."

What about the Bible? Jean Gibson thinks a moment, then replies carefully, "The Scriptures provide us with a guide for living. They're not infallible. That's the difference between the United Church and the Salvation Army, the difference between a thoughtful faith and blind acceptance. My understanding of God's will is experiential, how could it be otherwise? Many times I've prayed for guidance, and many times I've been answered. But the answers haven't always been what I expected. Surely that's where faith comes in."

During lulls in the proceedings at General Council, Jean Gibson got to know a young woman from the Youth Forum who sat next to her. Now she smiles. "She told me she didn't know what homosexuals were like because she'd never met one. So I showed her the picture of my daughter that I always carry. This is my daughter, I said, and she's a lesbian. The young woman just stared at me. Then she blurted out, 'But she looks normal, and so do you.'" Jean Gibson laughs. She does look normal, a grandmother, a United Church lady.

During these warm summer days in Victoria, other commissioners were trying to get on with other business. It wasn't easy. Rev Roy Demarsh chaired the sessional committee on agriculture, free trade, and the environment. Studying mathematics and physics at university, he found his way to faith through science. "I began to understand the entire universe as a set of interlocking energy systems. This planet earth and in fact all material substance is a vast and marvellous physical energy system. The gift of animate life is another kind of energy system, even less substantial than the atoms and molecules of the material world. Another energy system is human consciousness, the awareness of self and other. None of these happened by accident. So I came to the conclusion that there must be a divine energy or power, which we call God."

As Roy Demarsh understands it, this power is divine grace, or love. "Despite all kinds of evidence to the contrary in the world today – think of how much we're spending on armaments while three-quarters of the world's population starves – still I believe without question that this God, this power of love, is greater than the power of evil." This is a man who had polio as a child, and who has to plan his motions carefully through a Sunday service, so as not to fall. "To act in the name of this power, or of justice," says Roy Demarsh, "that's what it means to be Christian." To him The Issue is purely a matter of justice.

With a few exceptions, his congregation saw it differently. Trinity United in Minto, New Brunswick, serves one of Canada's oldest coal-mining towns. It's a tough place. One elder of the congregation, a military man, said of the self-declared homosexuals who had first sought ordination, "There's only one way to deal with people like that. Take them out and shoot them."

Roy Demarsh had just begun his term as the new elected chair of Maritime Conference when he went to General Council. At home in the manse, along the road from the beautiful little red-brick sanctuary where he serves, he talks about the church's conciliar system, calling it "a limited democracy. It's much more democratic than the Anglican system, where the bishops make all the major decisions. But by intention and tradition in our church, the delegates to any court are not bound to represent the views of the people who elected them. They have to listen very carefully to those views, but as a court they have to seek to understand God's perspective. Anyone who says that congregations can direct how commissioners vote is suffering a serious lapse of faith."

In Victoria he watched as General Council dispatched each of his sessional committee's complex, urgent concerns in no time at all. "The farm crisis – less than ten minutes' debate. I'd been working on free trade for a year and a half. It got ten to fifteen minutes of the commissioners' time. And the environment, probably the most important single issue facing humanity today, the same thing – a few minutes, then we were done." Roy Demarsh frowns and shakes his head. He's not alone in his frustration.

The Division of World Outreach presented a report to General Council that had major theological, economic, and political implications. For decades the church's traditional notion of Christian missions had been breaking down, with the recognition that missionaries had often done more harm than good, and that the "natives" whose souls the missionaries set out to save could teach them at least as much about life, spirituality, and even Christianity as they already knew. The new report urged the church to erase the last vestiges of paternalism and to move into a new relationship with what would now be called its partners in other lands. In effect, it would blur the distinction between missionary and development worker. The title "missionary" has such negative connotations in the field that it should gradually pass out of use. In some cases no such person would be required, perhaps only material aid – this would be the partner's decision. And both women and children would be more involved than ever before in these decisions. This World Outreach report passed with hardly any debate.

Some commissioners believe that another policy paper that was presented at Victoria, *A Place for You*, will have a greater long-term impact than anything the church has done on The Issue. It would expand significantly the role and rights of young people in the church. In a church-wide referendum, a majority of congregations had already rejected an impossibly complicated initiative that would have make it much easier for young people to become full members of the church. Some of its most vocal opponents also led attacks on the various human sexuality initiatives. But since many congregations had already put into practice some of the measures that were turned down in the referendum, the thirty-second General Council directed that a simplified version of the same question be submitted in a new referendum. After cursory debate General Council approved *A Place for You*, with few amendments.

Commissioners joked later that if anyone had wanted to get any really outrageous policies through General Council, this would have been the year to do it. Who would have noticed?

Outside the auditorium, commissioners had access to several information tables. On one side the United Church Renewal Fellowship showed its 1985 video, *Homosexuality: A New Direction*. Next to it was the Community of Concern, where one could still sign the Declaration of Dissent. Next door to that Homosexuals Anonymous offered "a healing ministry for homosexuals," under the auspices of John Howard.

At another table, irreverently decorated with pink balloons, Affirm and its friends served non-alcoholic punch, showed a video that argues for lesbian and gay ordination, handed out a list of answers to often-asked questions about homosexuality and ministry, and sold We Affirm buttons and pink triangles.

A few days into General Council, a gang of noisy American fundamentalists showed up to disrupt the proceedings. A few of them got into the hall. Local arrangements coordinator Rev Bill Howie dealt with them. He persuaded one of them, who seemed to have some authority, to go outside with him for a minute. Then he returned to tell the others, one by one, that the one who was outside wanted to talk with them. Eventually all of them were safely outside the hall, and debate could continue.

How did Howie know what to do? He smiles a little. He used to be a navy chaplain, and this was the method he'd learned to defuse rowdy drunks.

CHAPTER 14

Fear and Trembling

Sessional Committee Eight began each day's work with prayer. At this point twenty-four people from as many backgrounds and positions were searching desperately for common ground. If they could find it, then perhaps so could their beleagured church. And if they couldn't find it in prayer and worship, where could they?

One of those mornings Vera Sampson arrived a little early. She found obscene, violent, anti-homosexual graffiti scrawled across several blackboards, messages that none of the committee members can or are willing to recall. "It made me feel sick that someone would do that. I wanted to rub it off right then, before Alison Rennie or Tim Stevenson could see it." But Marion Best arrived and persuaded her to leave the graffiti.

That morning committee members sat for a while in silence. They said the Lord's Prayer, then they set about their work. "It was a strange feeling, like having your house vandalized," says Vera Sampson. "After that we decided we'd better not leave any of our working papers lying around."

Alison Rennie recalls that the graffiti was shockingly vicious, but for her the memory has faded to a minor detour in an amazing journey. "Working with that sessional committee was probably the most profound experience I've ever had in my relationship with the church. I'd expected that it would be a real trial, a head-to-head encounter with rabid bigots. But just as they did, I got some of my stereotypes blown out of the water. Some of the people who were polar opposites to me in perspective turned out to be some of the people I trusted the most." Before General Council she'd been studying some of Martin Luther's writings, and had been struck by his argument that the failure to assert one's beliefs is a failure to be Christian. "I heard some very conservative people on the committee speaking and demonstrating acceptance in ways I wouldn't have believed possible."

Twice the committee worked through the night, scrambling to find some patch of common ground. They talked and wrote, discarded and rewrote. Fortunately Rev Jim Beal had brought his laptop computer to Victoria. As the only member who had also served on the equivalent committee in 1984, he hadn't been keen to throw himself into the fire once again. But he was persuaded that he could contribute a unique continuity to the committee's work.

Jim Beal also brought five years' experience in human relations work and counselling, as personnel officer for the Bay of Quinte Conference. He ministers to the ministers, people who work under enormous stress. "God in the front office," says one. "That's what the people want." Experienced ministers claim the job calls for these qualities: the patience of Job, the wisdom of Solomon, the endurance of an ox, the voice of an angel, and the skin of an elephant. Almost every minister you ask says if you can get any other kind of work, do.

A rangy, soft-spoken man, Jim Beal admits that he still has remnants of bias against homosexuality. "How could anyone raised in this culture not? It actually helps me in dealing with other people, to know how hard it is to get over that kind of conditioning." In his work he had encountered a number of ministers he knew to be homosexual. "Without exception they're good Christians, faithful to the Gospel and to the church. As far as I can tell, most of their problems come from a culture that tries to force everyone to be heterosexual and get married." In his counselling work all the major sexual and relational problems he had dealt with occured in the lives of married heterosexual ministers.

Next day the sessional committee would face first reading before a General Council that was holding its collective breath. The system of first and second readings was new, an attempt to air in advance each topic that the Council would have to debate. In this case it was particularly crucial.

Finally by about 2:00 a.m., committee members found some basics principles on which they could agree. They concurred with existing United Church statements on marriage, confessed that the Church as an institution had participated in the oppression of lesbian and gay people, urged that human rights legislation for homosexual persons be extended throughout Canada, supported the existing system for ordaining and commissioning ministers, admitted to a lack of knowledge about sexuality in general, recognized the importance of a church-wide study on the authority and interpretation of Scriptures, and saw the need to focus on eligibility for church membership before making a statement on eligibility for ministry.

On the thorniest subject of all, the exhausted members finally abandoned consensus and voted, nineteen to five, that sexual orientation in and of itself should not be a barrier to ordination. The five were not prepared to support the statement without imposing conditions.

On the afternoon of the third day, chairperson Marion Best delivered the committee's progress report to General Council. The hall was hot, quiet, and very tense. One commissioner recalls the petitions piled on a table at the front, "like a mini-Mount Sinai we had to climb before we could see what the promised land might look like."

Marion Best outlined the results of two months' intensive analysis of these petitions, by her and other committee members. She identified the tensions in the process, between trying to be faithful to the church's conciliar tradition and addressing expectations that somehow the petitions, which contained six to eight thousand conflicting arguments and requests, could constitute a referendum. "What happens," she asked her fellow commissioners, "to a *Gift, Dilemma and Promise* which was passed at General Council only four years ago, with some very solid statements about marriage and family life?" She surveyed the hall over her half-glasses. "People who wrote some of these petitions sounded as though we had no policies at all, as if we were proposing an anything-goes kind of morality. What does that mean for us as a council when we labour and struggle and give birth to all these documents, and then congregations never hear of them or choose to totally disregard them?"

This was the one time when Marion Best betrayed a hint of impatience in public. She told the commissioners she didn't have answers to these questions, but surely for the sake of the church they would have to be answered. Then she concluded her report by requesting feedback, in writing or in the discussion that would follow, especially on the most difficult question of all – to ordain or not to ordain. Some of the sessional committee people had wondered whether it should be avoided altogether as too divisive. The General Council would have to decide for itself.

The first reading was a free-for-all without motions, amendments, or votes. Speakers covered most of the spectrum of opinion and all the areas of contention. Rev Stewart Robertson of rural Saskatchewan urged Council to pass the report and get on to more important things. "Our church will not break up or separate over this," he said. "Church union was born on the prairie. And we've withstood all kinds of things there: drought and grasshoppers and students from Eastern Canada." He got one of the few big laughs in the debate.

If the church were to condone homosexuality, Commissioner Morley Clarke said, it would be a disaster. What else might follow: bestiality, necrophilia? Commissioner Jean Gibson recalls her anger. "Either I had to get to the microphone, where I'm sure I would have lost my cool entirely, or I had to get out. So I went outside for a while." Later she told Clarke that she hoped he would have the decency never to say such ignorant, hateful things from his pulpit. "His wife was standing there beside him. They must have thought I was some kind of a wild woman!"

David Paul told the assembly of his dilemma, which others shared. Aged twenty, he was the youngest elder in his church at Almonte, a small town near Ottawa. Many in the congregation had told him to stop homosexual ordination. His minister told him he must vote according to his conscience, but made it clear that could only mean stopping homosexual ordination in its tracks. He came to General Council convinced that homosexuals shouldn't be ministers anyway because they'd make poor role models for young people. As far as he knew he'd never met one.

One afternoon between sessions in Victoria, David Paul was chatting outside with several Youth Forum delegates and a minister from the West. They were talking about sexual orientation and practice. The minister mentioned that until three years ago he'd been married, but since then he'd come to terms with the fact that he was gay – in the language of the debate, a practising homosexual.

"My jaw practically fell on the ground," says David Paul. Tall and lanky, he looks like a college basketball player. "I'd got to know this man at General Council, and I'd been thinking how much I'd like to have a minister like that in our church back home. Then suddenly I find out he's gay. So I started thinking about how God calls people to ministry – if He calls a homosexual, and they have to go through the same process of ordination as everyone else, how can anybody say that's wrong?" But, he told the court, even though he'd changed his own mind he didn't feel it would be right to ignore the wishes of the people back home. He couldn't vote against them. When it came down to it, he would have to vote against himself.

Some commissioners recounted personal experiences to make their points. Rev Brian Thorpe of Deep Cove, British Columbia, told the hushed auditorium, "In the early years of my ministry, I was called to a hospital room where a woman was dying. Another woman cradled her friend's head in her arms and stroked her hair." His voice cracked as he reconstructed the image. "They'd been together for over thirty years, they'd been strong church people and faithful disciples of Christ. Now here they were practising their relationship in front of me. I don't know what went on in their bedroom, just as with the straight members of my congregation I don't know. But I saw that expression of love between those two lesbians as a gift, a vehicle for God's grace." He asked the other commissioners not to shut out the possibility of doing the same.

Later in the proceedings Brian Thorpe would challenge Morley Clarke for claiming that AIDS proved homosexuals were unsuited for ministry in God's church. Others remember his intervention as blazing with anger but under control. "It was one of the most offensive things I'd ever heard," he recalls. "AIDS is no more a gay disease than sickle-cell anaemia is a black disease," he told General Council. "And no one has been more conscientious in combatting AIDS than the gay community."

Away from General Council and in retrospect, Brian Thorpe speaks of his church with some sadness. He grew up and was ordained in Saskatchewan, a province that's spawned many populist movements and a consistently progressive conference of the church. He had come to General Council as chairperson of a relatively liberal presbytery, Vancouver-Burrard. "I guess I'd been pretty naïve about the United Church. Somehow I'd assumed that the bigots and the literalists would have left already, to other churches that would offer them more attractive homes." He corrects himself. "I should say selective literalists. They don't seem at all concerned with what the Bible has to say about economic justice, peace and war, or any of that – only sex."

Standing on the deck of his home, set among towering West Coast firs, he traces the links between sex and spirituality. "In my experience, when people have a sense of wholeness about themselves – including their spiritual and sexual selves – it reveals itself in their willingness to be open and vulnerable. On the other hand when people are rigid and closed about everything else, it often seems to indicate that their sexuality's repressed or distorted. Such people tend to be intensely competitive, they have to win – even in their religion. They have to be holier than thou."

That same evening at General Council, the outgoing moderator delivered her parting sermon. She recalls the standing ovation she received that night as one of the most moving experiences in her life. Anne Squire's two-year term had probably been the most difficult in the sixty-five-year life of the church. This would be the first and the last chance she would have to speak to the church's highest court.

She talked about her United Church; what she'd learned about it, and what hopes she had for it. She had learned "that some of our members spend half of the time crying for leaders, and the other half nailing them to the cross." In hundreds of scheduled meetings and thousands of informal conversations, she had encountered "a depth of faith and breadth of vision that lift my spirits, and a superficiality of faith and an intolerance that shatters my image of what a Christian is."

Wearing a white robe and a dark stole, she set before the commissioners a series of questions on the most contentious issue that faced it. "The question is whether we in the church can accept the ministry of gays and lesbians," she said, "or whether we can tolerate erecting barriers to ministry." Quoting from the Basis of Union, which names no such barriers, she asked the commissioners "whether we plan to change that Basis of Union to place limitations on those whom Christ may call. The question is also whether we can close our eyes to the kind of suspicion that is already wrecking the careers of all suspected gays and lesbians, which in essence means all single candidates and indeed all single members of the order of ministry."

She asked General Council to consider how the United Church understood and interpreted Scripture, how it defined sin, whether it could learn to live with changing family patterns, whether it could learn to define human morality in more than simply genital terms. For Anne Squire the ultimate question was simple, "whether we as a church will be an inclusive or an exclusive body." As she reads it, the Bible records a long, tortuous journey "in which God has been continually pushing and prodding a stubborn people into communities that were more inclusive," from the concept of a chosen people, a people set apart, to the idea that all people are God's people. To be faithful, she said, the United Church must continue on that difficult journey.

With feedback in hand, including seventy-five written responses, the sessional committee retired to its classroom to begin again – not from scratch, but close enough for its weary members. For Jim Beal the process of first reading and feedback was crucial to their work, "It saved us from feeling we were operating in a vacuum." At least now they had a clearer picture of how the thirty-second General Council might react.

Until then Vera Sampson had felt only "fear and trembling" about the outcome. She had called home in New Brunswick to see how people were reacting to the election of a Korean-Canadian as their new moderator. "Apparently they were freaking right out. Oh oh, I thought, this doesn't sound good!"

The feedback that the committee received ranged from very negative to very positive. "I don't really know why," Vera Sampson recalls, "but probably for the first time in this whole process I actually started to feel hopeful that something good for the church might come of it." They'd already clarified and tested some of their assumptions. There was no question that the Council wanted to, or rather that most commissioners believed they had to, deal with the ordination question. Somehow over the next two days the sessional committee would have to produce a statement as broad and complex as the United Church itself.

Saturday night several members of the committee felt inspired to create a statement based on that year's General Council theme, the church as covenant community. The covenant was an undertaking to work together, to seek God's will and to act upon it. They worked through most of the night, and at breakfast the next morning they showed the results to the chairperson. They said they'd been moved by a charismatic experience, an encounter with the Holy Spirit. As Marion Best recalls it, the statement recommended blanket acceptance for homosexual people. She asked its authors if they could imagine presenting it to their congregations back home. Unnerved, they presented it to the rest of the committee instead. There, in an odd reversal of roles, the more liberal members found themselves diluting and rendering less radical the work of the self-declared conservatives.

While debates proceeded on other matters before General Council, intense strategy sessions about The Issue were taking place elsewhere. Self-declared liberal evangelical Clarke MacDonald, self-declared gay man Eilert Frerichs, and self-declared conservative evangelical Jim Somerville, a Community of Concern leader, met in the cafeteria to hammer out a definition of sexual orientation. "Sexual orientation in and of itself," an ambiguous term, could function equally well as a bridge or a barricade. But what did orientation include? Fantasies? Sexual acts? Relationships? The question wouldn't go away. The three men produced a handwritten two-page document that says, "We understand orientation to mean the natural inclination and direction of a person's sexuality." "Natural" is bracketed, and "given" written over it. Then "direction" is bracketed and "expression" written over it. Each of the words is loaded with possible and significant meanings. The document is another United Church verbal balancing act.

Frerichs took the draft to Affirm, and Somerville took it to the Community of Concern. Neither group found it to be workable. "It was ridiculous," says Frerichs, looking back. "All by ourselves the three of us were trying to save the church. Surely if it's up to anyone to save the church, it's up to God."

Another attempt to find common ground – any common ground – was a joint breakfast meeting of about thirty people from "the two sides," Community of Concern and the Renewal Fellowship on one side, Affirm and Friends of Affirm on the other. No one who was there can recall now what was said or what was eaten. Was it a waste of time? Certainly not, says one of its organizers, Clarke MacDonald. "It didn't achieve what we hoped it would, but I never think anything's a waste of time that is done at the behest of what the church needed at that time, and – I'll be pious enough to say – at what we believed to be God's will at the time. Nothing like that is ever wasted."

Sunday evening, August 21, the church installed its new moderator. This would be one of the few moments at General Council when commissioners could turn their attention from struggle to celebration. Members of the Vancouver Korean United Church choir sang, former moderator Bruce MacLeod preached a rousing sermon, then Children at Council and the Youth Forum presented gifts to the Very Reverend Sang Chul Lee. His wife – or spouse, to use inclusive language – Shin Jah Lee, joined him to receive best wishes from six former moderators.

Back in their classroom, Sessional Committee Eight laboured on through their last night together. First they shed a heavy burden they'd been carrying. Based on the feedback they had received, they decided that instead of asking the commissioners to vote on the March report, which had been the target of so much rage, they would draft an entirely new one.

Community of Concern member Rev Don Collett remembers the long trek. "I've never in my life worked with a more dedicated group, with people who were more committed to the survival and health of their church." One of his contributions to the document late that night were some thoughts on "the overemphasis on sexual sins in our society. There are all kinds of sins that are much worse. But few of them seem to have as powerful an emotional impact as sex."

Their search for answers led them back to the church's founding document, the Basis of Union. Vera Sampson recalls their route. "The vast majority of petitions asked us not to change the existing process for selecting ordained and commissioned ministers. That process is clearly set out in the Basis of Union. It isn't the role of General Council to say yes or no to any candidate for ministry. That power and responsibility has always been in the hands of each individual congregation, and there it should remain."

Jim Beal had to walk back and forth repeatedly from the classroom to the computer room, where he printed out the latest efforts of the committee from his laptop computer. On each of these journeys he would pass through the press room. "Each time I went through there I was carrying exactly what they wanted to get their hands on. But none of them ever noticed me." He grins, the successful conspirator. Like many other commissioners, he experienced the hovering press as more of a nuisance than anything else.

Members of the sessional committee had written up three different statements on the blackboard, now cleaned of graffiti. None of the statements was quite right. Marion Best recalls, "Someone – I don't remember who – went up to the board and somehow combined all three of them into one. We looked at it, we went round the circle, we made changes here and there, and then eventually everyone said they could live with it. We recognized that parts of the statement were ambiguous, but what else could we do in a church like ours?"

She also recognized the dangers of decision-making at three in the morning, by exhausted people working under terrific strain. She suggested committee members sleep on it, and see if their consensus still held after breakfast.

Apparently it did. In an unusual move, the members decided that Marion Best shouldn't be alone on the platform to present their collective work. They would all be there. They also agreed that from this point on, the statement – *Membership, Ministry and Human Sexuality* – would no longer be theirs. It would belong to General Council, to make of it and do with it what the commissioners would. As commissioners themselves, each of the people who had conceived the new statement would now be free to react to it as they saw fit.

The committee's last decision concerned its corresponding members – should they, too, be present on the platform? As they had done before, Alison Rennie and Tim Stevenson withdrew from the circle while the others worked through the question to consensus. (John Howard had left the committee for other commitments.)

The decision: They had come this far together. They would complete the journey together.

CHAPTER 15

On the Seventh Day

After a short break in the afternoon of the seventh day, the main event began.

The twenty-four members and two corresponding members of Sessional Committee Eight sat in two rows on the platform, facing their fellow commissioners. A few minutes before, Alison Rennie had been waiting outside the auditorium, waiting to go on with the others. She was fearful. "I'd checked out the platform that morning. It was very brightly lit, for the cameras, so you couldn't see very much out there in the hall. We'd heard rumours about busloads of fundamentalists coming down from Nanaimo to break things up. I was standing there waiting. Suddenly these two kids ran in the door with submachine guns pointed at me. I thought this is it, it's really happening!" But the kids were local, and the guns were toys. It was time for Alison Rennie to join the others on the platform, and face the hall.

Each commissioner had a copy of the new statement. Speakers would be allowed three minutes each. They would line up at microphones and hold up coloured cards to indicate on which side of the debate they would speak: green meant pro, red con, and yellow a point of privilege, or a challenge of debating or voting procedure, which took precedence. These cards allowed the moderator to indicate order of speakers, balancing pro and con. At each speaker's turn in front of a microphone, a spotlight came on and the cameras hummed. While church staff recorded everything, the news cameras selected the hottest speakers, the ones who made colourful points in thirty-second sound bites.

Within minutes the first shot was fired by the Community of Concern, a motion to define sexual orientation so as to exclude practice for all but the heterosexually married. The man who moved it, Rev William Wan of the Chinese United Church in Ottawa, quit the church soon after General Council. Community of Concern speakers argued that they needed a clear definition to take home to their constituents, one that excluded practice. They were defending the family, they said, which they believed to be in danger. As Bill Fritz puts it, "If you have an ethic that downgrades marriage and family life, then I can see on the horizon fragmentation and fracturing of families. I think if the family deteriorates and is no longer the norm, society as a whole will suffer. That's the price we'll pay for condoning homosexual practice."

Affirm spokesperson Erin Shoemaker told the commissioners that indeed orientation implied practice. When celibacy was enforced it wasn't a gift of God, she said, it was a punishment that limited the wholeness of being. Given the explosive nature of the question, why didn't she – or Affirm – leave it ambiguous? "We were afraid of being sold down the river, like the Anglicans who've settled for a double standard (marriage for some, celibacy for others). Many lesbian and gay people in the church are in relationships, and it's safe to say that many are sexually active. Why should we have to choose between our partners and our church? Why should we have to choose between our wholeness as human beings and our church?" As Erin Shoemaker spoke, her partner, Sally Boyle, listened from the gallery.

On the Council floor, Commissioner Brenda Ferguson also felt a particular vested interest in this question. Celibate by choice, she ministers to two small rural congregations in southern Manitoba. Her father was Catholic, her mother Anglican. As a child she attended Baptist and then evangelical churches, but quit at age twelve. When her brother was killed in an accident, Brenda Ferguson found that she needed church. In the United Church she found support, acceptance, and a new kind of freedom. These days she sees the boundaries of that freedom being tested, as church members struggle with abortion, inclusive language, and The Issue.

Before she went to General Council, many people told her she had to kill the March report. She herself had no great investment in it. In fact she felt it had gone too far, that people were nowhere near ready for the kind of recommendations it made. At the same time she believed that her duty as a commissioner was "to consider each issue in the light of my faith as a United Church person and the collective wisdom I would encounter at General Council."

Brenda Ferguson decided long ago that if she was to be a minister she wanted to devote all her time and energy to it. She would not marry and she would not have children. And as a single person she would not have sex. Genital sex, that is. "In the 1980 human sexuality report we learned that our sexuality is a very basic part of who we are, it's part of everything we do." As she speaks she's doing needlepoint, a rural scene. "Even in this – you can express your sexuality in anything you do. But if sex is something you only do in bed, that isolates and restricts it."

While she believes in celibacy for people who aren't married, and in particular for people in the order of ministry, she doesn't believe it should be imposed. For her it's a charism, a gift she accepted from God. "In one way it's the standard that

God sets for me, and in another way it's what I've chosen for myself." The way she talks, they sound like the same thing.

"As what might be called a practising heterosexual," Rev Ken Gallinger from Richmond Hill, Ontario, told the other commissioners he'd been puzzling over the difference between sexual orientation and practice. "My wife and I live together in the manse. Is that practice? If two men live together in the manse, is that practice? That's what I keep hearing. Nancy and I frequently enter church holding hands. Is that sexual practice? We're sharing an apartment with three kids, so I guess that's about as close as we get!" Laughter rippled through the hall – recognition, relief? He went on. "Now if two gays walked in here holding hands, would that be practice, when it's not for Nancy and me? When I can't figure this out for my own life, I don't see how I can ask a committee to come up with some kind of a restrictive definition."

Two questions came up again and again in this first round of debate. First, were homosexuals to be dealt with as equals or not? Second, to what degree should the church be regulating sexuality in general and homosexuality in particular? The government had removed itself from the bedrooms of the nation two decades back. Was the church now to take its place? Absolutely, said some. Absolutely not, said others, and the rest were somewhere in between. A majority of commissioners defeated the Community of Concern's motion, and sexual orientation wasn't defined.

Then began the first of many COC attempts to shoot down the main target in the statement, point three. In two parts, point three affirmed existing conditions for membership in the church, specifying that these should apply regardless of sexual orientation, as well as existing conditions on eligibility for ministry. The COC's first motion proposed separating the two parts. Together, the two parts made it harder to accept homosexuals as members but block them from ordination. People who opposed dividing the motion saw it as faithful to the church's stand on ministry of the whole people. Separate standards, they argued, shouldn't apply to lay members and ordained ministers. The motion was defeated.

Two members of Sessional Committee Eight moved that the March report, *Toward a Christian Understanding of Sexual Orientations, Lifestyles and Ministry,* be shelved. The motion passed. Most commissioners, regardless of their own feelings about the report, were greatly relieved. BJ Klassen, chair of the group that produced it, watched from the gallery as General Council debated how far to the back of the shelf it should be pushed. Was she disappointed? "By how the report was received and used, yes. Especially the accusation that we'd ignored theology. We thought the report was theologically very sound, but we avoided using academic language. We wanted to speak to people's own experience, not tell them what to think."

Whatever happened to it, she says, the exercise of producing and reacting to the March report clarified many issues which the church had to face sooner or later. "My philosophy of education is that there's no point in redoing these things, you might as well start fresh. This was an entirely new group at General Council, with its own dynamics and its own process." As a resource person she sat through the sessional committee's forty hours of wrangling, responding only when asked and then only to questions about the making of the original report. In her Emmanuel College office a year later, it's clear that she has moved on to other things. A student knocks at the door – usually it's open. They make an appointment, and she resumes. "It was nerve-racking to go through it all again, but it was also a privilege to watch those people work, to see how they struggled faithfully with the same dilemmas that we did."

The sessional committee presented their report to General Council in three stages. Since the March report had been lambasted for not paying enough attention to marriage, the new statement didn't make the same mistake. It affirmed Christian marriage at length, quoting verbatim from several statements that had been set into church policy at earlier General Councils. But by now some commissioners were so geared up for the attack, they wanted to change even those earlier statements, to rewrite history. After it was made clear that this couldn't be done quite so easily, debate proceeded on the confessional statement.

In the tradition of such documents, the first part set out the grounds, theological and otherwise, that led to the recommendations. In essence it argued that if we believe these things, then it's only right that we should be doing these other things. But in this case the committee acknowledged "our inability at this time, given our diversity in our understanding of the authority and interpretation of Scripture, to find consensus regarding a Christian understanding of human sexuality, including homosexuality."

Two Community of Concern members moved to add a line to the statement, that God expected fidelity from married people and "celibacy, chastity, sexual abstinence and continence" from everyone else. After discussion this was defeated. Earlier, at a press conference, Affirm spokesperson Eilert Frerichs had predicted both the motion and its defeat. The majority of heterosexual commissioners, he told reporters, wouldn't stand for such restrictive rules. For homosexuals perhaps, but for themselves, certainly not.

Then an attempt was made to remove from the confessional statement all references to injustice against gay and lesbian people, as well as a line that acknowledged their contribution to the church. One of the men who moved this last amendment was Leander Mills of Saint John, New Brunswick. He and his colleagues in the Community of Concern could see that such an acknowledgement might lead to acceptance. But their motion was defeated.

The commissioners went off to supper, gathering in discrete groups but crowded together in the cafeteria. In the auditorium, someone replaced the candle that would remain lit throughout General Council, next to the open Bible on a lectern, always in full view at the front of the platform.

When debate resumed after supper Leander Mills tried again, this time seconding an amendment to kill the entire confessional statement. This, too, was defeated, as were a flurry of other amendments to water it down. To orchestrate these manoeuvres, the COC leaders strategized continuously. Other commissioners recall seeing them run out of the hall, across the gallery, and back again, again, and again.

One amendment that the Council did accept indicates how complex the word games became in this debate. The original sentence was candid and reasonably straightforward: "We confess that we have refused to recognize and appreciate the effective participation of our Christian gay and lesbian brothers and sisters in all aspects of our church's life, including the Order of Ministry." It followed the tradition of the church's 1986 apology to native people.

After an unsuccessful attempt to throw this out, finally it ended up: "We confess that we have not all responded to the acclamation of appreciation of the effective participation of our Christian gay and lesbian brothers and sisters in all aspects of the Church's life, including the Order of Ministry, declared at the 30th General Council." This elaborate formulation would give permission to those who wished to maintain a clear conscience. It was moved by Rev Heber Elliott of Portugal Cove, Newfoundland.

Born in a Newfoundland outport, Heber Elliott taught school in Labrador for several years before choosing instead to work with adults in a faith community. Ordained to the United Church at age thirty-four, now he serves two congregations on Conception Bay. The population of Bell Island shrank from twenty thousand to five thousand after the iron ore mines there were shut down in the late sixties. Only twenty-seven United Church families remain. But the congregation in Portugal Cove is growing, it's a bedroom community for St John's, a little to the southeast.

Heber Elliott came to General Council with a clear sense that he was to vote down any attempt at permitting homosexuals into the pulpit. "The Portugal Cove congregation had already had one homosexual minister," he says. "He declared himself on TV after he'd left here for the mainland. The people were quite upset when they heard that. At the same time they realized that he'd been working here among them, they hadn't known, and his work was good. It was a bit of a quandry for some of them." Nevertheless the majority concluded that even though sexuality was a private matter, "certain moral standards had to be maintained, particularly for the clergy."

A few more amendments were made to the final section of the confessional statement. Given General Council's mounting anxiety to produce a statement that might fly back home, these changes affirmed marriage yet again, twice within the same short sentence, as if married people were an endangered species. Then the full confessional statement passed.

In the gallery Sally Boyle wept, as did other lesbian and gay members of the church. In a series of steps since 1985 she had come out – or self-declared – before two small Saskatchewan congregations. It cost her both ministries. Now she works as a hospital chaplain in Saskatoon and enjoys the work. But still she wants more than anything else to be in pulpit ministry, it's where she belongs. Why then did she reject the closet that so many other ministers accept? Isn't the cost of coming out too great? "I found the cost much greater in not doing it. I don't know how we can describe to folks how hard it is to hide one of the most significant parts of ourselves all the time, to hide who we truly are and who God created us to be."

For the next round, which everyone knew would be the even more bitter, Moderator Sang Chul Lee asked former moderator Clarke MacDonald to take over the chair. The new moderator feared he might make errors in a job he'd just entered the night before, keeping track of speakers at several microphones, points of order and privilege, and amendments piling on amendments in the hottest debate of any General Council in decades. Clarke MacDonald was an interesting choice. Of several former moderators present, he was not only an experienced chair but also the best-known opponent of the recently shelved report.

After a ten-minute break – for toilet, coffee, prayer, a moment outside in the flowered evening air, or frantic strategizing – the Council heard the committee's recommendations. Now reporters who had been lulled by the intricate verbiage of the earlier debate snapped to attention. Through all the reports, studies, and debates over the years, no matter how complex and tangled were the issues of sexuality, theology, society and politics, this question had remained the one central, abiding obsession – should homosexuals be allowed into the pulpit? On this question, many had come to believe, The United Church of Canada would stand or fall.

Section three said, in Part A: "That all persons regardless of their sexual orientation, who profess Jesus Christ and obedience to Him, are welcome to be or become full members of the Church." Part B said, "All members of the Church are eligible to be considered for the Ordered Ministry." The commissioners had already voted not to separate the two parts. The Community of Concern now moved to dump "regardless of sexual orientation."

Two years before, Margaret McPherson of Winnipeg had moved that the executive delay any further debate on The Issue until the church was better prepared for it. It couldn't be done, the executive didn't have the power. Now she was a commissioner, trying to decide whether or not to drop "regardless of sexual orientation" from the statement. She voted to cut it. "As far as I'm concerned when you say all persons are welcome, all means all. You don't have to qualify it." Later she would change her mind. Speaking in the precise tone of a former schoolteacher she says, "It turned out that to many people all doesn't mean all. I can't imagine what it does mean to them, but it certainly doesn't mean all."

Commissioner David Paul told the assembly that he had changed his mind again. Earlier he had said he couldn't vote contrary to the wishes of so many folks back home. Now he said he must. He had come to realize that for the church to close its doors on good potential ministers, just because they were homosexual, would do more harm than good. It wouldn't be right.

The atmosphere was so tense that the Chair asked commissioners to sit in silence for fifteen seconds before they cast their votes. After the silence, 160 voted to dump the "regardless" phrase, and 205 to retain it. This time several commissioners asked for a list to be circulated so they could record their dissenting votes, presumably for posterity. The rest of the voters on either side chose to remain anonymous. Of the sixty-one commissioners who signed the dissenting list, twelve were women.

In the next move, COC chairman William Fritz seconded a motion to delete section three entirely. Two commissioners from Ottawa announced that if this motion were defeated they would move for a church-wide referendum on the subject. It was. Then there followed a flurry of motions. One that would require "faithfulness in relationship which can only be expressed by two persons living in commitment to each other which is intended for life" was defeated. Another motion to replace the already approved section three with a new wording that excluded "regardless of sexual orientation," was ruled out of order by the chair, since the court had already voted to include the phrase.

Throughout this long, intricate debate Marion Best had been trying to be a peacemaker, doing a kind of Henry Kissinger shuttle on and off the platform. But she was getting increasingly distressed. "I watched all this procedural wrangling going on, a whole hour of it, with all these yellow cards being waved on points of personal privilege, mostly by male clergy." Recounting it a year later, her voice still rises with distress. "I kept thinking, is this how we've learned to make decisions? We were dealing with the life of our church!"

Imagining that she could somehow save her church, while the debate raged Marion Best negotiated privately for several hours back and forth between coc chairman Fritz and Affirm spokesperson Frerichs. She tested possible amendments, changes in wording, anything that might make peace. "One of them would agree to something, they'd check it with their respective group and then they'd tell me it wouldn't work. I guess I was pretty naïve about politics."

Earlier, one of the sessional committee members had suggested a Scripture reading, Psalm 131. At this point Marion Best sat down and read it: "Lord, my heart is not lifted up, my eyes are not raised too high; I do not occupy myself with things too great or too marvellous for me. But I have calmed and quieted my soul, like a child quieted at its mother's breast; like a child that is quieted is my soul."

Calmed and quieted, Marion Best spoke briefly to the Council, on the motion before it, to take an immediate vote on section three. The current wording, she said, was the very best the sessional committee could produce "with integrity and faithfulness." The motion carried. But before the vote could be taken, two COC commissioners moved to adjourn until next morning. Their motion was defeated. The majority of commissioners were determined to have it out then and there. The vote was taken, section three carried, and "regardless of sexual orientation" stayed in.

Journalists raced off to tell the world that the United Church had thrown open its pulpits to gay ministers.

A little after midnight Moderator Lee resumed the chair. Members of the Youth Forum gave their impressions of the day's debate. The Youth Forum is a kind of junior General Council, with its own parallel sessional ommittees. The ninety-five youth delegates at Victoria were corresponding members, with the right to speak but no vote. Some commissioners resented even that much say for a group they would prefer be seen and not heard. One commissioner called them "a noisy, uncontrollable mob."

They presented to the assembly a prepared statement on homosexual ministers as role models. Gen Creighton is eighteen. She worked on the Youth Forum sessional committee that dealt with The Issue. "We young people are supposed to conduct our lives according to these role models," she argues at her home, half-way up a mountain in North Vancouver. "But when did anyone ever ask us what we want our role models to be like? For myself I'd pick people who are caring and compassionate, people who don't just talk at you but really listen as well. Sexual orientation has nothing to do with it. For my kids the last person I'd want is a bigot, a person with a closed mind."

Since childhood Gen Creighton, like both her parents, has been deeply involved in the life of her church. She worked a summer at the United Church lay training centre in Naramata and served as a delegate to British Columbia Conference. She's also a member of the local board at Highlands United. "Whenever I say anything at a meeting the older people just nod and smile at me. It's pretty obvious they aren't listening."

She doesn't believe that God sits up on a throne in heaven. "God works through community, that's the whole point of having a church. Otherwise why not go off by yourself and have your own private thing with your own private God?" Under a wide-brimmed sun hat, her brow creases with annoyance. "I don't understand people who want the church to be a little club where only they can belong and someone else can't. I think that's very childish."

Long after midnight, many of the commissioners were wilting with fatigue. Graham Scott and William Fritz tried one last time to prescribe boundaries. They moved to insert into the statement, "in light of Holy Scripture our ideal for all being both faithfulness in marriage and faithful abstinence while single." The motion was defeated.

Why did the majority of commissioners defeat so many of these attempts at drawing lines? Graham Scott believes they had a vested interest. "A surprisingly large number of our clergy and lay people either live rather loose lives themselves, or they know someone who does." In his church office in suburban Burlington, Ontario, he says, "Some of them are divorced and living with someone, in other words they're living in sin. Naturally that would dispose them to an anything-goes kind of morality. I believe there were enough of these people at General Council to tip the balance."

Two commissioners moved to adjourn until morning. An amazing 118 others voted to continue working. But the motion carried, and at 2:25 a.m. the court adjourned.

CHAPTER 16

The Promised Land?

Wednesday, August 24, the eighth day. One more, then the commissioners could return home. Home to cities, towns, and congregations across the country where already the headlines had hit: UNITED CHURCH COUNCIL VOTES TO ORDAIN HOMOSEXUALS. UNITED CHURCH REJECTS CALLS TO AFFIRM "TRADITIONAL" VALUES ON MARRIAGE, SEX. POLICY WILL DRIVE PARISHIONERS FROM CHURCH.

Janice Scrutton, of Sessional Committee Eight, made the first move. Committee members had agreed among themselves that as commissioners they would be free to vote on the statement as they saw fit. Now she told General Council, "On some points our consensus was only reached because our statements were incomplete and unqualified, trusting the floor of council to amend and amplify or qualify." She continued, "However, since General Council in its wisdom has seen fit not to qualify or amplify the document by holding up a standard of fidelity within marriage and self-controlled abstinence – or some similar definition – in singleness, for my own integrity I feel the need to distance myself from the document and say I could no longer agree to consensus."

Marion Best made the second move, proposing to amend part of the statement the commissioners had already approved. Further reworded, it read: "that all Christian people are called to a lifestyle patterned on obedience to Jesus Christ." With this sentence the peacemakers hoped to build a bridge as wide as their church. The amendment passed.

Suddenly Leander Mills interrupted debate to call for fifteen seconds of silence for "those in pain and hurt." Then, with another commissioner from the Maritimes, he boycotted the remainder of the debate. He told the press outside that he was going to quit the United Church and probably take his Saint John congregation with him.

The majority of commissioners supported a motion to consign the March report to the archives. Since it didn't reflect "the present position of the United Church of Canada," it would become "an historic document." One of its authors, Dr Pam Brown, watched from the gallery as her work disappeared. She felt no regrets. "Whatever happens to it, we can still say that we created it. And there is no reason whatsoever to be ashamed of anything in it." General Council actually turned out better than she expected, she explains back home in Halifax. "From the sheer wielding of power I saw there by the Community of Concern, I thought they'd kill any chance for an inclusive policy. The new statement didn't really change anything, but at least it forbid the exclusion from our church of one whole group of people."

Sections of the statement were passed to affirm the present selection process for ministry, leaving the decision to the individual congregations. Next up was another section affirming that it was "inappropriate to ask about sexual orientation of those in the candidacy process, or those in the call/appointment/settlement process." Jim Somerville of the COC argued that unless orientation was defined for the committees that select ministers, "There's going to be discrimination against single members of the order of ministry. None of us would consider that appropriate." How would they know who was homosexual and who wasn't? Others argued that selection committees shouldn't be discriminating like that in the first place. The section passed. In a rage, Graham Scott ripped his shirt.

Alison Rennie listened to this verbal tinkering with some dismay. "I found all the procedural wrangling very frustrating, all the attempts to block good discussion. But when the issues were really addressed, the work that we'd done in the sessional committee seemed to have an effect on the court, signalling the direction that our church was going to take." She'd seen this one-step-forward-two-steps-back process before, in the women's movement, and wasn't discouraged. "Wherever the General Council went with it now, I knew how far we'd gone in the sessional committee. I knew that it could be done."

Another section passed that called for further study and dialogue on The Issue and urged the whole church to counter discrimination against homsexual persons inside and outside the church. A few more rewordings and changes of order carried, more attempts to head off negative reactions back home.

An eleventh hour amendment added to one of the new statement's many affirmations of marriage "the charism of celibacy, and the way of chaste singleness." Charism means gift. It's a classic United Church balancing act. The movers of the addition hoped it would incorporate at least some of the concerns they had heard from people in the pews, but at the same time avoid dictating that celibacy or chastity is the only permissible sexual behaviour for people who aren't married.

At some point in all this tortuous manoeuvring, Clarke MacDonald told the court that, though the new statement wasn't perfect, it had reached a point where he could live with it. In a voice that rings with easy authority he told the court, "I believe that what we have before us is the nearest we can come to honouring statements of the past, to honouring the appeals and petitions of the church, and to honouring the rights of persons regardless of their sexual orientation." Since Clarke MacDonald wasn't a commissioner he couldn't vote, but commissioner Ed Bentley recalls that the former moderator's words hit the assembly "like a wave. You could hear something like a sigh go through the hall, people were so relieved."

Then a vote was called on the whole statement, as amended. As usual it would be a show of hands. A variety of eyewitnesses – commissioners, observers and journalists – estimate that two-thirds to three-quarters of the commissioners voted in favour. The moderator turned down a request for a vote count, calling the majority clear and substantial. Seventy-one commissioners asked that their names be recorded as dissenting voters.

One of the no votes came from Heber Elliott. He recalls that as he voted he felt a certain tension. "I guess I'd have to say that deep down I believe the way the church is going is the way that Christ means us to go. But I also knew what I was going home to, the traditions and the expectations that people have." He had already told another commissioner that after the previous night's vote, he wondered if he would have a congregation to go back to at all. "I voted against the statement because I feared it would split our church, and because I felt a responsibility to vote according to the wishes and feelings of the conference that sent me to General Council."

The moderator told the court a Korean parable, and Marion Best read from the Psalm that had comforted her earlier in the debate.

As the exhausted commissioners were about to adjourn, John Sparling of Mississauga, Ontario, raised a point of order. He said that "regardless of sexual orientation" in the new statement changed the Basis of Union, the section that says "No terms of admission to full membership shall be prescribed other than those laid down in the New Testament." Therefore, he argued, a church-wide referendum would have to be called.

The general secretary, Rev Howie Mills, ruled the next morning, the last day of General Council, that the new statement's section on church membership did not violate the Basis of Union. On the contrary, he said, it actually reinforced the policy that stated no one who professed "faith in Jesus Christ and obedience to Him" should be excluded from membership. Then John Sparling moved that the Church's Judicial Committee review this ruling, and if it was overturned that a remit be called. Janice Scrutton seconded the motion. It passed.

The commissioners sang a hymn. One of the Third World guests, a nun from Uruguay gave her impressions of the day's events. She was impressed. At 5:30 p.m. Wednesday, August 24, the General Council adjourned, its work done.

The end-product was very Canadian, and very United Church. After reaffirming Christian marriage, confessing their faith, their sins, and their inability "to find consensus regarding a Christian understanding of human sexuality, including homosexuality," the General Council declared that "all persons, regardless of their sexual orientation, who profess faith in Jesus Christ and obedience to Him, are welcome to be or become full members of The United Church of Canada. All members of The United Church of Canada are eligible to be considered for ordered ministry. All Christian persons are called to a lifestyle patterned on obedience to Jesus Christ." They tried to give something to everyone: recognition and hope to lesbian and gay people, inclusiveness to people who want an inclusive church, but at the same time a battery of safeguards for people who want a church that's governed by strict rules and traditional images of marriage and family.

After consulting with his Community of Concern colleagues, Leander Mills decided not to quit the church. Instead he would "take direction from my congregation."

Youth Forum delegate Corinne Toews from Regina had seen a debate that was "dominated by forty-five to sixty-year-old heterosexual men. This whole thing seems to be such a blow to them, to the way they were brought up to see their masculinity." She found women at General Council more willing to talk about their own feelings and experience. "Men just give you their opinions, they seem to think that's all they have to do. I guess women have to fight so hard for the right to speak out, they may as well do it once they get the chance."

Bill Fritz, chairman of the Community of Concern, was disappointed. "We wanted a clear message to take to our churches back home, that the only acceptable standard for Christians is fidelity in heterosexual marriage and chastity in singleness. It's a standard that's served us very well for two thousand years. But we didn't get that. What tipped the balance was the most effective homosexual lobby group I've ever seen at any of the four General Councils I've attended. They worked very well, and influenced a great many commissioners to be sympathetic to the homosexual people. The very fact that they were allowed to articulate their position on the floor of Council gave them a considerable edge in the proceedings."

Don Gillies of Friends of Affirm told the press he had a sinking feeling in the final debate as he watched the new statement being "dismantled. Instead of just listening to the Spirit and passing the visionary statement that the sessional committee presented to us, the Council buckled to well-orchestrated protests and watered it down. How much are we prepared to give away," he asked, "to people who want it all?"

This was Ellinor Townend's fourth General Council, and of them all she felt best about Victoria. "We found the least disruptive solution that we could, without abandoning our responsibility to lead." She went home to Edmonton satisfied that she had voted "according to the two basic laws of Jesus Christ – to love God, and to love your neighbour."

Many commissioners said the Holy Spirit was at work there, at General Council. As Sharon Moon sees it, "All kinds of people were changed in ways that surprised and even terrified them. I don't believe there's any other way to explain that than to say it was the Spirit. It must have been an awful inner wrench for people to go through this kind of profound experience, and at the same time to know that they'd have to go home and face the folks who hadn't."

Graham Scott told the press that *Membership, Ministry and Human Sexuality* was "almost acceptable." Later he would call it "a poor compromise that satisfied no one." And a year and a half later he says, "General Council was the worst experience of my whole life. To see good people turning their backs on God, that was hell for me."

In the end there was little feeling of triumph, Marion Best told a press conference, only anxiety. She recalls, "Everyone was so tired. We did what we could, but most of us were fully aware of the deep predicament we were in. The headlines had already started, and the reactions back home. We also knew that you can't legislate welcome. All we could do as a General Council was encourage congregations to welcome people."

For Eilert Frerichs, the saddest thing about Victoria was that, even in that gorgeous flower-laden atmosphere, "We ended up talking about sexuality once again in a totally cerebral, disembodied way. It makes me sad that we're so afraid of our bodies." At his office in Hart House at the University of Toronto, he says, "That's what really fuels this debate – this terror that human bodies are these mindless, animal, passionate entities that have to be restrained or some kind of awful social anarchy will break out! If people could only name these terrors and these demons, they wouldn't be nearly so repressive and destructive to themselves and to others."

Rabbi Jordan Pearlson, one of the invited "theological reflectors," told the commissioners he hadn't believed they would have the nerve. The United Church had an admirable history of speaking out for the underdog. But for the first time the underdog was actually knocking at their own door. "I really didn't think you'd do it, but you have, you've done it. You had the guts to go across the border into the promised land."

As General Council closed, Erin Shoemaker told the press that even though she felt lesbian and gay church members had finally been included at the table, they had been given a stool so low they could hardly reach it. In retrospect her partner Sally Boyle believes that some ground was gained. "In 1984, General Council didn't have the nerve to say that no one shall be barred from ministry. In 1988 they did." She regrets that since everyone was so tired by then, Affirm didn't celebrate this major step. "And I think it's really sad that our church has chosen to batter itself for taking that step, instead of patting itself on the back."

Ed Bentley withdrew from the Community of Concern because he believed the commissioners did what the majority of petitions asked them to do. "We threw out the March report, we affirmed marriage as well as celibacy for the unmarried, and we maintained the status quo in the ordination process." In his eyes most of the media coverage gave the false impression that two small factions – "the ultra-liberals and the ultra-conservatives" – fought it out in Victoria. "When anyone from either of these two factions spoke, the lights went on and the cameras rolled. They couldn't care less what anyone else had to say. When I asked one reporter why not, he told me I wasn't news. No wonder people got such a distorted picture of General Council."

Dorothy MacNeill from Nova Scotia put her green "yes" card in the front of her Bible. "I thought it might be important one day, you know, for history." Then she went home.

CHAPTER 17

Back Home

Shortly after he got home from Victoria the new moderator wrote a letter to all congregations in the church. "Not all will agree with the General Council's statement," Sang Chul Lee wrote. "But it is important for everyone to know what Council said rather than to react to some distortion of it." A copy was attached. "For those who are concerned about too much 'head office' or 'staff' influence in this whole matter, I want to assure you that only five of the 391 voters at General Council are employed at '85' – and I and the General Secretary are two of them: we did not vote, except in the election process." He closed with a plea. "I think it is very important for all of us to go slowly in these excitable times."

Two powerful forces were busy heaping fuel on the excitable times, the media and the Community of Concern. To a public dependent on the media for its news and views of the world, the press presented an image of Victoria that's perfectly captured in these headlines from two major daily papers: UNITED CHURCH FACES BITTER SPLIT and GAYS IN THE PULPIT!

In some cases headlines like these were followed by more complex stories, usually written by correspondents who actually had attended the events that they wrote about. Editorials varied from outraged attack to cautious respect. But right across the country the message the media planted then has continued to be reinforced: the United Church had opened the doors.

Back in the pulpit, ministers throughout the church rediscovered both the power and the limits of their position. For their part, the people in the pews got messages so radically different from each other it's hard to believe they came from within the same church.

When Vera Sampson returned to her church in Saint Stephen, New Brunswick, people told her they were glad to see her safely home. And they weren't only talking about her well-known horror of flying. Most Labour Days the church is almost empty, but this time it was packed. Vera Sampson stepped out of the pulpit – she didn't want any barriers here – and quietly went over the statement, what it said, what it did not say. She completed this process the next Sunday. After that parishoners made it clear to her that they would find any more talk about sexuality disruptive to their worship. They had their own problems, a new roof for example, in a congregation with limited means.

Another sessional committee veteran, Don Collett, returned home to Taber, Alberta. He was exhausted but felt good about *Membership, Ministry and Human Sexuality.* A Community of Concern member since April, he didn't feel any doors had been opened or closed. "I was pretty sure that no church in southern Alberta was going to accept a homosexual minister without a lot of reflection, to say the least." Some members of his congregation were angry, but not with him. Now that he was home they managed to separate him from the decision-making process in which he had been so intimately involved.

In his private life Don Collett wasn't so lucky. His Roman Catholic wife consigned the United Church to hell, and demanded that her husband recant his part in making the new statement. He wrote a sermon in which he tried to do just that. The first Sunday after General Council he stood in the pulpit, his wife sat in her usual pew. "It was one of those times when the sermon I'd written refused to preach itself, it wasn't working. So I abandoned the text and just talked. I can't remember now what it was that I said. But after the prayer when I looked out at our pew, my wife was gone." A few hours later she informed him that he had betrayed her and the marriage was finished.

The church lost members right after General Council, and it's been doing so ever since. In fact the church has been losing members for years. At union in 1925 it has 600,502 registered members. It reached an all-time high of 1,064,033 in 1965, and then like other mainstream Protestant churches it began to shrink. In 1972 it dropped below a million, in 1982 below nine hundred thousand. In 1984 it slipped by more than ten thousand. Some blamed this unusually sharp decline on that year's turmoil over sexual orientation and ministry. Some now blame all of these losses on the church's failure to maintain biblical and Christian traditions.

By comparison, conservative evangelical churches boomed in the eighties, apparently by offering simple answers to complex and frightening modern dilemmas. But recent indiscretions by some of their leaders seem to be landing these churches in hot water, too.

In the United Church Christian charity began to slip as well, as angry members withheld their money either to punish or to put pressure on church leaders. By the end of 1988, givings had dropped nearly five per cent, and budget planners had to start revising goals. The 1989 budget was secure, more than $37 million, but in projecting beyond that it became clear that programs and jobs would have to be cut in all divisions of the church, at the national, regional, and local levels.

In the uproar following General Council, some ministers quit the church immediately. In British Columbia one departing minister told a TV interviewer that he had never really been happy in the United Church. The real trouble began in 1936, he said, when it disobeyed the Scriptures by starting to ordain women. In quitting the church, a minister forfeits some pension benefits. Some critics of the right-wing see this as a test of principle, and believe that the ministers who left are the only ones in opposition who've dared to take serious risks for their convictions.

In fact many ministers who opposed the new statement did not leave. Instead they would fight the church from within. In a church officially devoted for nearly a decade to reducing the height of the pulpit, some of the people in it would now rediscover with relish its good old-fashioned power.

In some cases the exercise of that power began at home. Over the last decade and on several working committees, one prominent churchwoman had been continuously supportive of the various human sexuality initiatives. As a commissioner at Victoria she had maintained this support by voting in favour of *Membership, Ministry and Human Sexuality*. Then she went home. Her husband had been active in the Community of Concern prior to General Council, and became more so after it. People who know this woman report that she virtually disappeared for several weeks. She didn't return calls. When she surfaced again, she had recanted. Her previous position had been a mistake, she told anyone who asked.

The Sunday after he returned from General Council to his Ottawa pulpit, Jim Somerville preached that "a very small but powerful lobby group caused the church council to ignore the wishes of its congregations." He announced later that he had met with lawyers to try and gauge how much of a threat the new policy actually posed, to what degree the church would now be subject to government human rights legislation. In his contribution to a *Chatelaine* "debate," Somerville wrote, "The United Church is in danger of losing its moral integrity, the people in the pews are losing their voice in church affairs, and society is drifting aimlessly in want of spiritual guidance."

Here were the stark outlines of a grim story that would be told in various ways over the next few months to many congregations across the United Church. The majority of commissioners at General Council were either sheep who had been brainwashed by a powerful lobby group, or agents of that group who had used the church's conciliar system to get themselves into positions where they could open up the church to depravity and immorality. The minority who opposed the statement were the true defenders of the faith, speaking out against those forces of evil on behalf of the grass roots, who felt exactly as they did. The church leadership in Toronto consistently ignored the membership, it was virtual dictatorship by a liberal, meaning radical, minority.

General Council had left the power to choose ministers where it had always been, in the hands of local congregations. So what was the problem? Rev Gordon Ross of the Community of Concern says, "Ordination doesn't just mean ordination to one congregation. When you're ordained you're ordained to the whole church. That means we can't just block this thing at the local level, it has to be stopped everywhere. Anyway, if a local selection committee can't ask about a candidate's sexual orientation, how are they to know what they're getting?"

The Community of Concern moved quickly to organize the disaffected. In Maritime Conference they moved so quickly that hardly any congregations had time to read the new statement – particularly congregations where the minister opposed it. Many people were led to believe that instead of shelving the March report, General Council had ignored the petitions and approved it. Early in September the COC called a rally, to take place in Sackville, New Brunswick. As one of the Maritime founders of the organization, John Moses chaired that meeting.

When he had heard part way through General Council that "regardless of sexual orientation" had passed, he had contemplated quitting the church. He knew that enough people would go with him to split his congregation. But he also knew that St Paul's church struggles to survive at the best of times, and now with their new building project it was far from the best of times. He decided to wait. His first reaction to the new statement was negative. It seemed to say in a more convoluted way the same things the original report had been attacked for saying. And it seemed to confirm that there were serious problems in the decision-making structures of the church. In this frame of mind John Moses took the chair at Sackville.

"There was tremendous undirected power in that room," he recalls nearly a year later. "In the right hands it could have torn the whole conference apart. I started to feel I was chairing a hate meeting, directed at homosexuals and anyone who dared to support them." As he speaks in his cramped office at St Paul's, his tone is dark. These aren't comfortable memories. "The people who were there didn't want to let anyone speak who opposed the mood of the meeting – they even tried to silence Roy Demarsh [chair of Maritime Conference]. When I tried to stop the meeting from turning into a lynch mob, I became their target."

For a while Moses didn't get much sleep. He took another look at the General Council statement. "On reflection it still seemed to me an imperfect document, but an honest one. It didn't hold homosexuals hostage to our inability to make a decision." To his congregation he said, "There are many things about the United Church with which I take issue. I would like to see more emphasis on spiritual growth and evangelism. I would like to see more sensitivity to local congregations and a less confusing and bureaucratic structure of government. On the other hand I am proud that this church seeks to hear the cries of the poor and the oppressed, and to care for a hurting world. The good outweighs the bad. If any of you finds a perfect church, please come and tell me about it. On second thought, don't bother. I wouldn't be happy there, because I am not perfect." This time he didn't get a standing ovation.

John Moses resigned from the Community of Concern steering committee, and withdrew from the public arena into the life and concerns of his own congregation. "Until then the press was calling me all the time for interviews." Now he looks puzzled. "From that day they stopped. I suppose I wasn't news any more." But most of his congregation stayed on, to build their new church.

The Community of Concern steamrollered on without him. Two weeks after General Council the steering committee met in a Toronto suburban church. They decided to retain legal counsel, "so that we may consider, as we proceed, all available options open to us," their press release said, "including the option of seeking injunctive relief in the civil courts." Spokesperson Rev Gordon Ross, himself a lawyer, told the press that the COC would prefer not to go to court. It might depend on what happened to their drive for a church-wide referendum. Then again it might not. "What we were trying to do at this stage was avoid the kind of walkouts that were already taking place across the church." At the same time they intended to force the executive to do what the General Council had refused to do, to close the door.

In Vancouver Rev George Morrison rejects the new statement as "very little different from the March report. It's a dangerous move away from the clear, unanimous viewpoint that's prevailed down through history and right across the whole Christian church, to one of ambivalence. The next inevitable step is acceptance." It's typical, he says, of the inexorable slide to the left that he's observed in church leadership over the past twenty years. "The norms that were in place when I became a minister are now seen by this leadership to be conservative. But that's certainly not where the vast majority of people in the pews are."

In Saskatoon Rev Dick Hetherington launched his own personal crusade, both within the Community of Concern and beyond. He's an on-again-off-again minister in Saskatoon, and something of a maverick who is convinced that Jesus Christ was entirely human and not divine. It shocked him that the General Council statement supports civil rights for homosexuals. "It's very hard to show compassion for homosexuals when they refuse to admit that there's anything wrong with them." The church should be clear, he says, that homosexuality is immoral – biblically, anatomically, and biologically. In his small apartment in a Royal Canadian Legion building he says, "No Christian has a right to views which are contrary to the Bible." One wall of his living room is lined with file cabinets, overflowing with documents on homosexuality and other battles lost and won.

Some AIDS victims are innocent, says Dick Hetherington, but most are not. And homosexual relationships don't count. "There's only one kind of real family, that's a father, a mother, and their children. Any other kind is artificial." Then there's the danger of role models if homosexuals are allowed to be ministers. "Young people are predisposed to experiment. If they try homosexuality and they have an orgasm, they'll get caught up in it. Orgasms are addictive. It's almost impossible to break that pattern."

The Community of Concern had almost eclipsed the United Church Renewal Fellowship, but not quite. The UCRF lost some of its leaders and about a third of its membership – some left the church, some moved into the COC. In September the board of directors issued their statement rejecting *Membership, Ministry and Human Sexuality* in its entirety. The General Council had contradicted "the Scriptures of the Old and New Testaments," and "seriously placed at risk the peace and welfare of the whole church." The UCRF statement recognized the need for "an independent association of congregations" to be established outside the United Church, and said there were UCRF leaders who would help. To this day each issue of *Renewal Fellowship Magazine* continues to carry an ad for Homosexuals Anonymous in Barrie, Ontario, offering "healing for the homosexual, healing for the church."

In Winnipeg, Rev Wing Hei Mak ministered to the Chinese United Church. "The General Council faltered," he says, in his office at the end of the small A-frame church. "It ignored the basic question, whether homosexuality is a sin." Wing Mak came to Canada in 1957 to study aerospace engineering here and in the United States. An agnostic then, he converted to Christianity in the Baptist Church, then went to an evangelical theology school. When the Chinese United Church in Ottawa was looking for a minister, he got the job. "It was a Canadian couple who helped me to find Jesus Christ, so I was glad to return here and give back some of what I had been given by them." Later he moved to Winnipeg.

"There is no split in the Winnipeg congregation," he says. "We support the Community of Concern. Chinese people are very family conscious, and the Bible promotes that. God designed male and female for sex, not man and man or woman and woman. The only natural form of sex is between man and woman in holy wedlock. Unfortunately the United Church has allowed social trends to change our way of thinking. That is clearly unchristian." On the wall behind him a poster announces the Chinese Mission '89 in Washington D.C. "Equipping the Force for God's Kingdom," it says.

Wing Hei Mak has returned to Ottawa, to replace a minister who quit the church. With such grievances, why didn't he leave himself? "If you leave, you lose your power," he says. A smile lights his face, then passes. "If we want to change the church we have to stay in it. The United Church is quite influential in society. So it's very important that we reverse the process that's been set in motion." How? "At the next General Council we have to get a remit [referendum] on self-declared practising homosexuals. We have to make sure that the authority of scripture is respected, that the theology schools are reformed, and that the structure of the church is changed so that its decisions reflect the wishes of the grass roots. A Community of Concern task force is working on that." The organization is nothing if not ambitious.

The COC's most spectacular event in 1988, mid-September in a Toronto church, attracted over eight hundred people. It opened with a rousing evangelical worship service. Shortly before noon the assembly was informed that people would have to sign the new COC statement of conviction if they wanted to participate in the debate that afternoon. Clarke MacDonald protested: They hadn't even seen the document. At lunch he told others that in fourteen General Councils he'd never felt as manipulated as he did that morning.

Then he saw the Declaration of Intention – the plan of action, which proposed class actions by departers to retain church property, closer relations with the UCRF and Church Alive, withholding funds from the Mission and Service fund, closer relations with the splinter Congregational church to which some of the departing ministers had gone, and a separate theological school. "All of these proposals could only have divided our church," says the former moderator. "So all of them were anathema to me."

In the afternoon he was invited to make a statement. He told the meeting he'd joined the Community of Concern to get the March report shelved. Now that the General Council had done exactly that, he was leaving. Since then he's been invited several times to rejoin. "At this stage," says Clarke MacDonald, "the only thing I'd join is anything that promises to be a reconciling force in the United Church."

The sound of church doors slamming echoed across Canada. In Maritime Conference, the executive decreed at its September meeting that "in light of scripture-based concerns expressed by Presbyteries, Pastoral Charges and individuals," only those people would be ordained, commissioned, or settled in ministry "whose lifestyle includes faithfulness in marriage to a spouse of the opposite sex and celibacy in singleness." Ironically, this action did exactly what the General Council had been accused incorrectly of doing: It limited the power of congregations and presbyteries to choose their own ministers.

One member of the Maritime Conference executive, Dorothy MacNeill, noted that if the new policy's three arguments were taken literally, it would make all of her heterosexual children ineligible in one way or another, not only for ministry but even for membership in her church.

Another executive member, Barb Rumscheidt, was also a commissioner at General Council. For her the Maritime action came as a shock. "It was the first time I've seen such blatant capitulation to a mob. I was amazed at how much power people were willing to give up for so little gain." In the peace movement, the women's movement, and on a number of other fronts, she devotes a considerable portion of her life to opposing abuses of power. "Have we forgotten so easily how Hitler came to power? Not by force. The Germans *voted* for him. They liked him because he gave them *autobahns* and restored their national pride. They refused to believe that all his other stuff could affect them."

Barb Rumscheidt believes that the new policy clarified the lines of struggle in her part of the church. "General Council's refusal to say no means a potential yes. If the doors aren't open, then at least the windows are. That's how conservatives in this conference read the statement, and so do I. In other more liberal conferences I understand things are a little hazier, which makes them harder to pin down. Here it's absolutely clear what's at stake."

Nova Scotia Premier John Buchanan belongs to the United Church. He's also believed to be the most powerful opponent of the movement to include sexual orientation in the province's human rights code, a campaign Barb Rumscheidt helped to organize. "Politicians know that if the United Church has an open policy, that makes it harder for them to exclude lesbian and gay people," she says. "On the other hand if the government includes them in human rights legislation, it makes it that much harder for the church to deny them civil rights."

In many parts of the country, commissioners were invited to church meetings. They expected to give their impressions of General Council and the creating of the new statement. But in many cases before they could give anything they were attacked, personally blamed for letting in the queers. Commissioner Margaret McPherson had never experienced anything like it before. "People started shouting at me, 'We told you to get rid of that report!' I said we had. They called me a liar, they said I was brainwashed. No one's ever said things like that to me before. They were bloodthirsty!"

After one meeting a man told her he would never let a homosexual near the pulpit in his church. It turned out that as a child he had been sexually molested by his uncle, who was married with kids. Margaret McPherson told him she was sorry, then asked if he realized how many women had been assaulted by heterosexual men, including ministers? Should that disqualify heterosexual men from the ministry, she asked. It wasn't the same, he said. "People weren't prepared to hear any kind of reasonable argument," she says. "One woman in her thirties actually came right out and said the only people we should ordain were married men!"

Another available target was Jim Beal from the Bay of Quinte Conference of eastern Ontario. He had three counts against him: he had been a commissioner, he had worked on Sessional Committee Eight, and as a minister he should have known better. He attended meetings so angry that he feared physical attack. "Suddenly I saw forces at work in my church that I hadn't been aware of. I guess I'd been pretty naïve. The whole thing really shook me, I was depressed for months." A whole year later, he still sounds shaken. It seems the only thing not shaken was his faith in the Gospel. "There seem to be a significant number of people who want the church to keep things the way they've always been – or how they imagine they've always been – in a moral straitjacket. But that's not what the Gospel's about, not at all. Jesus spent most of his life challenging the way things were."

One prospect, which both the sessional committee and General Council tried to avoid, has already come to pass – a witch-hunt against homosexual people. According to Jim Beal and to others in similar positions across the church, the climate of escalating fear has forced lesbians and gay men already in ministry to be more secretive than ever. Some of them couldn't stand the added tension, and left. "We're losing good ministers. Unlike the people who are leaving in protest, the homosexuals who leave don't want to hurt their church, and they don't hit the headlines. They just leave quietly."

The mood in the pews seems to have varied according to what people had heard about the Victoria meeting, and from what source. In New Brunswick Vera Sampson and Doreen Kissick, another commissioner, were invited to speak to a congregation on the verge of quitting the church. Some members wanted to know if there might be another side to the story they had been getting every day in the media, and from the pulpit Sunday after Sunday. The two commissioners discovered that, even though copies of the new statement had been sent to every minister and local church board, no one in this congregation had seen it.

They passed out copies of the statement, described the debates that shaped it, and answered questions about its contents. They showed how it differed from the March report. General Council had not opened any doors, Vera Sampson said, it had simply refused to close them. Later she got a thank-you letter from the congregation. They had appreciated the opportunity, they said, to be informed.

In Morris, Manitoba, former sessional committee member Bill Fulford reported to his congregation. Almost all of them had signed the Community of Concern's Declaration of Dissent in the spring. Bill Fulford went through the new statement point by point, showing how it met each of the concerns expressed in that declaration.

Later the elected board of the Morris congregation voted unanimously to disengage from the Community of Concern.

Since it had served its purpose, they said, it no longer had any reason to exist. At the same time, the board said that it would be inappropriate at present to ordain a homosexual minister in Morris. "A small town can be very unkind," says Bill Fulford. "A Mennonite friend told me the reason you don't see any homosexuals in Morris is because they chased them out."

As for the whole church Bill Fulford believes, "We'll move on, with new knowledge and new understanding." Surrounded by plants at the garden centre he operates in a Winnipeg mall, he says, "If we admit – and I think we'll have to – that people can't change their sexual orientation, then we'll have to look at how we can encourage committed, exclusive relationships. Doesn't that mean we should be covenanting people together, in some equivalent to marriage? I never could have accepted that before General Council, but I do now."

Many commissioners were accused of not listening to the folks back home. Otherwise how could they have voted the way they did? At a Vancouver Island meeting, commissioner Jean Gibson compared it to the capital punishment vote in Parliament. "Poll after poll said seventy, eighty per cent of the people want capital punishment. But even in a conservative-dominated Parliament a solid majority of MPs voted against it. What happened? They had the opportunity to study the information, to debate all the implications, and to ponder their own responsibility if they approved killing by a state that they represented. They said no." The analogy was a familiar one to Jean Gibson. For years she and her husband volunteered as prison visitors, and for six years she worked on a community parole board, weighing the fitness for parole of inmates in federal penitentiaries, often people with life sentences.

One of the indicators of rage in the church continued to be letters, mainly to the *Observer* but also to church officials. After General Council some of them contained a new theme. *Observer* editor at the time, Hugh McCullum, wrote in an editorial, "A small but steady stream of letters began to arrive – some hiding their bravado behind anonymity, others signed and traceable – calling our Moderator some of the vilest names I've heard in many years of receiving racist letters and hearing bigoted statements about non-Anglo Saxons."

Strangely enough, the only person who wasn't getting this kind of mail was the moderator himself. When Hugh McCullum and others told him nervously about the letters they had received, Sang Chul Lee felt his supporters needed more comfort than he did. "All my life I've met racism – as a Korean in China, then in Siberia, then under Japanese occupation, then as an Asian in Canada. So what's new?" He laughs. "It doesn't frighten me. But it does make me sad to know that our church has attitudes in it like that. We should have gone beyond that by now." In response to the *Observer* editorial, another stream of letters poured out from quiet corners of the church in support of their spiritual leader.

The newsletter of Metropolitan United in London, Ontario, implied that Lee's election had been orchestrated by Toronto Conference, and that his short time in Canada (twenty-seven years) and inadequate English made him less than suitable for the job. This is the congregation where Morley Clarke, another candidate for the moderator's job, had been minister and is still a member. Clarke himself added fuel to the accusations in a *Toronto Star* interview. In response Toronto Presbytery resolved to censure the instigators of the story through regular church channels. The moderator asked them to stop.

"All my life I've been fighting many things," he says in accented, but clear English. "But I've always tried to avoid attacking individuals – it's not mature and it doesn't help. It's like jumping into the mud."

There would be no shortage of mud.

CHAPTER 18

Panic

By November 1988 Canada's largest Protestant church was paralyzed, on the verge of disintegrating. So the press was saying, and so the Community of Concern was saying. Much less was heard from the many congregations where the majority of members appeared to be satisfied, more or less, with the decisions of General Council. These were going about their usual business – church on Sunday, choir practice, meetings, repairing the roof, and so on. But right or wrong, the perception of impending doom helped shape one of those strange events that the various participants interpret in such contrary ways it seems not to have been one event at all, but many.

Friends of Affirm requested a post-General Council meeting with the new moderator and the general secretary. The latter replied that it would be inadvisable at this time for senior church officials to meet with any lobby groups. Unlike the United Church Women groups or the men's association, neither Affirm, Friends of Affirm, the Renewal Fellowship,

Church Alive, nor the Community of Concern is recognized as an official body within the church, since none are accountable to its decision-making courts.

But shortly after their highly publicized Toronto meeting, representatives of the Community of Concern did meet with the general secretary. As a result the moderator proposed a more official meeting, a kind of summit with six representatives each from the COC and the General Council. Here occurs the first critical difference in perception, or memory. People on the General Council side called this meeting a dialogue, people on the Community of Concern side a negotiation. The gap in understanding is wider than words. Dialogue implies an attempt to find common ground; negotiation an attempt to win territory. As it turned out, the Community of Concern team arrived with a back-up caucus in the next room of nine people, including two lawyers.

Executive member Margaret McPherson is candid about the decision to meet with one group and not the other. "The COC were the ones who were doing all the screaming. We had no problems with Affirm. They weren't trying to pressure us, they weren't threatening to leave the church and withholding their money."

The meeting lasted ten hours, at Cedar Glen, a United Church conference centre in gently rolling hills north of Toronto. Leaves were falling, the oaks and maples were nearly bare. The two dialogue/negotiation teams shook hands and set to work. The COC had brought a full agenda: the Victoria statement had to go; inclusive language had to go; the theology colleges were too liberal; church decision-making structures had to be changed to reflect "the grass roots."

At the end of the day, the two sides had hammered out a document, which both would take back for their respective executive bodies to consider. The Community of Concern side called it an agreement, the General Council side a proposal. The document's central point was the conducting of a mail-ballot in which the statement approved by the thirty-second General Council would be reopened. All the commissioners would be asked whether they would accept the substitution of the phrase "without exception" for the present wording, "regardless of sexual orientation." If they did, it would read, "All persons, without exception, who profess faith in Jesus Christ and obedience to Him, are welcome to be or become full members of the United Church of Canada."

From here on the stories differ more and more.

According to Gordon Ross, one of the lawyers on the COC back-up team, the General Council representatives wouldn't even acknowledge for the first few hours that there was a problem. According to Glenna Beauchamp, a commissioner at Victoria and a member of the church's dialogue team, the General Council representatives spent the first few hours dealing with hostility and intimidation from the other side. "It was like agreeing to go to a marriage counsellor and then without warning one side shows up with a really aggressive lawyer."

Into this already simmering soup was thrown another ingredient. At Victoria the General Secretary had ruled that since the new statement did not change the church's constitution, a church-wide referendum on it would not be required. Commissioner John Sparling demanded that the church's Judicial Committee review that ruling. He and his lawyer presented their arguments to a panel of seven, which included lawyers and a justice of the Supreme Court of Canada. The panel also heard two more appeals, both from Oshawa Presbytery, asserting that the new statement had altered conditions for membership and ordination, and that it limited the power of congregations and presbyteries in interviewing candidates for ministry.

In November the Judicial Committee released its judgement. By a margin of six to one it ruled no in all three cases: a referendum was not justified, conditions for membership had not changed, and General Council had not limited the power of congregations and presbyteries.

Here again there are two versions. In a detailed explanation of its ruling, the Judicial Committee said it was incorrect to assume that the clauses under question in the statement had opened the door to ordained ministry for homosexuals. The chief COC lawyer interpreted this to mean that the committee had removed any ambiguity on the matter. They'd made it perfectly clear, he told the press, that no practising homosexual person could be ordained or commissioned. He didn't mention the next sentence in the Judicial Committee's ruling: "On the contrary, in terms of ordination or commissioning, the clauses go no further than to say that any member has the right to apply."

The Cedar Glen document would be tested at the General Council executive and at the Community of Concern. In the Church Alive *Theological Digest*, editor Reverend Ken Barker reports that the "agreement" was formally endorsed by the COC at its general meeting on November 24. Ken Barker was one of the group's negotiators at Cedar Glen. But this endorsement carried a rider; it would only be binding on the COC if the General Council executive endorsed "the statement of recommendations which were negotiated by both parties."

That COC meeting was timed to coincide with the regular meeting of the General Council executive: seventy-five representatives from across the church who are responsible for decision-making between General Councils. Normally the executive gets through its agenda in three days of hard work. This time two more were added at the beginning to deal with the turmoil in the church, and the executive hardly got around to dealing with anything else the whole week.

Reports from some regions were grim. Glenna Beauchamp recalls, "In the western conferences it looked like we could weather the storm. But some of the eastern conferences were close to panic, especially London where they were saying if something isn't done fast we'll collapse." In this panicky atmosphere, at first it seemed that the executive might accept the Cedar Glen document. Ellinor Townend from Edmonton spoke in favour of the central point, the mail-ballot on substituting "without exception" for "regardless of sexual orientation." "It seems to me we've already made the point at Victoria, and we don't need to keep on making it," she argued.

Part way through their week-long meeting, the executive called an interim press conference. Since the Community of Concern was making such effective use of the media, why shouldn't the church? Four people – two executive spokespeople, the moderator, and the general secretary, Howie Mills – faced the press.

Margaret McPherson recalls, "The journalists directed every one of their questions to Howie Mills. Since there was nothing for him to do, Sang Chul Lee just left quietly at the end of the presentation. The crazy thing was, we were making the decisions there, not Howie. When I asked one of the reporters why they ignored the rest of us, he said, 'It's easier that way, people know who Howie Mills is. We don't want to confuse them with too many strange faces.' No wonder people out there think all the decisions are made by a few people at 85 St Clair!" Rev Mills agreed to sit out the final press conference.

Then the Community of Concern sent three members to the executive meeting, to announce that they weren't sure any more whether "without exception" would fly with their membership. Were there to be barriers or weren't there, executive members asked. The COC leaders couldn't say. Ellinor Townend began to feel more protective of the Victoria statement's original phrase, "regardless of sexual orientation."

Executive member Ralph Garbe argued that until the whole church had time to react to the new General Council policy, it should be suspended. A member of the Renewal Fellowship and of the Community of Concern, he ministers to Byron United in London. Others responded that to suspend a General Council decision would be improper, in fact it would significantly undermine the authority of the church's highest court. Here was an irony: a man who said he spoke for the grass roots was urging an executive body to suspend a policy that had been approved by the closest thing the church has to an elected parliament. The proposal was rejected.

At the final press conference, spokespeople Ed Bentley and Margaret McPherson announced that the executive recognized "the high degree of distress and confusion currently in the church," it acknowledged that all statements were "subject to review and reconsideration by any future General Council," and it formally invited congregations to consult and respond to the Victoria statement, *Membership, Ministry and Human Sexuality*. The insights arising from this process would be reported to the executive and then to the next General Council. Somehow all of it sounded very familiar.

Why on earth did they want to reopen that Pandora's box yet again? "We didn't," says Margaret McPherson, "But what else could we do? The only ones we'd heard from up to that point were the screamers. We wanted to hear from the whole church." She hesitates. "Time may prove us wrong."

Almost immediately Glenna Beauchamp had second thoughts. "We got so caught up in all the talk about how many people were hurting from the Victoria decision," she recalls. At home in Shoal Lake, Manitoba, she's limping from a farm accident. "But there's hurting and there's hurting. Lots of white people were hurt when black people got civil rights. It seems to me the people who are really suffering in our church are the ones who've tried to be faithful and sensitive through all this – they've been really crunched by it. You don't hear about them. And that kind of hurt is very hard to fix."

Heber Elliott of Portugal Cove, Newfoundland, who served on the executive committee, doesn't know what else they could have done under the circumstances. At General Council in Victoria he had told other commissioners he wasn't sure whether he'd have a congregation to go home to. People in Portugal Cove had said that if General Council let homosexuals into the pulpit they'd quit the church. Then the thing happened with the priest.

The sad story that unfolded in St John's, and in the national media, started in the autumn of 1988 in Portugal Cove. "When it came out that the Catholic priest here had molested more than twenty boys, it was a terrible shock to everyone," says Heber Elliott. "We have three churches in the community, and the clergy are all well known. People were very bitter. It's taken a lot of hard work, months of it, to separate homosexuality and perversion in their minds."

He hasn't entirely made the separation himself. "After what's happened here, I'd still be very uneasy if I knew my son had a homosexual teacher or a homosexual doctor." Even so, things have settled down in Portugal Cove. No one has quit the church, in fact the congregation has grown. And their contributions to the Mission and Service Fund, a weather-vane for popular mood in the United Church, have increased.

Two months after General Council, Newfoundland and Labrador Conference enacted a policy similar to that of Maritime Conference, barring self-declared, practising homosexuals from the pulpit. Heber Elliott believes it kept things from boiling over in Newfoundland. At the same time, he fears that reopening the statement for debate threatens once again to mislead congregations into thinking that petitions constitute a referendum. "If they think the statement will be rescinded at the 1990 General Council, it's quite possible they'll be disappointed again." He doesn't believe it will be? "I don't see that happening. If it does there'll be just as big a backlash on the other side. I don't see how there can be any real winners in this."

In the chaplain's office at the University of Toronto, Eilert Frerichs calls the executive action "unfaithful to General Council. The *Membership, Ministry and Human Sexuality* statement called for dialogue throughout the church. But the executive refused to offer its most vulnerable members the kind of protection that would allow us to enter into dialogue without risking our jobs and our place in the church. On the other hand they caved in to pressure and agreed to dialogue with the so-called Community of Concern." Why does he say "so-called"? "The leaders of that organization have proved that they have no real understanding of community, nor do they seem to be especially concerned about anything except maintaining their own privilege and power."

On the Community of Concern side, the executive action was immediately labelled a profound disappointment, a betrayal and further proof that the church hierarchy wouldn't listen to the grass roots. Gordon Ross was particulary upset that in its statement to the press, the executive hadn't once mention its negotiations with the coc. "That was a very tacky performance." But neither did the executive once mention homosexuals in its statement. In fact this was another United Church balancing act.

In its press release, the Community of Concern urged the faithful to support the COC, to press for a reversal of the Victoria statement, and to elect representatives "who will genuinely reflect your concerns and wishes in the courts of the church." It sounded like the opening of an election campaign.

To Gordon Ross, now executive director of the COC, the whole affair was a waste of time. "I never thought this crisis could be resolved through nit-picky legal procedures, and it was an illusion to think it could be." He leans back in his chair, rocking a little. "What the church needed was what the Community of Concern asked for, a binding referendum on this matter, in which every member of the church would have a vote. That's what we still need." The executive argued that a referendum on this matter wouldn't be consistent with United Church tradition, and it would only increase divisions in the church. "So what?" asks Ross. "Do we want to resolve this crisis or don't we?"

He believes that, in effect, "The executive's action said now we've given the Victoria document a second reading, and we expect the church to give it third and final reading at the next General Council."

If that happens, it happens August 1990, in the very heart of COC country – London, Ontario.

CHAPTER 19

A Block in a Grove of Trees

A grey Sunday morning, summer in Halifax. Rev Anthony Ware preaches his first sermon at St Andrew's United. This is one of the "big pulpits" of the Maritimes. Presbyterian before union, it still looks it today – solid, no frills. Like the fill-in minister he's replacing, the new man appears as many people imagine ministers ought to: middle-aged, silver-haired, and robed in black.

The pews are packed, unusually so. Some people came out of curiosity, to see how the new man would do. There are lots of grey, white, and balding heads – some hats and gloves. The service moves along in a formal, dignified manner, with nothing in it to upset or embarass. Anthony Ware seems a touch nervous. He calls the stool in the pulpit "the most uncomfortable seat in the whole church." No wonder. In waves of unwelcome publicity, St Andrew's has been called one of the major bloodbaths in the current turmoils.

Eric Mercer is an elder here. In his seventies, he's an old-fashioned man who objects to elders counting the Sunday collection during the service, just so they can get away faster when it's over. "If they aren't joining in the fellowship of the service, what's the point in being there at all?" He's retired from the navy, and works half-time now as secretary-treasurer of the Atlantic School of Theology. It's a unique experiment in ecumenical theology education – United, Roman Catholic, and Anglican – initiated in the 1970s by the United Church.

Eric Mercer was born Presbyterian and became United at union. Catherine Mercer has been involved in the church since she grew up in New Brunswick. When study materials on The Issue first hit St Andrew's, a subcommittee of the governing board ruled that since they were too humanist and not spiritual enough, they would not be studied by the congregation. Dr Pam Brown, an active member of the congregation and one of the authors of the materials in question, protested at this arbitrary end to a debate that hadn't even started. Though Eric Mercer himself considers homosexuality "a disgusting habit, and a characteristic I wouldn't want to invite into our pulpit," still he agreed with her protest on the grounds that things hadn't been done as they should. The Mercers initiated a small study group themselves. It met first in their home, in a fine old Halifax neighbourhood.

After some weeks, the people who attended – all heterosexual, married couples – arrived at different conclusions. So did Catherine and Eric Mercer. She believes that no group should be ostracized in the church. "It's hypocritical to claim that you love all of mankind, then turn around and say you don't want someone to move in next door because property values might fall." She knows of two homosexual men she could accept as ministers. "They live together as a couple. They're exceptionally fine people, very caring."

Eric Mercer wonders if they're *practising* homosexuals, for him that's a crucial distinction. "I don't know anything about that," she replies. "And I wouldn't want to know. But I don't see why they shouldn't have every opportunity in life that I have." These are people she knows. What would she say if a stranger came along asking to be a minister, and acknowledged being sexually active and homosexual? "I'd say" – she stops a moment – "I would say that I'd rather you didn't come to our pulpit."

Every morning Eric Mercer reads his Bible, and various scholarly commentaries along with it. "I suppose with all this reading I've become a little more discerning. You realize after a while that we don't know everything we think we know." Take the Sodom and Gomorrah story in the first book of the Bible, where God rains down fire and brimstone on the twin cities of sin. The question is, what exactly was the sin? Some believe the Bible indicated clearly that it was homosexuality. Others believe the Bible indicates it was gang rape. Still others that it was a refusal of hospitality to strangers, who also happened to be messengers from God.

What does Eric Mercer believe? "I don't believe all those men could have been homosexuals as we understand the term – some of them perhaps, but not all. What happened there wasn't a homosexual situation, it was gang rape. It was one of those situations where men acted as beasts, as men sometimes do." At the same time he isn't sure whether homosexuality is God-given, or whether it's learned and therefore closer to the realm of sin. "The trouble is, if we agree that they're born that way, we may condemn them to never getting out."

Aside from The Issue, St Andrew's already had its own troubles. Prior to General Council two of the ministers seemed increasingly at odds with the majority of the congregation. Partly it was a matter of style, partly an indicator of much deeper rifts in the United Church. One Sunday the senior minister suddenly issued an altar call, the faithful were to come forward and declare their commitment to Jesus Christ. People were shocked. "It was like Billy Graham," says Eric Mercer. "We don't do things like that at St Andrew's. I'm not saying we shouldn't, but to do something like that you have to consult with people first, you have to prepare them." About a hundred concerned people formed a committee and asked for dialogue with the senior minister. Instead he quit, and took some members with him.

Shortly after General Council two more ministers quit. They said in their parting sermons that the United Church had moved beyond redemption. Until then Eric Mercer had never paid much attention to the regional or national structures. St Andrew's was his church. "When I heard those men talking on the radio about splitting our church, I was horrified. For the first time my own security was threatened," he says in the Mercers' comfortable house. It sits on a quiet street lined with a variety of tall old trees.

St Andrew's didn't collapse. It lost about eighty-five families, "some of them good givers," says Eric Mercer, and gained about fifty. "A whole new leadership has come forward, people who sat back before and let others do it." But both the Mercers see problems with the national church leadership, "the civil servants up there in Toronto," Eric Mercer calls them. He believes some of them have been there too long. "Most of them are ministers. Why not move them out into pastoral charges, and let someone else take a crack at it?" Who would decide on the replacements? "Ah," he says, "That's another problem."

"It's our own fault," says Catherine. "When people go to presbytery meetings – *if* they go at all – often they just sit there and won't open their mouths." She's been to enough presbytery meetings to know, and is not said to be inhibited about opening her mouth. "Most of them don't bother to report back to their congregations, and the people back home don't bother to ask," she says. "Then something happens, and everybody wonders where on earth it came from."

In 1989 Eric Mercer went for the first time as a delegate to Maritime Conference. Despite his own reservations, he disagreed with the policy that was affirmed there to bar self-declared practising homosexuals from even being considered for ministry. His reservations had less to do with homosexuals than with established church practice. "I have faith that congregations will have the sense to make the right choice, and I wouldn't want to take that freedom away from them." He chooses his words carefully. He's seen enough fighting for a while. "The Community of Concern takes an authoritarian approach. They say we have to cut a few freedoms in order to be secure. But surely being a Christian involves taking risks. Look at the kind of risk that God took, sending Jesus Christ among us. His own son was executed – that's the kind of risk I believe you've got to take if you're going to be a Christian."

On the other side of Canada, in Victoria, if a few dozen folks show up for Sunday service at Pilgrim United, Rev Bill Taylor calls it a good day. One January morning in 1989 the 9:30 service was packed, with the choir and the minister in top evangelical form. Then all of them disappeared – to form a new branch of the Congregational Church. A former minister at Pilgrim, Bill Taylor had been asked to preside at the 10:30 service.

"We had eight people. Two were there by mistake, two had got the time wrong, and one was a visitor from Ottawa." Bill Taylor smiles, remembering. Then he continues, with the easy rhythms of an experience preacher. "But we sang, we prayed, I doubled as organist and preached a new year sermon. What could have been more appropriate than a new year sermon?" In his living room he has an old church organ, which he plays for sheer delight in its wonderful sounds.

Pilgrim United isn't far from the University of Victoria, where the thirty-second General Council forged its famous statement. The United Church was particularly hard hit on Vancouver Island, with a number of congregations splitting. Before they departed, some of the faithful left their mark. Pilgrim and several other church buildings were defaced, usually by scratching out the "united." Throughout most of 1989, area staff worked virtually full time on damage control. Retired ministers were called in to heal the torn remnants. They were known and trusted by congregations they had served in the past, as Bill Taylor was at Pilgrim. But this time his congregation consisted of one man who had stayed behind, loyal to the United Church. "He wondered what was going to happen to him, where would he go? I told him to stay where he was, he'd be looked after." His voice radiates calm assurance. "Even if it was only him and me, Pilgrim would continue to be a church."

At seventy, Bill Taylor has nearly lost count of the number of times he's retired. After he retired from his pastoral charge in Saskatchewan, he worked as a navy chaplain, then as classification officer in a British Columbia penitentiary, steering inmates into rehabilitation programs. After that he took on the pulpit at Pilgrim, then went back to prison work as full-time chaplain. When he retired from that, he expected to stay retired. Then Pilgrim broke up.

Where does he stand on The Issue? By way of answer he tells a story. "I was sitting in my office one day. The door was open. Suddenly there was a man in my office with a long knife. He told me to move. When a large man with a knife tells you to move, you move." Three inmates held Taylor and several others hostage for four days. He seemed to come through it better than the others, who were all younger. "I tend to distrust it when people claim God has talked to them, telling them to do this or that. But in this case I definitely did hear something. It wasn't words, but there was a very clear message, in the form of a question: can you love these people who are threatening to take your life? As far as I'm concerned there can only be one answer to a question like that, or you might as well get out of the whole bloody business. It's not by our words, our prayers, our singing, or our temples that we'll be known, but by what we do for others."

He knows homosexual people in ministry, and says he has no problem with that. But he believes lesbians and gay men made a tactical blunder "when they started shouting from the parapets and asking to be ministers. The way things are, how many congregations would call a lesbian or a gay man to be their minister? And how many congregations could survive if they did?"

A ship passes. The Taylors' sunroom overlooks the Juan de Fuca Straits, and the Olympic mountains of Washington state. Bill Taylor doesn't believe "the sexual thing" is the big issue for his church. "That's just a blip," he says. "The big issue is the authority of Scripture, whether the United Church continues to take a reasoned, critical approach or allows itself to get pushed into a literalist approach. I don't know where some people leave their minds when they go to church."

This is not a new struggle, says Bill Taylor, it's been going on since the birth of the Christian church. "It's okay with me as long as people don't presume to put words into God's mouth. Anyway the literalists aren't as literal as they pretend to be. They pick and choose quite freely among the Scriptures. In the New Testament they always choose the Epistles [the letters of the missionary apostles] over the Gospels, where you'll find the really hard commands of Jesus."

What's become of Pilgrim United? Between them, Bill Taylor and the one man who stayed have kept it alive, with help from Victoria Presbytery. For them it's an act of faith. On any Sunday ten to forty-five people show up for service. A few families who left have returned. And the church is well situated in one of the fastest growing parts of Victoria. But people are shy about entering a large, nearly empty church. So presbytery secretary Bill Howie came up with a lend-a-family campaign, in which one family from each congregation in Victoria would volunteer to join the Pilgrim congregation for a year, in a concrete gesture of support.

Bill Taylor would like to retire again, walk his dog and watch the ships go by, but only when he can leave the church in good hands. "I know from prison riots how dangerous it can be when a vocal minority carries along the rest, who aren't asking the right questions. We have to be asking ourselves what Christ would be doing in this situation. That's all we have to know. What would Christ be doing?"

Will the church survive? No question, he says. "A church is a fellowship of people with a shared belief in God. And the expression of God's personhood is Jesus Christ, a man who was tempted just as we are. Yet somehow or other this man was still God – he was a reconciling force between God and humanity. Wouldn't you think that's what we're called to be now, reconcilers? It makes me cross to see so many wreckers in our church." He sounds it. In the warm sunroom his robe and his stole, hand-woven by a friend, hang to dry after being washed. It's an odd juxtaposition of the sacred and the practical. "But when you think about it," he says, "do we really need a building or an organization to do His work? I don't think so. If it comes to that, I believe we could sit on a block in a grove of trees, and still be the church."

In their November 1988 decision, the General Council executive asked congregations to study and discuss the Victoria statement, then to send in their reactions via the executive to the thirty-third General Council. To avoid any charge of interference, the nervous officials declined to suggest any method for responding. Some presbyteries have prepared questionnaires, others have recommended structures, but these were optional. By the November 1989 deadline the executive had received a stack of assorted documents: obscene letters, photocopies of earlier petitions, statements from official boards, and individual members saying they approve of the General Council statement, or they aren't thrilled with it but they can live with it, parts or all of it have to go, or they're tired of The Issue and have nothing more to say on it.

To prepare their response, after service the last Sunday of May 1989, about a third of the congregation stayed behind at First United in Ottawa. Their inner-city church had been through its own kind of resurrection. Like a species facing extinction, its numbers had shrunk well below the critical level that's necessary for survival. Rev Sharon Moon arrived with a clear assignment: build up First United or close it down.

Sharon Moon went to Sunday school in a fundamentalist Baptist church. "Grim, gruesome stuff," she recalls. Then the United Church came to town. As it opened up, so did she; she played the organ, taught Sunday school and led the CGIT – Canadian Girls in Training, an ecumenical church variation on Girl Guides. At seventeen she told the minister she wanted to be a minister, too. He informed her – incorrectly – that as she was female she wouldn't be eligible for ordination. This minister is now a Community of Concern leader in British Columbia.

Over the next few years Sharon Moon found that she couldn't believe any more in God, at least not in a God "that was way out there, up there, sitting on a throne." As a teacher in Ghana, she met Roman Catholics who acted out their faith in hospital work and building irrigation systems. Then, inspired by the birth of her first child, "a deeply mystical experience where I was suddenly, powerfully aware of the presence of God," she returned to church, taught Sunday school, rediscovered the Bible, resisted but then eventually answered the call to ministry that she'd heard when she was seventeen.

First United, a large church built of city-darkened bricks on a downtown street, had just enough money to last three years. Sharon Moon made a deal with the aging congregation. Together they would either find ways to renew their church, or they would help it to die with dignity. In three years it had become a model for inner-city churches, alive and growing. Was it a miracle? Of sorts, she says. "All you have to do is make people welcome, challenge them to ministry, help them discover their own gifts, then get out of their way." The congregation and its minister work with local peace groups, Salvadorean refugees, a lesbian and gay group, an affordable-housing network. Prayer groups, guided meditation sessions, and "What on earth do we believe?" meetings help to draw people into an ever widening, all-inclusive community of worship and action.

As for The Issue, Sharon Moon speaks for herself, "Several lesbian and gay people have come out to me, and for some of them it's been the first time in their lives that they've done that." Excitement rings in her voice. "They've been through a great deal of agony and soul-searching, and finally they're coming to their truth. Watching someone go through that, it's literally like a struggle to be born. To me it's a moment of healing, a very holy moment."

What should be the role of the church? "Religion has great power to heal, and it has great power to destroy," she says. "Homosexual people have experienced that destructive power much more than the healing. So have women, and other people who are power poor. But that's not what Jesus is about. Jesus reached out to the power poor, he always reached out to empower people. To me it's a question of how we can recover that original impulse, and transform some of the distortion that's happened."

After the congregation studied the March 1988 report on sexual orientation and ministry, they decided not to send in a petition. With a wide range of opinions and feelings on The Issue, they didn't want to risk dividing their community by declaring a position. "We agreed that what holds us together is more important than our differences," says their minister. "That way instead of having winners and losers, we keep the dialogue open." At their May 1989 congregational meeting, First United supported the Victoria statement. Some felt it should have said that sexual orientation wouldn't be a bar to ministry, others that it might already have gone a little too far in that direction. The dialogue continues at First United.

When a rural eastern Ontario congregation met, ostensibly to consider the same Victoria statement, there was only one item on the agenda: joining the Community of Concern. Several influential members were pushing for it, hard. One speaker after another denounced homosexuality, the national church staff, the executive, and General Council. The only way to stop this slide into perdition was to join the Community of Concern. Applause and cheers.

A young woman – in her mid-thirties, but in a crowd like this she would still be called young – sat quiet, listening. She had grown up in this church, then left for a job in the city. But it hadn't been so long that people didn't remember her – in Sunday school, the youth group, the junior choir. She was sitting with her parents, her mother a past president of the women's group, her father an elder. It was for their sake that the young woman held back from speaking. Besides, now that she had left it wasn't her place to say what was right for this congregation. But finally she had heard enough. She stood. People smiled – though she'd been away for a while, she was still family. Small towns are like that.

"The people you're talking about," she said. "Those sinners, deviants, perverts, and child-molesters that you'd never let anywhere near the pulpit here? Those people – that's me you're talking about." She took a breath. The smiles faded. "I'm a lesbian."

The silence in the church hall was breathless. When the votes were counted, the congregation as a body had decided it would not join the Community of Concern.

CHAPTER 20

Some Folks in Duff

Duff is a dot on the map of Saskatchewan. Up close it's a brown and yellow grain elevator, a handful of houses at a bend in the highway, a garage, an old store boarded up, and a couple of tiny white churches. For supplies folks have to go to Melville or Balcarres, a few miles down the road either way. The signs here say kilometres, but the people say miles. That's how the roads were set up, three roads along means three miles.

The United Church in Duff was built by its members in the first year of the Depression. Downstairs there's a meeting room, a small kitchen, a tiny bathroom, and the heater. The sanctuary can seat about ninety people, but rarely does. Most Sundays Pat Krug and her husband are there, so is Dorothy Frick.

Dorothy Frick and Pat Krug are prairie United Church women to the core. Both are married to farmers, growing wheat and canola a few miles from the church. Each of them has raised a crop of kids. Both grew up in the church, taught Sunday school in it, and served as delegates in several of its decision-making courts. Both of them believe in God, read the Bible, and care deeply about the fate of their church. They also happen to be on opposite sides of The Issue. That's not easy in a congregation as small as Duff. In a place where your closest neighbours are half-way to the horizon, church means a lot.

A third person belongs in this story, minister Gordon Jardine. But he's no longer there. He could be called a victim of The Issue. Gordon Jardine grew up in a remote part of Manitoba, "where we only saw a student minister now and then in the summer. The rest of the time church wasn't something we went to on Sundays, it was right there at home and it was all the time." The village was so small, they had to get along with their neighbours – Scots, Germans, and Italians. That's where he learned the meaning of community.

Before church union, Dorothy Frick's pioneer family was served by a Methodist circuit-rider, a travelling saddle-bag preacher. When she left home to get a job, she went church shopping – Jehovah's Witness, Anglican, Baptist, and United were available. She chose the United, "because it was more open and because action was part of the faith," she says. She has a long list of church credentials: Eighteen years as a Sunday school teacher, active in United Church Women, the memorial fund and several other committees, president of the parish, chairperson of the local board, delegate to presbytery and conference. "It got to the point where, if I didn't have the church, my life would be empty."

Forty years ago, Sunday school and CGIT formed Pat Krug's vision of church. Ten years older than the United Church, Canadian Girls in Training was created by Anglicans, Baptists, Methodists, Presbyterians, and the YWCA. Nearly every United Church girl got involved during its peak years, 1930-75. Long before such concepts were widely accepted even in the church, CGIT stressed small-group dynamics, cooperation over competition, and leadership training for young women.

Like Pat Krug, many women who've moved into church leadership roles credit CGIT as a major influence. Its motto:

"As a Canadian Girl in Training, under the leadership of Jesus, it is my purpose to cherish health, seek truth, know God, serve others, and thus with His help become the girl that God would have me be." For Pat Krug here was a clear path that integrated faith, mission, and community.

Later, when she was married with kids, she took further leadership training at the church's Prairie Christian Training Centre. There she learned to risk speaking out what she believed and to accept challenges to her faith. She studied, served on committees, wrote petitions, and was elected president of Saskatchewan Conference in 1978. She's been a commissioner at eight General Councils, including Victoria where she worked on Sessional Committee Eight. An NDP candidate in the last provincial election, she's offended when people claim her faith is directed by her politics. "It's exactly the other way round," she argues. "Everything I do, including my political activities, is motivated almost entirely by my faith."

In Gordon Jardine's first pastoral charge, a minister came to him asking to be married. The minister admitted he was gay, and the prospective bride knew it. She believed she could straighten him out, he craved the security of marriage in a society that demanded it. Jardine agreed to marry them. "Those people lived together for twenty-five years and raised a couple of kids. For most of those years they had to go to marriage counsellors, and both of them lived in continuous personal torment. If I knew then what I know now . . . " He doesn't finish. This is a man who bears his particular cross – shame for what might have been – quite heavily.

Dorothy Frick encountered The Issue several years ago, when study materials arrived at Duff. She read everything on it that came her way, and concluded that "while a few may be born that way, most of them choose it – they turn that way." And the Bible tells her it's a sin. "Of course they have our sympathy. But the church shouldn't be condoning it, we have to take a harder line." She speaks quietly in the church hall, no bigger than an average living room. Upstairs in the sanctuary, a brightly coloured banner that Gordon Jardine made proclaims "a gift of the Spirit."

Dorothy Frick quotes *Reader's Digest*, "One of the greatest sins of the twentieth century is permissiveness." She nods in agreement. She acknowledges that Jesus forgave our sins, but continues pointedly, "He also said go and sin no more. After all, the United Church doesn't accept alcoholics, does it, unless they try and change." From her reading Dorothy Frick believes most homosexuals want to change. "They aren't happy, how can they be? They know that they're wrong, so naturally they have all this guilt and insecurity." What would she say to ministers who turn out to be homosexual? She hesitates, then says firmly, "It's a sin, there's no two ways about it. You have to mend your ways."

Pat Krug began to study human sexuality when she joined a group preparing for the 1980 General Council. She also knew a few lesbian and gay people who had viable ministries, and got to know a woman who was just then coming to terms with her sexual orientation. "With her I was able to work through all kinds of questions that I had," she recalls, settled into an ancient, collapsing sofa in her porch-cum-pottery studio. "That was a big step for me."

In March 1988 when the report came to a Duff congregation meeting, Pat Krug, her husband, and one other person supported it. Everyone else opposed it. But what about the Bible? "The echoes that its stories set off in me are so exciting, if I read it before I go to bed I can't sleep! But it's not simple stuff, it takes an incredible amount of thought and reflection." For her the key elements in it that pertain to The Issue are "the call for hospitality and inclusiveness, community, and the unavoidable element of surprise in human life."

She's puzzled by the charge that in supporting civil rights for homosexual people, the United Church is caving in to social trends. "Lesbians and gay men aren't accepted by society, far from it. If they were, we wouldn't have to push for civil rights!"

For more than a decade Gordon Jardine worked at the church's Prairie Christian Training Centre, in the deeply etched Qu'Appelle Valley of south Saskatchewan. In workshops which he had helped to organize, he learned firsthand how structures and attitudes can keep people in their place, women and homosexuals in particular, and how heterosexual men like himself can help to maintain these structures. With his head full of such radical notions, he went off to be minister at Duff and three associated congregations about an hour's drive from Fort Qu'Appelle. "I was naïve, to say the least. I assumed that a majority of the members would have at least some sympathy and respect for gay and lesbian people. That was the year when I lost what was left of my innocence," says Gordon Jardine. His tiny basement office is a cool, crowded cave in a house he built himself, where he lives with his wife and children.

Dorothy Frick was delighted when Duff United took a firm stand against the March report. Then at its 1988 annual meeting Saskatchewan Conference arrived at a more liberal position. Bitterly disappointed, she joined the Community of Concern. "I saw it as a lever, to get the report defeated at General Council." But they failed to close the door at Victoria. For the first time in her life, says Dorothy Frick, she began to question her church. "For years we've been asleep in the pews, never questioning the decisions that were made. That's not true any more. When they opened the door to homosexuals, that was the beginning of the end of the United Church as we know it."

In the summer leading up to General Council, Pat Krug got an anonymous letter signed "a member of the church," accusing her of wrecking it for the sake of the queers. One Sunday a man told her husband he couldn't stand talking with homo-sympathizers, then he turned his back. A meeting of the United Church Women scheduled to be held at the Krugs' place was suddenly shifted to another house, without telling her. After General Council no one asked her what happened there. The Krugs continued to be shunned.

When the March report came out, Gordon Jardine was asked to give his opinion on it, at each of his three congregations. At Balcarres there was deep division, but there was also dialogue. "That was the only one of the four congregations that I thought behaved in a Christian way," he recalls. At Duff only a few people, including Dorothy Frick, were willing even to discuss the issue. At the other two, "I didn't get five seconds into my answer when they told me to shut up. With no further discussion they took a vote that they'd never let a homosexual into their pulpit. It was unanimous. They closed the door on any possibility of dialogue that I could see. That kind of behaviour didn't seem Christian to me, it seemed more like what you'd expect of Nazis."

One Sunday in June 1988 he was in the pulpit, preaching about the famine in Sudan. "I started to weep. I just lost it, I couldn't stop." A year later, his voice is unsteady as he recalls that morning. "I realized that I was in real trouble, and had to get out."

Dorothy Frick's husband, who doesn't go much, keeps telling her to quit the United Church. He'd been raised a fire-and-brimstone evangelical. When they were married they went to the United Church because she preferred it and because it was closer. They didn't have a car then. But Dorothy Frick won't give up on her church, not yet. "There's no other church I'd feel comfortable in. It's a way of life for me."

So far Pat Krug has hung on at Duff. "All I can be sure of is that I'm saying what I believe, and I'm hearing what others believe – as much as they're willing to tell me." But why do she and her husband stay in a congregation where they're treated like pariahs? "You have to live with things for a while," she says, "As long as I'm there I have to be dealt with, face-to-face. Most of us are too polite, we don't like conflict. Worse than that, we see diversity as conflict and want to do away with it."

What has to happen for Dorothy Frick to stay in the United Church? "We have to take a firm stand on homosexuality like the Anglicans did." The Anglican bishops of Canada decreed that homosexuals would only be eligible for ordination if they took a vow of celibacy. But how could such a policy be brought about in the United Church, which is not run by bishops? "We have to be much more careful whom we send to presbytery and conference," says Dorothy Frick, carefully. "That's the only way we're going to get more control over General Council."

Gordon Jardine is back living in Fort Qu'Appelle. He works with wood now. "Ever since I was a kid I've loved the smell and the feel of wood – especially its sculptural qualities." He makes bowls, small decorative boxes, as well as baptismal fonts and sacramental objects for churches. "I find it healing, the most personality-unifying thing I've ever done. For now anyway, it seems to be my soul's calling. I guess you could call it my ministry."

He goes to church along the road in Balcarres. "I don't think I could ever go back to serving a congregation which acts in direct contradiction with the Gospel." He's talking about a calling that's shaped most of his adult life. "Christianity isn't an exam you pass so you can get into heaven. And I certainly don't believe it's what the Community of Concern says it is, something you can define by majority vote. More often in history it's been a small remnant that's been faithful, able to see injustice and have the courage to fight it."

In the end neither Dorothy Frick nor Pat Krug may have to decide whether to carry on at Duff United. Among many items facing cutbacks in the shrinking church budget are mission support grants. These are subsidies from the national church that keep alive hundreds of small, isolated, and inner-city congregations that can't generate enough revenue to be self-supporting.

Duff could be one of the first to go.

CHAPTER 21

Into the Storm

Who should and who should not be a minister, that is the question. Or is it? Some believe the question ought to be: who's to decide who should be a minister? The congregations? The Community of Concern? God?

According to the United Church Basis of Union, "We believe that Jesus Christ, as Supreme Head of the Church, has appointed therein a ministry of the word and sacraments, and calls men and women to this ministry; that the Church, under the guidance of the Holy Spirit, recognizes and chooses those whom He calls, and should thereupon duly ordain them to the work of the ministry."

Nothing in there about homosexuals. In fact many have already served as ministers. Many still do. In the current jargon, some of these have been practising homosexuals, some not. Some have been caught, some suspected, some driven out of pulpit and community. Some committed suicide, another way out. Some were married, produced and raised children. Others remained "bachelors" or "spinsters." Some were known by their congregations to have companions, particular friends or "personal assistants." Some of these partners even shared the manse. And in some cases they've been welcomed into the life of the community, almost as if they were husbands or wives. And so it would go, for years. This was the conspiracy of silence, delicate but strong.

Brian Burke doesn't believe in the conspiracy of silence, at least not for himself. In official church talk, Brian Burke is a self-declared practising homosexual. In his own words, he's a gay Christian living in a committed relationship, out of the closet. He believes that to be a Christian means "to be a whole person in right relationship with God." Among other things that means being out of the closet. Brian Burke also believes that he's called by God to be an ordained minister in the United Church. He's taken the first official steps toward ordination: his Vancouver congregation agreed to sponsor him as a candidate, and the local presbytery approved. Now he's in theology school.

Like many candidates for ministry, he came to his calling by an indirect route. He was raised an Irish Catholic in Quebec, but in his teens rejected the rigid, archaic dogmas of that church. The more he learned of official Christian history – the Crusades, the Inquisition, the conquests – the less he liked what he heard. Then at university he met United Church people "who went to church not because it had all the answers, but because it encouraged them to ask questions, to explore and to progress in their faith." Among others he met Bill Siksay. They live together now, in Vancouver. They go to South Hill United, a predominately working-class and elderly congregation. Both of them serve on its board.

Brian Burke worked in Ottawa for a year, as executive assistant to MP Margaret Mitchell. He believes strongly in Martin Luther's concept, the priesthood of all believers, which holds that every Christian is a minister. But over the years he's become increasingly aware that he wanted to make the church his whole life. The Issue was the catalyst.

"Obviously it's polarized the church. But at the same time it's clarified many things, including what it means to be a minister," he says, at home in the small apartment he shares with Bill Siksay. "I've seen the pulpit used in two ways. I've seen it used as an instrument of power, to lie, manipulate, and keep people in the dark. On the other hand I've seen pulpits used to shed light into some very complex, frightening aspects of life, to help people think for themselves and explore their faith in an active, conscious way." If that's what a minister can do, that's what Brian Burke wants to be.

He knows what he's up against. His partner went through it a decade ago. Bill Siksay grew up United Church in Oshawa, Ontario. From childhood he had an unfocussed notion that he'd like to be a minister. At the University of Toronto he encountered theology students whose faith found active expression in the struggle for justice. They inspired him to follow a similar path. His old Oshawa congregation was delighted to sponsor him. Bill Siksay was bright and well respected, and their first candidate for ministry in half a century. The area presbytery approved. In 1978 he entered the Vancouver School of Theology as an intended candidate for ministry, the first stage in the process.

By then Bill Siksay had been actively gay for four years. "Actively gay" is what the church now calls "practising homosexual." His fellow theology students were supportive, but urged him to maintain the conspiracy of silence. He did.

Then in 1980 a friend back in Toronto was murdered by a man he'd picked up in a bar. Bill Siksay heard about it on TV. "It was a terrible shock, especially the way the cops and the media dealt with it. They more or less said that he got what he deserved. Just before he was killed Duncan had come out to his family, United Church people. They told him to see a psychiatrist. And then he died. Here I was going into the ministry with a sense of the Bible and Christianity that was rooted in the seeking of justice, and I couldn't say a word." He broke the conspiracy of silence.

He told his family, wrote to his minister in Oshawa, and informed the presbytery committee that he was gay. This was a first, and no one knew what to do with him. One minister on the committee asked him how he would do marriage counselling. When he began to respond, the minister interrupted. How could *you* do marriage counselling, he asked again – it was a rhetorical question. Bill Siksay answered anyway. "I've probably learned a lot more than you have about keeping relationships going, with none of the support structures that heterosexuals have to help them all their lives."

Presbytery passed him on to conference. The conference executive decided that no lesbian or gay person would be accepted as a full candidate – the next stage for Bill Siksay – or for ordination, not until the national church had a policy. The buck was being passed, and along with it the intended candidate. Presbytery passed him back to the congregation that sponsored him. After a long meeting, twenty-five of thirty elders voted to continue sponsoring him.

Back to presbytery. This time there were people on the committee that he had never seen before. The chair asked him what he believed in. "I believe in God," Bill Siksay began. "Don't be flip," said the minister. "What do you believe in?" Another rhetorical question. "The rest of it went downhill from there," he recalls. "It was a third-degree grilling where they asked me all these questions, but they weren't interested in any of my answers."

Through this turmoil he fell so far behind in his work at theology school that finally he withdrew. Presbytery claimed he had been expelled. The school denied it and recommended that he continue his studies. So did his congregation. But by now the relationship between Bill Siksay and the presbytery overseeing his candidacy had collapsed. Thoroughly discouraged, he withdrew as a candidate for ministry.

Now he works as executive assistant to Svend Robinson, Canada's first openly gay member of Parliament. It's a good job for Bill Siksay, but despite everything that happened the first time, and the current state of his church, he still wants to be a minister. Why? "The Christian message still provides the basic framework for my life, for all of life. I still want to live and work in a setting that fosters that message." He speaks with quiet conviction. "I don't know of any institution that's struggled harder than the United Chuch has to be open and responsible and faithful to that message. And I still think I have skills for ministry."

Both these would-be ministers know they've got an uphill climb ahead of them. It may be even steeper today than when Bill Siksay tried it the first time. His presbytery committee asked him back then how he'd deal with a hostile congregation. "I wouldn't," he told them. "There's this fallacy in the United Church that to be a minister you have to be able to minister equally well to every person in every congregation in the country. That's baloney, there's no minister practising who'd be acceptable to everyone in the church. Ministers who don't know that are fools, and probably cause more problems than they solve. That's the whole point of the selection process, isn't it, where a congregation and a minister are supposed to find each other."

To become ordained ministers, Bill Siksay and Brian Burke are willing to adapt and adjust in many ways. But not in the one way that their opponents want, not unless something is given by the other side. Says Brian Burke, "As long as our critics refuse to allow that a lesbian or gay relationship could have the same intrinsic value, the same human worth as a heterosexual relationship, how can they turn round and demand of us the same behaviour that they supposedly demand of themselves – fidelity, the intention of permanence, and so forth? The only word for that in any language is hypocrisy." His voice peaks then settles, as it might in the pulpit. "Once we've agreed that the relationships have equal value, then it's reasonable to talk about what ethical systems we can share."

At South Hill United one Sunday, a woman in her eighties was talking with Brian Burke. She is what's called a pillar of the church, and she's a conservative on most issues. She patted him on the arm. "You have to be patient," she said. "Some people take longer than others to understand."

It took Darlene Young two decades to understand. She was raised in Cape Breton, Nova Scotia, by fundamentalist Pentecostals. The Bible was the rule, and life was grim. In her teens she jettisoned all that, decided there wasn't a god and that it was a waste of time to go to church. She hung around with people whose ultimate goal was the next party. "But I was always a reflective person, and I guess all along I was looking for something beyond that." One Easter she found it, "a conversion experience," she calls it, in a United Church, of all places.

"Suddenly I could see that there was a god, there was a plan, and there was a place for me in that plan," she recalls, in the small Halifax co-op apartment she shares with her partner. "In the Pentecostal sense I felt compelled to acknowledge my sinfulness, and give my life to Christ. This was a very personalized faith, just me and Jesus." Once again for her the Bible was God's word, infallible, without contradictions. And Darlene Young realized that the only place she could fulfil her commitment to Jesus was in ministry.

But where? She had serious doubts about the United Church. "I saw it as very liberal, not enough centred in the Bible and too much in the world." She tested her call as a summer fill-in with a conservative congregation in rural Nova Scotia. She loved it, the lessons, the preaching, all of it.

But she wasn't at peace. "From my early teens I knew I was a lesbian. But the Bible said it was a sin. So I ran away from myself, I got deeper and deeper into my religion. I became incredibly homophobic, what else could I do? Any time the subject of homosexuality came up I'd just bombard people with Scripture." By then she was studying at the Atlantic School of Theology in Halifax. Another student minister and an Anglican priest both confided in her that they were gay. "All I could tell them was 'you're sinners, you've got to repent.'" She shakes her head, uncomfortable with the memory.

Darlene Young's first summer internship took her into a charismatic congregation in northern Ontario. The people there believed in miracles and speaking in tongues. This was far more pentecostal than anything she'd ever encountered, especially in the United Church. "These people were so conservative they actually forced me to react, to question my own way of thinking. Against my will I started to open up. My faith started to grow."

At the same time her internal war escalated. "I prayed and prayed and prayed for the desires to be taken away. They weren't. And it was taking more and more energy to hide them." During her last year of theology school she met a woman in New Brunswick. They became lovers. "Finally I had to come to terms with who I was, and what the Bible was. Instead of a list of rules, I found the living spirit of God there, in the poetry and the insights and the wonderful stories of people's faith journeys. I knew if I was to take the Bible seriously, I had to believe that I was created in God's image, and that God had graced me with my life, which included my sexuality."

It was the start of another conversion experience. This one would cost her dearly.

In her last year of theology school Darlene Young told a few close friends, classmates, about her relationship. "They were far more supportive than I'd ever been." But they asked her some hard questions. How could she function in ministry while maintaining a relationship in secret? Or, on the other hand, how long would she survive in ministry if she was honest and open about her sexuality? She and a gay friend at theology school actually contemplated a marriage of convenience, but settled for using each other as social cover. As the need arose, each could refer to the other as the absent boyfriend or girlfriend.

"As things turned out, my first pastoral charge was in New Brunswick, so I was able to maintain my relationship – but in a *very* discreet manner. The strain was incredible. Your first experience as an ordained minister totally on your own is hard enough." She was ministering to five separate congregations. "On top of that my church was forcing me to lie about who I was. This was my most important relationship, the person I was relying on for support, but I couldn't tell anyone. I'd have to go out of town just so we could be together."

When the March report came out, people in her congregations started talking about homosexuals, "as if they were alien creatures from another world. I wanted so much to tell them, wait a minute, there are people right here in your congregation, there's one in your *pulpit!*" In a study meeting she sat quietly while one of her parishioners said, "I'd know if one of them was preaching. I could spot one of them a mile away." On more than one occasion she heard people say, "They should all be taken out and shot."

The strain became intolerable. "I didn't see how I could stay in ministry and live out my orientation with any kind of integrity." In the summer of 1988, after two years in Sussex Corners, she resigned from her pastoral charge to study for a year and plan her next moves – in or out of the ministry. A friend persuaded her to give two radio interviews, one before the Victoria General Council and one after. In the second of these, on the same day the Community of Concern held its big rally at Sackville, Darlene Young came out on the CBC."People kept saying this was only an issue in Toronto and Vancouver, thank God we don't have any of them here in the Maritimes. So I felt it would have to be me."

By the rules that govern ministry, the local presbytery – Saint John – was supervising her studies back at the Atlantic School of Theology. Since she was studying, she was taken off the list of ministers available for pastoral work. By spring 1989 Darlene Young knew that she was still called to congregational ministry, whatever the risks. Her studies complete, she applied to be listed again as available for call. "Given the climate here I wanted to be on the national availability list so congregations elsewhere would have the opportunity to consider me."

Saint John Presbytery refused. It acknowledged that in every way Darlene Young was eligible to be listed for call, except for one thing – she was what they called a self-declared practising homosexual. According to the Maritime Conference policy enacted in autumn 1988, self-declared practising homosexuals would not be ordained, commissioned, or transfered within the church in that region. Darlene Young was assigned to limbo.

She decided to appeal. "Ultimately in my mind what they were doing was impeding my vocation." As she says it, she doesn't sound angry, but determined. By vocation, she didn't mean the employment they were denying her, she meant the call to ministry which she believed had come to her, not from the United Church of Canada, but from God. "I know I have gifts and talents in preaching the Word – helping people to make connections between their daily lives and God, in leading groups, and in pastoral care. I feel I have the right to exercise that call, at the very least to see if there's a congregation out there who'll consider me."

The wheels of justice grind slowly. She couldn't even go back to school until the conference appeal committee clarified her status. She worked with mental patients at the Nova Scotia Hospital. "This was totally outside the context of what we usually think of as church, but it was a very spiritual, faith-filled experience for me." Also she helped organize the Halifax visit of the Names Project, the huge and ever-growing quilt whose segments recall the lives of AIDS' victims around the world. "That was a ministry in itself, to show solidarity with people who suffer from such a terrible disease."

Finally in August 1989 the appeal committee heard her case. A month later they delivered their verdict, finding "that there has been a substantial injustice in the disposition of this matter by Saint John Presbytery." It directed that Rev Darlene Young's name be placed on the General Council availability list, and recommended that should she receive a call or appointment it be supported by the presbytery "because of the lack of consensus in the Church as a whole as to whether the practice of homosexuality is in every circumstance a bar to effective ministry, and because there may be pastoral charges, presbyteries, or conferences which would approve such a call or appointment."

CHAPTER 22

Some Folks in Penticton

About twenty-five thousand people live in Pentiction, British Columbia. It sits on a land bridge between two long, narrow lakes deep in the Okanagan Valley. The surrounding brown hills are terraced with orchards and vineyards.

You can't miss the United Church, it's painted bright blue. Two proposals to tone it down have been rejected by the congregation. In a recent census almost a quarter of the people in Penticton claimed allegiance to this church. The actual membership is about seven hundred, and average attendance about a hundred and fifty. This includes a wide range of ages and, particularly when it comes to The Issue, a wide range of views. As in most congregations there are homosexual members, and parents of homosexuals who are known as such to very few. Sunday mornings you can choose between two services, one fairly structured and traditional in its tone, the other looser and more contemporary, often organized and led by lay people.

When the March report hit the press, a meeting was called at Penticton United. Before the congregation saw the report they all received from one of their members a copy of an editorial from the March 28 issue of *Western Report*, a right-wing magazine based in Alberta. The heading captures its tone: "And now a word from Canada's No. 1 ecclesiastical freak show."

The editorial is signed by Ted Byfield, chairman of the family company that publishes *Western Report*. The Byfields, who don't belong to the United Church, love to use it for target practice. Almost every one of its public positions offends them – on peace, economic justice, women's rights, inclusive language, abortion, and now worst of all, homosexuality.

In his March 28 editorial Byfield predicts that the Church, which he calls "the Rhinoceros Party of Canadian Theology," will soon be marrying men and dogs. He concludes by agreeing with those who believe that "their church has been taken over by a bunch of trolls, and is being destroyed in the service of causes that are either not Christian at all, or wholly alien to Christianity." Coming from a committed business vision of life, his advice is simple. "Just cut off the funds to head office. In almost no time at all you'll be amazed at the changes that occur."

Not surprisingly, the Penticton congregational meeting was a highly charged affair. Five petitions resulted. One demanded rejection of the report, one called for its acceptance, one had doubts about it, and two affirmed existing procedures for ordaining and commissioning ministers. All were passed on to presbytery, conference, and General Council. At a second meeting, about a third of the membership turned up to vote on whether they would allow the ordination of self-declared practising homosexuals. A number of people boycotted the meeting, objecting to such a narrow and loaded question. About three-quarters of the people who came voted no.

After General Council, The Issue moved to a back burner. Life went on at Penticton United. But not for the local Community of Concern chapter, whose members feel isolated, unheard, and misunderstood. When a committee was struck in 1989 to select an interim minister, none of the four COC nominees was elected to it. Some members have already left the church, but they stick with the COC, clinging together for comfort and reassurance.

Their chairman, Ed Chyzowski, gathered them together one summer night in 1989 to air their grievances in the back room of Mickey Finn's, a steak and seafood restaurant he owns and operates in Penticton. Here's some of what they had to say:

Alma Petkau: We came to the United Church ten years ago, looking for a church with old-time values, the values we were brought up with. For a few years it was all right, then it started slipping away from us. The thirty-second General Council was the final straw.

Phyllis McIntosh: I've been in the Church for sixty years. When the report on homosexuality came up, I wrote to everyone from the moderator on down, telling them if they passed it I'd have to leave. I resigned from the Church right after General Council, from the UCW and everything. It's not my church any more.

Ed Chyzowski: I've had fifteen happy years in this church. But now I have no sense of belonging any more. We're hungry and we're not being fed. So we've turned to the Bible, the Renewal Fellowship and the Community of Concern for our spiritual needs.

John Yost: I've been a member since I was born. There's no way I want a homosexual in the pulpit telling me it's okay. The church has been trying to please too many people. The time has come to get off the fence, to go one way or the other.

Bernice Wish: I joined the church in 1941 believing in the Basis of Union, the twenty articles, many of which are now being flaunted and ignored. It's reached the point where I don't have anything in common with the church any more, so I've resigned and joined the Presbyterians.

Eleanor McDonald: I was organist and choir director for eight years, but I resigned from the church four years ago. I was upset when I went to church and didn't feel any religious uplift, and because lay people were doing things in the church that they're not qualified for, like interpreting the Scriptures. We pay professionals to do that for us.

Harold Myers: I've been a member of this church for forty-one years, and in every one of those years I've held some office. You look to the ministers for leadership, and all they do is present both sides of the issue and leave you up in the air not knowing which one is right.

Merv Petkau: I grew up a Mennonite, but I joined the United Church during my thirty-six years in the Royal Canadian Air Force. I'm not against a homosexual coming to church, but according to the Good Book he shouldn't be in the pulpit teaching morals to our young people – they're bad enough already.

Why do they feel so strongly that lesbians and gay men shouldn't be ministers?

Bernice Wish: You wouldn't expect a blind man to be a bus-driver, would you? If a married couple or a teenager was having problems, what kind of counselling could a homosexual offer them?

Harold Myers: I can imagine one of them wanting to have another man living with him in the manse. Society's set up for procreation, and homosexuals can't do that.

John Yost: And now they want the church to marry them! Marriage is a sacred vow between a man and a woman. There's no way it says in the Bible that a man can be married to a man, or a woman to a woman.

Ed Chyzowski: Until two years ago I didn't know anything about homosexuality, and I didn't want to – I still don't. I haven't associated willingly with homosexuals and I don't want to. I wouldn't go to their home, and I wouldn't invite them to mine.

Phyllis McIntosh: One of the items in the report is that you can't ask about a candidate's sexual orientation. I know from experience that there are homosexuals all about us, and they won't admit it.

Harold Myers: Everything's run by minorities these days. Ten years down the road you won't be able to turn down a homosexual. We have to build it into church rules now, so we can protect ourselves.

Alma Petkau: In all of history there have been moral standards. In those places where moral standards went down the drain, so did the civilization. If we don't follow what the Bible says, our society, too, will go right down the drain.

Merv Petkau: It's not just the United Church, the other churches have to come to grips with this thing, too. We have to get the churches back to doing what they're supposed to be doing – teaching morals. What we have now is closer to devil-worship.

Eleanor McDonald: I believe the Antichrist is taking over our church, its tentacles are reaching out in every direction. All the people who work at head office are under the influence. It's very discouraging. We've got to fight the whole church.

What other issues do they have to fight besides homosexuality?

Merv Petkau: I don't like the church being involved in politics. They should leave that to the government.

Bernice Wish: A few years ago they wanted us to support the grape boycott, for the unions. Where does this fit into religion? Christ said, "I am not of this world." He didn't go out trying to change the Roman Empire.

Merv Petkau: They shouldn't be telling me what I can buy and what I can't.

Bernice Wish: I was very upset when they started calling God Mother as well as Father. I was brought up with God the Father Almighty – it didn't say anything about Mother.

Merv Petkau: The majority don't want it, but they brought it in so quietly no one noticed. Now they're talking about rewriting the Bible, with that new Authority of Scriptures study.

Peggy Clarke: If they change the Lord's Prayer to "our parent who art in Heaven," I will not pray it that way.

Eleanor McDonald: I despise inclusive language, and I despise feminists who need government regulation or unionism or whatever to make their way in the world. Nobody has to use inclusive language to make me feel good.

Phyllis McIntosh: I never minded being called chair*man* of the council. It's a position, that's all, it has nothing to do with the person.

Peggy Clarke: If you got back to the ABCs of our faith, the Ten Commandments, the Lord's Prayer and all that, if you learned that and taught it and preached it, then maybe a lot of our problems would be overcome.

Harold Myers: Taking care of the spiritual needs of the people is a big enough job by itself that you wouldn't have time for anything else.

Phyllis McIntosh: How many of the kids today can say the Lord's Prayer? They're not even allowed to say it in school!

Eleanor McDonald: The children aren't being taught right. The closest they get to learning religion is when they compare Christianity with some of those other religions – Buddhism and the others – I believe to the detriment of Christianity.

Alma Petkau: So much money and effort is spent on young people, but they just use it for recreation instead of a learning experience. And they're not coming into the church.

Anything else?

John Yost: What bothers me is the people down in Toronto who govern the church think they know how we should perform and what we should believe. When we have a vote that we think something is wrong, those so-called educated people just ignore us.

Phyllis McIntosh: The powers that be at head office are so far removed from the grass roots, which I think is the most important part of the church. Without the grass roots we wouldn't *have* a church.

Bernice Wish: We're the backbone of the church.

Phyllis McIntosh: They've got to come down off their high horse. and see what it's like being the grass roots.

Eleanor McDonald: We're told that we're a democratic church. But as organist and choir director, when I tried to get a ruling on something, the minister wouldn't take a stand one way or the other. Someone somewhere is sure taking a stand, and they're inflicting it down the throats of everyone else!

Alma Petkau: The delegates that we send to conference and council aren't even bound to represent our opinions, they can follow their own ideas, which might or might not agree with ours.

Phyllis McIntosh: That's our fault. We should make them state their platform before they go.

Bernice Wish: After a while you started to realize you're being brainwashed. Look at Darwin, he was touted and promoted because of his great ideas about evolution, but I don't believe we came from the apes. If we came from the apes, why are there still apes?

Ed Chyzowski: We formed the Community of Concern to lobby General Council. If congregations all across the country do the same then General Council will have to listen to us. If they don't, General Council will continue to have its way.

Why is homosexuality the fuel that makes their anger burn hottest?

Ed Chyzowski: All my teachings, from my family, my church, the laws of society, and the Bible, tell me that homosexuality is sinful, it's criminal, it's an aberration, and a malady. After sixty years of believing that, how can you suddenly accept them just because someone in Toronto says love thy neighbour?

Bernice Wish: They claim that they're ten per cent of the population, but I don't believe it. I've lived sixty-six years, I've come in contact with hundreds of people in business, and in all that time I've never met a homosexual.

Merv Petkau: In the military we had names for them, and we knew how to deal with them. They knew what would happen to them if they acted up. The military has a way of looking after these things.

Bernice Wish: They say we persecute them, but how could I persecute them when I've never even met one?

Ed Chyzowski: What it comes down to is that it's a totally unacceptable lifestyle.

Harold Myers: It always has been, for the whole life of the Bible.

Ed Chyzowski: And that's why we have the Community of Concern, to stop the kind of changes from happening that would make all of us very, very unhappy.

Everyone applauds.

CHAPTER 23

Against the Tide

Critics charge that the United Church leadership and the commissioners elected to General Council have been swayed by a small, powerful lobby group of homosexuals and their supporters. The church also stands accused of bending to current fads, going along with the social tide. With a lot of help from the press, these two ideas have gained wide currency in many parts of the beleaguered church. Both charges warrant a closer look.

For homosexual Canadians these can be called the best of times and the worst of times. In the seventies they won civil rights in some jurisdictions, a lot more media attention, and the early warning signs of a fundamentalist backlash. Three provinces and one territory – Quebec, Ontario, Manitoba, and the Yukon now include sexual orientation along with other protected categories in their human rights codes. In the rest of the country, this move continues to be strenuously resisted.

As conservatives and Christian fundamentalists gained power in the eighties, the backlash escalated. The toll that

AIDS has taken, in North America primarily among gay men, compounds the problem. In the same way that church authorities blamed earlier epidemics on their victims – the poor, or in church terms, the sinful – so, too, conservative Christians have tended to blame this new epidemic on homosexual men, or in their terms, the sinful. In many jurisdictions civil rights came under attack and, in some places, have actually been reversed. Like other minorities, lesbians and gay men appear to be increasingly subject to physical attack by gangs of bored, disillusioned youth. So it appears that rather than following a trend, General Council may actually have resisted a tide.

As for "head office," the United Church doesn't have a non-discriminatory workplace policy for lesbians and gay men. Nor does it have the kind of policy that a number of other large employers have instituted, protecting the jobs of people who get AIDS. When parts of the church, such as the Naramata Centre in British Columbia enact non-discriminatory hiring policies, these apply only within their own small jurisdiction. Some argue that when it said "regardless of sexual orientation," the thirty-second General Council created such a policy for its ministers. If so it doesn't seem to have provided much real protection.

In November 1988 the executive sent to congregations a document answering many of the questions that critics were asking. Among other things, it says that "religious bodies are consistently exempted from some provisions of human rights and labour legislation. . . . it [the church] is not vulnerable to civil prosecution as long as it applies its procedures fairly and bases any 'discrimination' decisions on clearly stated policy approved in its formal beliefs and theology." In other words, "regardless of sexual orientation" in the Victoria statement makes it more difficult, but not impossible, to discriminate.

The stakes are clearly identified in a book called *A Crisis of Understanding*, published in Burlington, Ontario. It sets out the conservative Christian agenda on The Issue – homosexuality is a sickness and a sin, the family is threatened, the solution offered is the United Church Renewal Fellowship's: repentance and conversion to heterosexuality. Appendix C tells churches and other organizations how to avoid getting in trouble with the sexual orientation clause of the Ontario Human Rights Code. The advice originates with two legal advisers to the Coalition for Family Values, formed by several right-wing lobby groups, including the National Citizen's Coalition and REAL Women. The authors suggest restructuring doctrinal and policy materials to take advantage of exemption clauses in the Code. In effect, a clearly stated policy of doctrine such as the one the Community of Concern wants, manditory celibacy for unmarried people in ministry, would legalize discrimination, which already occurs de facto in the church.

Under seige, nervous church officials have backed away from any public action or statement that could be construed as supporting homosexual people, particularly those in ministry. The Victoria statement calls for "all courts, congregations and appropriate divisions of The United Church of Canada to become active in support of human rights for lesbian and gay people." This initiative appears to be on hold.

A senior church official told Eilert Frerichs that "in these difficult times, gay and lesbian people are called to bear the cross for the church." Frerichs replied that he thought someone had already done that. "In any case it's unfair for the church to assign that role to some of its weakest members," he said. "Surely if there's a cross to be borne, the whole church – the whole people of God – should be bearing it."

The thirty-second General Council called for "pastoral care of individuals and groups in our United Church of Canada community, who feel unheard, manipulated, or estranged." Allen Hall of Friends of Affirm says, "While the church has been giving all kinds of attention to people who've threatened to quit the church or withhold their money, as an institution it's provided none at all to the people who are most likely to be 'unheard, manipulated, or estranged' – lesbians and gay men. Instead of owning the Victoria statement proudly, they've run away from it. Staff people who've been supportive in the past have now been told to keep their distance. That means the institutional church is giving the whole field over to the Community of Concern." Allen Hall's brother, Carl, is a COC leader in New Germany, Nova Scotia. Theirs is one of many divided family stories in the United Church. At times The Issue looks like a civil war.

Witch-hunting appears to be on the rise, against suspected gay or lesbian ministers and candidates. And the campaigns appear to be working. Ministers in personnel work report that a number of lesbian and gay colleagues have left the ministry. They didn't leave in anger, but in fear. One personnel minister calls it "a reign of terror." In a church with a chronic shortage of ministers, fewer and fewer apply as the screws get tighter.

In Ontario a Community of Concern phone campaign threatened to block one candidate for the ministry at the conference annual meeting, where candidates are usually ordained. As a matter of principle he refused to disclose his sexual orientation. No one had any right to ask, he argued, and in any case it had no bearing on his fitness for ministry. At the same time he didn't want the ordination service to degenerate in mud-slinging and name-calling. Instead he withdrew, until a later date. Since then he's received a letter from one of the COC people, expressing her shame and regret over her part in what happened. She had come to realize, she said, that she could no longer associate herself with a group that engaged in such tactics.

A minister in the Maritimes had an overnight visit from her sister. First thing next morning a parishioner arrived on the doorstop of the manse, demanding to know who that woman was that had spent the night with her. A minister in Ontario has heard from several members of her congregation how grateful they are to have her in their pulpit, rather than "one of those queers." This minister is a lesbian.

A Prairie minister – divorced, with kids – says, "When you're gay you get used to living on edge, always half-prepared to be exposed and thrown out. That makes you flexible in some ways, less likely to get set in your ways. But it also makes it hard to give yourself completely to a congregation, the way I believe a minister should. It's for their safety as much as mine, should there be a sudden forced break. But I find that kind of holding back very painful."

A minister on the West Coast has served several parishes and worked on church committees at all levels. A former co-chairperson of Affirm, he lives with his lover. Many of his parishioners know it. Together they maintain the strange conspiracy of silence that continues to govern most of these situations. But he says he will never again accept a call to a congregation while concealing such an important aspect of his life. This minister is prepared for the possibility that his present congregation could be his last.

All in all, the door doesn't seem to have opened quite as wide as critics claim. But then the critics have made it clear that as far as they're concerned, if the door is open at all it's wide open.

What about this powerful lobby group, Affirm and its friends?

Friends of Affirm has members across the country, but no office, no organizational structure, no revenue, no publication, and no membership list. A loose association, it includes supportive heterosexual people, and homosexual people for whom Affirm is too public. With the national offices of the church and the Community of Concern both located in the Toronto area, spokespeople for the Friends of Affirm group in that city often end up speaking for the whole network. It did so at a press conference in April 1989, when the COC distributed its controversial questionnaire on the Victoria statement to United Church congregations across the country.

Friends of Affirm spokesperson Rev Lawrence Pushee, of Glen Rhodes United in Toronto, called it "an amateur survey composed of leading questions designed to elicit predetermined responses. And to make certain all the responses conform to COC policies, the surveys are numbered allowing for identification of respondents."

The final two questions in the survey asked whether the church should welcome practising and non-practising homosexual persons as ordained or commissioned ministers, lay leaders, members, or adherents. Lawrence Pushee told the press, "For gay and lesbian people in the church it must be a frightening prospect to have congregations being asked whether they should be written off entirely."

Aside from giving the occasional press conference, what is Friends of Affirm about? Says Allen Hall, "We're here to support Affirm, to provide a safe place for lesbians and gay men in the United Church, and to encourage face-to-face encounters between heterosexual and homosexual people. Also we want to help keep alive a vision of an inclusive church and to encourage people to think for themselves." In his own congregation, a woman told Hall she was quitting the church not only because of the homosexuals, but also because she couldn't remain in a church "that has a Chink as moderator."

Some Friends of Affirm advocate a stronger approach. In his office next to the church's Sunday school, Rev Don Gillies of Bloor Street United says, "The Moderator keeps asking us not to fight fire with fire, he wants us to take the high road on this. At least the liberal camp are tending to respect that. But not the other side. It makes me furious when they go round witch-hunting, keeping files on people, blocking people from their legitimate work as ministers, doing all kinds of harm to all kinds of people. Don't they know they live in glass houses? We have information about incest in the family of one COC leader. Do they think we'll not be tempted to respond in kind?"

Affirm has no office and no dues, but it does have elected officers, a small bank account, and national meetings twice a year. Even so, when Bill Siksay went to the 1989 Affirm annual meeting in Ottawa he wondered if the organization would survive. After Victoria the members were exhausted, and they've been worn down further by the turmoil that followed. Apparently Affirm survived its annual meeting. Bill Siksay was elected co-chairperson.

"Affirm consists of five or six small groups scattered across the country," he says. "At our largest national meeting ever, we managed to bring together maybe forty-five people. One Community of Concern mailing costs more than our entire budget for ten years! And unlike the COC we can't funnel donations through the church's charitable status number. This is what they call a powerful lobby group?"

The function of the group varies from place to place, according to the needs and resources of local members. In Toronto it tends to be a support group for United Church members and clergy who feel isolated in their congregations. In Vancouver it's more of a lobby group, but even there it's extremely low-key. And in other communities it has so few members it barely holds itself together.

A couple of years ago Barry Mills decided it was time to start an Affirm group at his church in downtown Edmonton. Perhaps it might grow into a group for the whole city, even the province. But Barry Mills doesn't look like a high-powered organizer. He's a soft-spoken, middle-aged man who teaches comparative literature at the University of Alberta. From his childhood in Saint John, New Brunswick, he remembers church as a very formal affair, a little grim, with elders in morning coats. In the early sixties when he recognized that he was gay, he went into exile from the church. It didn't seem to have a place for him.

Then he discovered Garneau United, in downtown Edmonton. He describes it as "a happy, active church, not rich," and much more open than he had expected to a variety of people and a range of social issues. He told the minister he was gay – no problem. In a discussion group on The Issue, some people were upset, a few even quit the church, but most were either supportive or at least open. After General Council a series of forums gave people the chance to thrash out the implications of the new statement. Mostly it was women who attended. "We've had some lively discussions, and people were very frank. The church owes it to its members to facilitate encounters of this kind with all sorts of people, lesbians and gay men, Third World people, people of other faiths."

When Barry Mills attended a post-Victoria meeting at another congregation, he felt as if he'd stumbled into another world. "I was really shocked to discover how sheltered I am at Garneau. At this other church a few really hateful people dominated everything, they ruined any possibility of free discussion. Mostly they seemed to be fifty-five-year-old men, and you could hear the fear and the rage in their voices. Men seem to be very threatened these days, with so many changes going on around them that they can't control. They seem to have such outmoded ways of dealing with the world."

Even when he was in exile from the church, "I never felt I was outcast by God. I have dialogues with the Holy Spirit. Since I was quite young, I've always felt the Holy Spirit was a friend." He smiles, as one might at the thought of a friend. "The Holy Spirit and I are at peace, on many issues. That's why I feel it's a dialogue." Do these issues include sex? "I believe you can love somebody with your body, as well as with your mind and your spirit. It's a very natural way of loving someone. For a Christian sex means love and concern for the other, even if the encounter is what some people might call casual."

Garneau United seemed a good place to start an Affirm group. Its congregation includes a solid core of people who are committed to a social-justice vision of Christianity. And like most congregations it also includes lesbian and gay members. "I don't need to have a gay minister in the pulpit," says Barry Mills, "and I wouldn't want the gay issue to overwhelm everything else. The more the church reaches out for understanding in all areas – spiritual, sexual, economic, women's issues – the better. I want my church to be open in every way that it can."

So Barry Mills wrote the board of the church telling them of his intentions. He got a reserved go-ahead. From others in the church whom he knew to be gay, he got no reaction at all. That saddened him. "Partly I suppose it's due to our own fears, which are perfectly justified, and partly it's due to the way people see Affirm. They're afraid that if they join it they'll have to come out and be on TV or something like that."

Garneau United in Edmonton, Alberta, has an Affirm group of one. Barry Mills fully anticipates that things will get rougher in the United Church. "But I won't abandon it, not so long as there are Garneaus in it, and not unless the whole church became something quite different from what it is now." He speaks with the careful precision of someone who respects language. "I expect my church will continue to evolve, even if some of the fifty-five-year-old men can't."

Adam Con is spokesperson for Affirm in British Columbia, and secretary-treasurer for the national network. That means he keeps the membership list and the books. He's an organist and choir director in Vancouver and teaches music in a suburban high school. "My ministry is music," he says. Raised Presbyterian in a Chinese-Canadian family, music brought him to the United Church, into his first paid job as organist.

One Sunday morning he met The Issue head-on. The minister of his church, St John's, preached a sermon on sin and punishment. Seated at the organ, Adam Con sensed trouble and took notes. Many types of people have been judged as unworthy, the minister said, "But there is one group that stands out today: AIDS' victims. . . . We may cringe at this notion, but we cannot dispute it. The Bible condemns homosexual acts as sin, and the wages of sin are death!" Adam Con finished the service, then wrote an article protesting this act of bigotry in his church. It was printed in *Angles*, a community paper for lesbians and gay men. Somehow the *Vancouver Province* picked it up, and ran the story under the headline: GAY ORGANIST IS UPSET AT SERMON. Whether he liked it or not, Adam Con was suddenly and thoroughly out of the closet.

Rather than investigating his complaint, the governing board at St John's tried to get the presbytery to discipline him as a church employee. In the midst of this uproar he went to his first Affirm meeting. Nothing came of the move to punish him at St John's, but he moved to a more welcoming congregation, St James. In Affirm he reorganized the shambles of its membership list, and because he was now one of the few people who felt he had nothing to lose by speaking out in public, he became a spokesperson. "It's important for as many of us as possible to be out, saying we're proud to be gay, we're the children of God." After church on a summer morning, he sheds his tie and talks in his Vancouver apartment. "We have to keep reminding the church that we're here and we belong. We're not talking about policies or positions here, we're talking about our lives."

Many people who could benefit from Affirm are afraid to join for fear of exposure. They risk losing their ministries, their jobs, their place in theology school or the community, especially in smaller towns. The membership list is kept with a certain amount of security, but Adam Con admits, "If anyone is determined to infiltrate and get people's names so they can blacklist them, we can't really stop them. But you can't help wondering what kind of malice or evil would make someone want to wreck someone else's life."

Sex. If it's not only for procreation, then what else? "It's like eating – a very important, life-giving, re-creating experience that's meant to be shared with others," he believes. "It's one of the gifts given to us by God. Sometimes the dilemma is how to use it responsibly. Though I love and respect them, my parents aren't an adequate role model for me. My relationships are different from theirs. The church could help a lot with this, but not by just trying to define or prescribe our sexuality."

At a British Columbia Conference annual meeting, he heard a United Church minister complaining about the kind of people they're letting into Canada and the United Church these days. "Some people want to be surrounded by other people who look and behave exactly the same as they do. I've found that racism works the same way as heterosexism. You get the impression that if people accept you at all, it's not for who you are but for what you can do, so you have to do 150 per cent to be as good as the rest."

What is Adam Con's vision for the United Church? "There's space for all at the Lord's table – even for those who've left, if they want to come back. The United Church has to continue on the forefront, seeking to understand what religion means for people today, not four hundred years ago. Our God is a living god, not a dead one. What we need is a living church."

In some ways Affirm itself resembles a miniature United Church, with its own internal wrangles and strains. Some of its members believe that diversity is their strength, just as it is for their church. But in a widely scattered organization with few resources that makes its decisions by consensus, there's endless, wearying debate.

Some of these strains arise from the pressures of the closet. "Kim" is a United Church minister with a Prairie congregation. She's also a former co-chairperson of Affirm. She feels the constant tension of passing, staying underground. "When you come out you've played your last card, from that moment on you're pegged. As it is I can be very clear in my public stands, in my sermons and worship. That's my bottom line in terms of integrity. But by letting people assume that I'm heterosexual, I figure I can make my best contribution, trying to bring the church from where it's gone this past year back to the open, caring community it ought to be." On the other hand, "Sometimes you feel like you're suffocating. It's getting harder every day."

Those who've come out remember their own fears and tend to be patient with those who haven't. But sometimes the patience wears thin. Erin Shoemaker and her partner, Sally Boyle, have both experienced the stress of public scrutiny, which is rarely sympathetic. Even so, Erin Shoemaker argues, "It's pretty evident that we'd have a lot more strength, civil rights, and all the things that other people take for granted if we had more of a public voice and public presence. The more of us are in the closet, the easier it is for people out there to deny that we exist." The two of them dream of a one-Sunday walk-out by all lesbians and gay men in United Church congregations everywhere. "Can you imagine?" says Sally Boyle. "Organists, choir people, ministers, Sunday school teachers, elders walking out? Do you realize how many churches would have to close?"

Eilert Frerichs went public in the media prior to the 1984 General Council, and he's been there ever since. "It's the safest place to be, out of the closet. Once you're out there, what can they do to you? Their main leverage is fear. Once you've got past that, you're free." Not that being out there doesn't cost. "It's a strain," he admits, lighting another cigarette. "You have to balance your own beliefs with a whole host of others'. On top of that you're forced to be a spokesperson for the conscience of the United Church. Since the officers of the church have failed so consistently to support General Council decisions in public, it's left to us to do it."

As their church struggles with Christian lifestyle and responsible sexuality, so apparently do the women and men in Affirm. For most heterosexuals, marriage continues to define their relationships – they're single, married, or divorced. For homosexuals the field is more open, and thus more difficult to define. Eilert Frerichs sees no reason why lesbian and gay people should imitate heterosexual marriage. "People who choose to make a commitment to each other don't need marriage. Two forces maintain that institution, and they certainly don't include the will of God. One is the terror of being alone. The other is socio-economic – modern marriage was a product of the industrial revolution, designed to make men more reliable workers and women more dependent in the household." In 1989 Reverend Frerichs's son was married, with his blessing.

If not marriage for gay people, what would he put in its place? "Relationships that create new community, in which people can learn to deal justly with each other, as equals. Covenants – agreements based on mutual trust – it's a most extraordinary thing to give yourself to another person, for life or six years or six months, even for an hour with a stranger."

"Glen" is an ordained minister in the United Church, "Jim" does community work in a large city. Both are members of Affirm, and Glen was one of its founders. When the two of them made a covenant with each other, they knew they wouldn't have any of the economic or social structures that support the institution of heterosexual marriage. Instead they invited about twenty friends, lesbian, gay, and heterosexual, to make commitments that they would provide various kinds of support. An older, married woman in Glen's congregation offered them her kitchen table. Says Glen, "That kitchen table is famous as a place where people can go and pour out their hearts to her. Maybe we'll never need to do that, who knows? But it's good to know she and her table are there."

Despite external pressures and internal differences, enough optimists hang on to keep this "powerful lobby group" alive and functioning. Toronto Affirm has launched a "let's talk" campaign. People are asked to wear a "let's talk" button to church on the first Sunday of each month and at church meetings. The campaign has two goals: to invite discussion and to make it harder to single out lesbians and gay men for attack. With each "let's talk" button goes a leaflet. It says, "Let's ask each other questions about our values, our faith and our beliefs regarding ministry and personal relationships. Let's explore with each other the meaning of God's presence among us. We won't always find the answers, but we can work with the questions together."

Weariness and hope – these two feelings come up constantly in talking with homosexual people in the church.

Sally Boyle agreed to work on the moderator's theology dialogue group. One of the founders of Affirm in Saskatoon, she's already lost two pastoral charges because she could no longer endure the closet. With experience like that behind her, and with all that she knows about the opposition, why does she still believe that dialogue is possible? "A good question," she says with a sigh. "Maybe because it's Sang Chul Lee who asked. I've seen him in action, he has such a tremendous sense of calm about him. If anyone can make something like this work, it has to be someone like him. And I think we have to be open to dialogue as long as we possibly can."

Sally Boyle has a lot invested in the United Church, in fact most of her life. "Of course we may not get anywhere with yet another attempt at dialogue. But if we don't at least try we certainly won't get very far, will we?"

CHAPTER 24

A Very Different Ballgame

By the end of 1988 the Community of Concern could properly be called the official opposition within the United Church. By the end of 1989 it had an executive director, offices in an Oshawa, Ontario, United Church, and a staff of three. Its 1989-90 budget is close to a third of a million dollars, impressive for a grass-roots organization in its second year of operation.

What is the Community of Concern, and what is it about?

The impact that it has had is easier to gauge than its actual size. By the end of 1989 its leaders were claiming one thousand clergy and thirty-two thousand lay signatures on their Declaration of Dissent. How many of these have left the organization since they signed, whether satisfied with the Victoria statement or alarmed by COC policies, is unclear. President Bill Fritz says many new chapters opened in 1989.

The Community of Concern has a new image, at least at the official level. Earlier there was much talk of theological battles, the war to be won, the war-chest to be filled. Such military talk has largely been replaced by gentler words:

tragedy, grieving, pain, and hurt. The new image is more conciliatory and uplifting. The tactics are the same ones the federal Conservatives used to turn free trade around and win the last election: marketing and PR.

Says a February 1989 COC advertisement: "Many people within our society are hurting because of disintegration of Family and Moral values. Today the Church has a great opportunity to preach good news to the poor, to help those hurting because of social turmoil; to free those in prisons of self-despair; and to proclaim God's eternal goodness." The advertisement closes with an ingenious numerical conjuring trick: "If you wish to become active or seek further information about the Community of Concern, join the hundreds of thousands of United Church members who are concerned for our Church's well-being." Donations are payable to Bill Fritz's Collier Street United in Barrie, Ontario, to take advantage of the church's tax-exempt charitable status. As a political pressure group, the COC itself lacks such a status.

COC advertisements and publications carry the title "Community of Concern within the United Church of Canada." Its place was tested when Rev Gordon Ross resigned his ministry at Knob Hill United in Scarborough, Ontario, to become the COC's first executive director. He asked that his new job be recognized as an official United Church ministry. When the local presbytery asked for guidance, the general secretary replied that the ministry could only be recognized officially if the organization was. That would mean the COC would have to be accountable, financially and otherwise, like any other official organization within the church, to its various elected decision-making councils. The executive declined to recognize Gordon Ross's new job as a United Church ministry. He's still listed on the ministry rolls, but without appointment. That leaves his pension intact.

Three major Community of Concern initiatives give a sense of where the organization is headed. One of these is the ten-point questionnaire it distributed across the church early in 1989, asking that responses be sent to Collier Street

United. Accompanying each questionnaire was a copy of "Reflective Notes on Membership, Ministry and Human Sexuality," by Professor Terry Anderson of the Vancouver School of Theology. He is introduced by a COC imprint on his paper: "Dr Terry Anderson is one of the leading thinkers in the field of Christian Ethics in the United Church of Canada. He is not a member of 'Community of Concern,' nor affiliated with it in any way."

The eight-page document begins: "I think that these actions taken by the 32nd General Council are, on balance, unwise, and deeply troubling." Professor Anderson argues that the Victoria statement contradicts both traditional Christian moral standards and the "social organization of sexuality." As far as he's concerned both of these are givens. "The Christian tradition is very clear that heterosexual marriage, with the alternatives of chaste abstinence and celibacy, is understood to be the pattern of sexuality that is most in accord with God's intention."

At one point he asks, "Should the church sanction and even promote homosexual orientation in the formation of the young and hold it up as an ideal equal to a heterosexual orientation, especially as we learn more about what causes sexual orientation and increase our human ability to determine it, either genetically or through environmental factors?" He doesn't question whether genetic tinkering might contradict God's intention.

Terry Anderson believes the question of moral standards should have been dealt with before the question of ordination. He accuses General Council of moving from "the clear moral standards of the tradition regarding homosexual behaviour, to ambiguity." As a result he calls into question "the whole process, ground and criteria by which our church makes decisions concerning basic beliefs and morals."

In September 1989 the COC released the results of its survey to the press. Executive director Gordon Ross commented, "Obviously a wide segment of United Church people find the teaching of the MMHS [*Membership, Ministry and Human*

Sexuality] statement unacceptable. I am hopeful that the General Council will take this and similar data seriously and withdraw the statement at the 1990 General Council."

Questionnaires were sent to the minister, the chairperson of the board, and the president of United Church Women in each pastoral charge, a total of almost seven thousand questionnaires. Eighty-four per cent were not returned. Of the 1,070 that were, in some cases more than one from the same congregation, 76 per cent agreed that the Victoria statement should be withdrawn. Sixty-five per cent of the responders said they would welcome homosexuals as church members, but 88 per cent rejected them as ordained ministers and lay leaders.

The numbers game is intriguing. In the absence of alternative data, the survey was intended to indicate a tidal wave of opposition. But what constitutes "a wide segment of United Church people"? One thousand and seventy people out of 850,000? What percentage of members would oppose a homosexual minister in their own pulpit, but wouldn't much care what happened elsewhere in the church? For that matter, what percentage of church members are homosexual, and what percentage of the clergy? What percentage of members are parents, friends, or supporters of lesbians or gay men?

A second COC initiative worth watching is its attack on the current state of United Church theology schools. This campaign is led by Rev Allen Churchill of Dominion-Chalmers United in Ottawa. In February 1989 he presented a detailed brief on the subject to the church's Committee on Theological Education for Ministry. It accuses the theological colleges of steering students in a direction that's "different from and incommensurate with the Articles of Faith of the Basis of Union or more generally with the traditional faith as is probably held by the majority of members of the UCC."

Allen Churchill initiated his study when the March 1988 report appeared to find support in theology schools. Even though this report was dumped at the thirty-second General Council, it's still very high on the COC agenda. It's by far the easiest way to start a fire. Churchill says homosexuality itself is a minor issue. The real prize is leadership of the whole church.

The brief refers to complaints by theology students that "their own somewhat different theological views" were not being respected by the faculty. It also charges that biased hiring practices keep evangelical professors out of the church's theology schools, and thus slant the education offered there in an exclusively liberal direction. Examples are cited where faculty or principals have made statements that contradict traditional teachings – for example, that some other world religious leaders may be worthy of equal respect alongside Jesus Christ.

Allen Churchill's passion on this matter is based on his understanding of the role that ministers play. "God calls people to be leaders of the church," he says in his office at Dominion-Chalmers. "He calls them to be faithful, and to make the church well. But too often they make it sick, even unto death." How? "By forgetting that their leadership is a subordinate leadership. We must always be submissive to Christ and the Word, and fulfil the function of any leader in any organism, which is to give direction but not to be tyrannical, and not to be disloyal." In precise, measured tones he defines what constitutes disloyalty. "One can demonstrate disloyalty by misreading, or misquoting, or misapplying the Word as it is given to us by Jesus."

The brief recommends ten changes, including the establishment of a new theology college, to meet the COC's specifications. "This may be the least offensive and most effective means of solving our problems," it concludes. In the meantime, Churchill's own congregation, Dominion-Chalmers, has agreed to finance a kind of embryonic theology school on its own premises for the next three summers on a trial basis. The first Ottawa Summer School of Biblical and Theological Studies ran for ten days in July 1989.

A spectacular COC project, "Faithfulness Today, A Lenten Conference on Jesus, Scripture and Justice for All People," happens March 1990 at the Hamilton Convention Centre in southern Ontario. Timed to precede conference annual meetings and then General Council in London, this extravagant event is clearly designed to put pressure on the United Church. A combination of born-again rally and intensive workout in conservative theology and sexual politics, its cosponsors are the Community of Concern and Church Alive, both of whose annual meetings take place the first day of the conference.

The sponsors' original star attraction withdrew shortly after he had agreed to participate. A theologian himself, Dr Markus Barth is the son of legendary German theologian Karl Barth, whose many volumes line the bookshelves of United Church ministers with widely varying views. Conference organizer Graham Scott issued a press release announcing that Dr Barth had to withdraw due to ill health. But the theologian had already made it clear in a letter that his reasons for withdrawing did not include ill health. He had changed his mind when it came to his attention that he might be used in a cause that had serious implications beyond his control. When challenged, conference organizers hastily issued a second release omitting any reference to health, and replaced Dr Barth with Dr Colin Gunton, professor of Christian Doctrine at King's College in London.

The titles of three final workshops at Faithfulness Today sum up its message: Can homosexual orientation be changed?; Loving faithfulness in marriage/loving chastity in singleness; Is the United Church capable of reform? Workshop leader for the last of these is Reverend Frank Lockhart, who also chairs the COC strategy committee. He is clear about the stakes. "Hopefully we will have changed the church by next summer [1990]," he says, "so that the General Council will be a very different ballgame." The convention climaxes with a banquet and a worship service, also described as a mass rally for the Community of Concern.

Registration cheques are payable to Church Alive, at Reverend Graham Scott's Appleby United Church in

Burlington, Ontario. Church Alive is still small and egghead-ish, as Graham Scott describes it, but it's still very much alive. An article in the July 1989 issue of its *Theological Digest* gives a sense of what its members are about. In it British historian Paul Johnson targets the temptation of idealism as a primary threat to contemporary Christianity. "Christians have the insight to grasp that man, in his earthly existence, is an incorrigibly flawed creature, that his earthly constructs inevitably end in disappointment at best, that he cannot, in fact, attain satisfaction and fulfillment on earth, and that the utopian kingdom is not of this world." But, he argues, "a large proportion of mankind . . . will continue to feel the itch to utopianize on earth."

As examples of this dangerous idealism, Johnson names the legitimizing of homosexual behaviour, the legalization of abortion on demand, the removal from their parents of children who've been "classified as abused by newly-invented and controversial techniques of detection," the systematic pursuit of women's rights, bilingualism and multilingualism, multiculturalism, and environmental and health politics. To exemplify "upholders of the traditional moral order," he cites Margaret Thatcher.

Like Allen Churchill, Scott dismisses The Issue as a minor one. "The gay ordination issue is the knife-edge of the new morality. I suppose it's unfair in a way that gays have to bear the brunt of the reaction." He has no problem, he says, with the pursuit of justice. On the other hand, "Some people in the United Church have too narrow a view of justice. Justice is only one aspect of the biblical concept of righteousness. Unfortunately that's got mixed up in a negative way with *self*-righteousness. In Biblical terms righteousness means being in right relationship with God, with your family, with your neighbours, and with the world."

The problem with the church, he says, is "the group in power. They're like the apostate kings of Israel and Judah. They've built up their power structure over years and decades, stacking all the courts and committees with like-minded people. Now and then they'll throw in a conservative or two, but I consider that to be tokenism of the grossest degree."

Graham Scott is one of twelve ordained ministers invited by the moderator to form a theology dialogue group, yet another attempt to search for common ground in the church. His only comment: "God help me."

Whatever COC leaders say, the issue that continues to generate the most heat for the vast majority of their members is The Issue. Joe Brinton is an accountant and chair of the COC at Bethany United in Halifax; Bill Piercy a lawyer and one of the leading COC members. Both grew up in the United Church. Their kids have been baptized in the United Church. Joe Brinton believes that for a long time, "United Church policies have been moving us away from fundamental Christian morals." To Bill Piercy the church is "a rock, an anchor. If the church endorses homosexuality you'll have no rules left. If homosexuality's okay, then why not adultery, incest, prostitution, and everything else? What we're talking about here is a total breakdown in moral values."

For both these men, the primary source of morality is the Bible. In the factory boardroom of another COC member, Joe Brinton says, "There are many passages I don't understand, but the truth is there. If you read it enough, you'll find the moral guidelines." Bill Piercy sees the Bible in continuity "with what our parents taught us, and what we know in our hearts. I just can't believe that God intends practising homosexuals to be in the pulpit." Joe Brinton adds, "We have nothing against homosexuals, we're not against the person. It's the behaviour which is unnatural and immoral. The Bible makes it very clear that man and woman were created for a specific purpose. It's inconceivable to us that homosexuality could ever be part of that purpose. That makes it an absolutely unacceptable lifestyle."

In a mellow voice that's remarkably like Brian Mulroney's, Joe Brinton admits, "All of us are sinners. But we can only be forgiven if we repent. If we don't think what we're doing is wrong, how can we repent?" Bill Piercy adds without pause, "People today think that guilt is a bad thing. It's not. In its place it's a good thing, if it leads you to repent."

Though some of their friends have left the church, Bill Piercy and Joe Brinton are hanging on, at least for now. Joe Brinton is banking on a full retraction of the Victoria statement at the 1990 General Council. "If we don't get that at least, many people will feel we've lost the battle. For most of us it would take too much effort to start infiltrating the presbyteries and conferences all over again." His brow furrows with concern. "People won't bother any more, they'll just drift away."

"Christ is testing his people," says Bill Piercy, "He wants to see if the majority will stand up and be counted. That will determine whether this church is worth saving."

CHAPTER 25

For the Bible Tells Me So

Homosexuality wasn't an issue at church union in 1925. But the Bible was. And it has been ever since.

Already at the fifth General Council in 1932, after a heated debate on divorce, the following conclusion was reached: "We cannot stake a vital decision (whether Jesus himself allowed adultery as a grounds for divorce) on a verbal uncertainty (that is, Jesus' teaching in Mark 10:2-12 in contrast with Matthew 5:27-32); and, therefore, we must consider the particular direction in the light of our Lord's attitude to life as a whole." For some that was radical talk back in 1932. It still is today, for some.

In his critique of United Church theology schools Allen Churchill charges that the principal of one college stated in a panel discussion, "he is doing everything he can to remove Jesus Christ from the centre of the Church's theology so that the Church can move forward into the modern era!" There's no doubt the accused said what he said; it's recorded on a videotape that has been widely circulated by the Community of Concern. The accused is Rev Garth Mundle, principal of St Stephen's College in Edmonton, Alberta.

Already as a child in Pugwash, Nova Scotia, Garth Mundle talked so much that he earned the name Preacher Mundle. He was ordained in the United Church, worked in a number of parishes, specialized in psychosexual and spirituality counselling, picked up three theology degrees and eventually won the job of principal at St Stephen's. Since part of the St Stephen's mission is to be on the frontier of theological thinking and educational methodology, one of the principal's duties is what Garth Mundle calls "visioning, the dreaming of dreams."

One of the dreams he's dreamed for the United Church is what he calls "a theological revolution." He doesn't think the church will survive without it. "I don't believe we can live whole, complete lives without a conscious religious framework and a faith community, these are as essential to human beings as breathing." At his home in Edmonton, he's seated but always in motion – face, hands – pulling ideas together and sorting them out. "But this worn-out religion that we insist on peddling – more and more people find that they can live without that. It's no more use today than the spats people used to wear to protect their shoes."

What might this revolution look like? "Over the centuries we've built up this enormous superstructure we call The Church. But that's not the real church, not if you believe in a living faith. We need to dismantle all of that mediaeval theology, stone by stone, save some treasures from it and some good building blocks, see what other materials we have, and from all of that we have to construct a new theological edifice in which we can liv

But what will it look like? "I don't know," says Garth Mundle. His partner, Dorothy, protests. She's a diaconal minister, and the current president of Alberta and Northwest Conference. "Surely people will want to know what the new thing looks like," she argues, "before they'll be willing to take apart the old one." Her work brings her into daily contact with people in the pew.

"That's what it means to be living in faith," he replies. "If I knew the future, why would I need faith, what need would I have of God? To live in faith I have to let go of whatever I'm clinging to now, without any guarantee that what replaces it will be any better or more secure."

And Jesus, does he have any place in this vision? "Of course. But instead of sitting around forever at the feet of a crumbling historical statue of Jesus, we need to recognize the living Jesus who beckons to us from the future. I'm not dismissing Christ or the Biblical tradition. On the contrary I'm looking at it in a different way, in a way that makes Jesus much more real, much more significant." Preacher Mundle is now operating at full throttle. "I don't see how we can truly accept the living Christ of the resurrection unless we're prepared to give up that dusty old statue. Why can't the whole church contemplate moving forward into the future to meet this Jesus who's there already, way ahead of us and full of life?"

Allen Churchill's Jesus, on the other hand, is the traditional sovereign Lord, a magnificent and radiant vision. This is a classical Jesus, the Jesus of the Apostle's Creed who rose from the dead to sit on the right hand of God the Father Almighty, from whence he'll come to judge the living and the dead. "God is the one who reveals himself in Jesus Christ," says Churchill. "I knew God before I realized who Jesus was. But there was a quantum leap in my understanding of God when I began to and as I continue to try to understand who this formidable character named Jesus of Nazareth was and is. I'm inclined to believe that Jesus of Nazareth is incomparable, and therefore that courses on Christology and on Jesus ought not to be taught under the rubric of comparative religions." Allen Churchill's Jesus is *the* Messiah, for all the world and for the rest of time.

Garth Mundle's Jesus, the Jesus of Palestine, is "dark and unshaven, probably in a grubby Arabic *djellaba*." Mundle has just returned from leading a tour of Israel and Palestine. "I'm sure that Jesus would be turned out of many United Church congregations today." This Jesus is not *the* Messiah, the final and ultimate word of God for everyone. He is the Messiah for Christians who accept him as such, as he calls them forward into a faith that's yet to be imagined.

Allen Churchill's Jesus and Garth Mundle's Jesus coexist in the Holy Bible. Are these two men reading the same Bible?

Debate on The Issue has caused a good many United Church Bibles to be dusted off and re-examined. Some people acknowledge willingly that they interpret the Bible, bringing to it their own experience of faith and the world around them. Some are ambivalent; they appear to accept parts of it as God's infallible word, other parts as subject to interpretation. And some claim that they simply take what's there, word for word, and live by it. Presumably this is one of the reasons this book called the Bible has been such a runaway best-seller for so many years. To say that people find in their Bibles exactly what they need to find is not an attack on it, but a compliment.

The church is currently engaged in a major study which some believe should have happened years ago, at least before The Issue overtook all else – the authority and interpretation of Scripture. A preliminary document released late in 1989 was cautiously worded, but gave little comfort to biblical literalists. "The experience of early Christians, who went for some time without a written text, reminds us that it is the Living Word, not the text, that is infallible," it says. "The text is only important insofar as the Living Word of God comes to us through it." An interim report goes to the 1990 General Council.

When he discovered the Bible, Moderator Sang Chul Lee was a Korean schoolboy living in China, a Korean exile under Japanese rule. In his autobiography, *The Wanderer*, he recounts how alien the writing style and cultural setting of the Bible seemed to him. But as he read, "I became more familiar with this Jesus person. He was poor, like me. He was harassed and persecuted, just as we Koreans were. Yet he cared for others, loved them, helped them, healed them. And finally he was put to death, though he had committed no crimes, just like my brother-in-law." His brother-in-law, a Korean nationalist, was executed by the Japanese.

"The story of Moses was a revelation. The children of Israel suffering under the unjust oppression of Egypt seemed exactly like the Koreans under the Japanese. The story echoed in me. Sometimes I could not sleep. I had to read it over and over again. The God described in these passages did not try to get the better over mortals, like the gods my parents had tried to appease. This God *helped* people in their struggle. He *liberated* them. Perhaps he could do the same for all of us. . . . The Christian God seemed always to change history. This meant that tomorrow things do not have to be the same as they are today. There is reason for hope."

No one in the United Church would admit to speaking for God. Yet this is exactly what happens when anyone says that such-and-such is God's word, God's plan, God's intention for humanity. It seems a very risky business. At the same time it's a typically human act. And we are, after all, only human.

Aside from the Sodom story, the favourite anti-homosexual passage in the Old Testament is Leviticus 18:22. "You shall not lie with a male as with a woman; it is an abomination." Nothing is said about women lying with women; presumably such a notion was inconceiveable to the male authors of the Scriptures. Also the male was considered the real propagator of the species; the woman merely a vessel. Chapter twenty prescribes the punishment: "They shall be put to death." Also condemned to death are men who sleep with their father's wives or their daughters-in-law, men and women who commit adultery, any person "who turns to mediums and wizards," and "everyone who curses his father or his mother."

These are among the hundreds of laws that, according to the Bible, were handed down by God via Moses to His chosen people, the Jews. Some of these laws are still fought over today in contemporary Israel. Chapter eleven of Leviticus contains the dietary laws: It's unclean to eat animals which do not both chew their cuds and have cloven hooves, for example the camel, the rabbit, or the pig. It's an abomination to eat anything from the waters of the earth that doesn't have fins and scales, which would exclude all forms of shellfish. Locusts, crickets, and grasshoppers are acceptable as food, but "all other winged insects which have four feet are an abomination to you."

The laws governing health follow. Chapter twelve decrees that all male babies must be circumcised on the eighth day. The same chapter says that a woman who bears a male child is unclean and can't enter the temple for one week; if she bears a female child she's unclean for two weeks. A woman is also unclean when she's menstruating, and mustn't be seen naked. Also unclean is anyone who touches her or her bed.

Chapter nineteen forbids the interbreeding of different kinds of cattle, the sowing of fields with two kinds of seed, and the wearing of garments "made of two kinds of stuff." In chapter twenty-five it says you can buy male and female slaves from other nations, and that these slaves are your property, which you may bequeath to your children as you choose.

Except for its final apocalyptic books, the New Testament is somewhat gentler. Recounting the life and teachings of Jesus, it's attributed to some of the disciples who were close to him in his lifetime, and to others who followed his teachings after he was executed by the Romans. The most prolific of these, and by far the most quoted, is Saul of Taurus. According to the Book of Acts, he was a Jew who participated in the imprisoning and stoning to death of early Christian converts.

One day on the road to Damascus Saul was suddenly struck down by a flash of light from heaven. Blinded, he heard the voice of Jesus, "Saul, Saul, why do you persecute me?" A few days later "the scales fell from his eyes," and Saul became a Christian. He changed his name to Paul, travelled widely, wrote prolifically, and virtually overnight became his former enemy's most powerful exponent and interpreter. When the Roman emperor had him executed, his central place in Christian theology and mythology was guaranteed. He became Saint Paul.

Since Jesus himself said nothing in the Gospels about homosexual people or acts, Paul is a very important source for people who rank homosexuality high on their list of sins. A warning he wrote to Christian recruits in Corinth is a favourite text to prove that point, in chapter six: "Know ye not that the unrighteous shall not inherit the kingdom of God? Be not deceived: neither fornicators, nor idolaters, nor adulterers, nor effeminate, nor abusers of themselves with mankind, nor thieves, nor covetous, nor revilers, nor extortionists, shall inherit the kingdom of God." That's how it reads in the King James Version. In the Revised Standard Version the list reads: ". . . neither the immoral, nor adulterers, nor homosexuals, nor thieves, nor the greedy, nor drunkards, nor revilers, nor robbers . . . " A later edition of the Revised Standard changes "homosexuals" to "sexual perverts." One German version of the Bible says "child molestors" and makes no mention of homosexuality.

Almost single-handedly Paul inspired the extreme split between body and soul that has tortured Christians in one way or another ever since. "The works of the flesh are plain: immorality, impurity, licentiousness, idolatry, sorcery, enmity, strife, jealousy, anger, selfishness, dissension, party spirit, envy, drunkenness, carousing, and the like . . . . But the fruit of the Spirit is love, joy, peace, patience, kindness, goodness, faithfulness, gentleness, self-control; against such there is no law. And those who belong to Jesus Christ have crucified the flesh with its passions and desires."

If Paul had mixed feelings about sexuality, in his first letter to the Corinthians he was quite clear on the status of women. "I want you to understand that the head of every man is Christ, the head of a woman is her husband, and the head of Christ is God." Paul expands on this theme in a later chapter: "As in all the churches of the saints, the women should keep silence in the churches. For they are not permitted to speak, but should be subordinate, as even the law says. If there is anything they desire to know, let them ask their husbands at home."

On the subject of slaves, Paul writes to the Colossians, "Slaves, obey in everything those who are your earthly masters, not with eyeservice, as men-pleasers, but in singleness of heart, fearing the Lord." In his letter to Titus, he further advises: "Bid slaves to be submissive to their masters and to give satisfaction in every respect; they are not to be refractory, nor to pilfer, but to show entire and true fidelity, so that in everything they may adorn the doctrine of God our Saviour."

As easily as opponents of the Victoria statement can find their justifications in the Bible, so can people more inclined to be tolerant. From the Old Testament, many quote this rhetorical question of the prophet Micah: "What does the Lord require of you but to do justice, and to love kindness, and to walk humbly with your God?"

In the remarkable story of the peasant David – the hero who killed Goliath – and Jonathan, son of King Saul, Bible readers find this: "The soul of Jonathan was knit to the soul of David, and Jonathan loved him as his own soul." Jonathan's sister Michal, David's wife, plays a minor role in the story. To protect David, Jonathan defies his own father. Says the enraged King Saul, "You son of a perverse, rebellious woman, do I not know that you have chosen the son of Jesse to your own shame, and to the shame of your mother's nakedness?" Even so, Jonathan keeps his secret appointment with David, who's gone into hiding. "David rose from beside the stone heap and fell on his face to the ground, and bowed three times; and they kissed one another, and wept with one another until David recovered himself."

Later when David is King of Israel, and both Saul and Jonathan have been killed in battle, David laments both their deaths, but most keenly Jonathan's. "I am distressed for you, my brother Jonathan; very pleasant have you been to me; your love to me was wonderful, passing the love of women." As with other passages in the Bible, readers will continue to find in this one exactly what they need.

Most Christians derive their inspiration and guidance primarily from the teachings of their Messiah. They find this directive, among others, in Matthew's account of the sermon on the mount: "Judge not, that you be not judged . . . . Why do you see the speck that is in your brother's eye, but do not notice the log that is in your own eye? . . .You hypocrite, first take the log out of your own eye, and then you will see clearly to take the speck out of your brother's eye."

Some Bible readers find their direction in Jesus' reply to a lawyer who asked him how he could attain eternal life. "You shall love the Lord your God with all your heart, and with all your soul, and with all your strength and with all your mind; and your neighbour as yourself." Some interpret "with all your mind" to mean continuous, conscious, critical questioning of all their beliefs, all their actions, and all their relationships.

What constitutes a neighbour? the lawyer asked. As he often did, Jesus answered with a parable. A man was robbed and left for dead in a ditch. First a priest and then a Levite – a strict, law-abiding Jewish sect – passed by without offering any help. But a Samaritan gave the man first aid, carried him to an inn and paid for his lodgings there. Since they didn't follow all the laws of the Torah, Samaritans were considered by more pious Jews to be unclean and inferior. "Which of these three," Jesus asked the lawyer, "do you think proved neighbour to the man who fell among the robbers?"

When a group of men asked him if, as prescribed in Mosaic law, they should stone to death a woman they accused of adultery, he responded: "Let him who is without sin among you be the first to throw a stone at her."

Even from the stern St Paul, some Bible readers have found a message that, for them, settles the question of biblical literalism versus interpretation. On the role of Christ's ministers, he wrote: "Our sufficiency is from God, who has qualified us to be ministers of a new covenant, not in a written code but in the Spirit; for the written code kills, but the Spirit gives life." To the Romans Paul wrote: "I am sure that neither death, nor life, nor angels, nor principalities, nor things present, nor things to come, nor powers, nor height, nor depth, nor anything else in all creation, will be able to separate us from the love of God in Christ Jesus our Lord."

But the Biblical argument doesn't end here, not in the United Church. Far from it. Very few Christians would argue that God's love was a simple matter of *carte blanche*, anything goes. Some see it as a kind of original tough love, the traditional image of a father's love, which demands obedience, rather than a mother's, which is supposed to be full of forgiveness.

But obedience to what or to whom?

To God, of course. God makes the rules.

How can we be sure exactly what God's rules are?

God's rules are set out clearly in the Bible.

But – And so it goes, round and round and round.

CHAPTER 26

The Power and the Glory

A clique of liberal-radicals runs the United Church from its headquarters in Toronto. They pack all the decision-making courts with their allies, being careful to include one or two conservatives as a token opposition. They ignore the grass roots, the people in the pew, and they silence ruthlessly anyone who is brave enough to dissent.

Through battles over The Issue, variations of this theme have come to haunt Canada's largest Protestant church. Ironically, it is also the most democratic of all the mainstream Christian churches. In fact this may be one of the sources of its present difficulties. Over the years some very different assumptions have grown up between people who lead the church, who have engaged actively in its life at all levels, and the people who follow, or at least who form the bulk of its membership. In many ways this has made disappointment and disillusionment on all sides practically inevitable.

Historian John Webster Grant describes the problem in the September 1988 issue of *Touchstone*, a theological journal. "The United Church has been self-consciously

Canadian, reflecting national moods and distrusting old world subtleties of theology. It has been predominantly liberal, reluctant to discourage diversity of opinion but prone to favour ideas that are seen as progressive. It has been strongly task-oriented, more concerned with problem-solving than with definition, and pragmatic in its readiness to borrow solutions from business and social science. At the same time it has sought in the tradition of the social gospel to be prophetic, declaring the will of God without fear or favour. Committed to a conciliar system and asking much of it, it has both inherited and generated a bewildering variety of ways of operating within it. The resulting combination of sometimes incompatible elements worked fairly well so long as a measure of consensus existed, but deep-seated differences of conviction have imposed a severe strain on it."

Here are some glimpses inside this tangled, disunited church, as it enters the last decade of the millenium.

The moderator has a pleasant office, with a decent view, on the top floor. He has a new blue carpet and an impressive dark wooden desk. On the cabinet behind him are gifts he's received in his journeys through the church, including a wonderfully comic stuffed-doll version of himself made by a teenager in Ontario, complete with glasses and white beard.

The Right Reverend Sang Chul Lee's desk is covered with letters – from the daughter of a lesbian wondering if her mother is a sinner, from a lifetime United Church member demanding that the moderator do something to haul the church back from the brink of hell, from another lifetime member pleading, why can't we just get on with other things? He gets thousands of letters, and meets thousands of people in his travels. Some of them ask him to perform miracles. "Many people seem to think I'm the Pope," he says, with a wide-eyed smile. "But this church doesn't give me any such power as that. If it did, I wouldn't want to be in it."

In a strange way he may actually have less power as moderator than he did, or will have again, as an individual. "My job is to be spiritual leader of the church, like a pastor to all the pastors and congregations. When an issue is as divisive as this one, our tradition says the moderator shouldn't make quick statements on one side of the issue or the other, at least not until the term ends."

What does he do then, what does he say to people? An angry United Church member phoned to tell him that if the church ordains homosexual ministers the same thing will happen as in Newfoundland, where Roman Catholic priests have been charged with sexual assault. "I tried to remind him that there are thousands of priests in the Catholic church, but very few in that situation. You can't label everyone like that. It's the same with heterosexuals, some are unstable and get into trouble."

Invited to an Affirm meeting in Toronto, he counselled its members to be patient. Some protested. They'd been waiting for centuries, how much longer did he expect them to wait? "You have to play the game with wisdom," he told them. "Your critics are looking for excuses. Provoking their emotions doesn't help anything." He knows – he's been in the hands of torturers. "You must continue to demonstrate that you are very serious," he told the Affirm members. "Also that you love the church, and that you want harmony with other members." Seriousness and harmony rank very high in Sang Chul Lee's sense of what's important.

"It's my wish at this moment that everyone in our church not learn how to confront but how to construct," he says. This is a man who's been called communist for opposing the South Korean dictatorship, and reactionary for opposing the North Korean dictatorship. "I want for everyone to learn something from this struggle – the clergy, the members, the homosexual people, and the critics – so that we can find the most healthy way for our church to develop."

Often to make a point the moderator tells a story. Each time he tells this one, people listen very quietly, he says. An eighteen-year-old man came to his office not long after his term began, in autumn 1988. This young man wasn't a church member, but he had read about General Council and the new moderator. He had no one else to talk to. "He told me when he was six or seven he realized he was different from other boys. Several times he was beaten up in the schoolyard. Later the boy's parents sent him to a psychiatrist, who confirmed that he was gay. When he heard this he attempted suicide, more than once." He tells the story slowly, recreating his own feelings at the time. "I just listened humbly, I had no answers to anything he said. When he was at the door to leave, he turned and said, 'It's not my fault, I was born this way. Is that a sin?' He fell into my arms – I had no words – we cried together like that for half an hour."

This moderator's power doesn't reside in his office. It radiates from his story.

Along the hall from Lee's ninth-floor office is the general secretary's. The sign says "Howie Mills," omitting his degrees and doctorates. His dark wooden desk is covered even deeper in paper than the moderator's. Front and centre are requests for rulings on the constitutionality of two conference policies that bar homosexuals from the order of ministry. (In January 1990, he ruled that there is nothing in the church's rules and procedures that allows the exclusion from ordination of a whole category of people.) One of the general secretary's functions is to be the official interpreter of the church's book of rules, the *Manual*. He can be overruled, either by the Judicial Committee or the General Council.

Each of Mills's other functions sounds like a full-time job, especially these days: caring for the wholeness of the church, ensuring that the personnel of the church fulfil what General Council intends, and seeing to it that the complex balance of professionals and volunteers who direct the life of the church can get on with their jobs. A fifth duty has been overwhelmed by the uproar – enabling the whole church to envision and plan for its future.

Surely this is a powerful position. "Well," says Howie Mills, "if the church were the hierarchical corporation that many people seem to think it is, then indeed this would be a powerful position. But it's not, it's built on a conciliar system. The decisions aren't made here, they're made in presbytery, at conference, and at the General Council." Perhaps people grown accustomed to hierarchical structures in other spheres of life crave the same in their church. "Yes and no," the general secretary replies. "Some people want to have it both ways at the same time. When it's convenient they want a corporate model, with a tough executive laying down the law. And when that doesn't suit them they want exactly the opposite, a free-church model like the Baptists have, where each member who can get to the convention has one vote and twenty seconds to speak. Those two systems are contradictory, and neither of them is faithful to United Church tradition."

During the stormy days immediately after the 1988 General Council, a number of presbyteries asked the general secretary to clarify whether ministers should be subject to discipline if they deliberately misrepresented General Council policy or undermined its authority as the highest court of the church. Several of these presbyteries had specific ministers in mind, in fact they believed that in several cases ordination vows had been broken. But true to United Church tradition they remained discretely nonspecific in their inquiry.

The presbytery is responsible for the immediate supervision of church staff, which includes ministers. As the top executive of the church, the general secretary is responsible for interpreting and conveying its policies. In a letter to all chairpersons and secretaries of presbyteries, Mills replied that the presbyteries' disciplinary role – which includes a range of informal and formal hearings, as well as an appeal process – should be exercised "when presbyters [ministers and other paid staff] evidently misrepresent the action of General Council, or promote disrespect for General Council, or seek to undermine members' respect for or serious wrestling with the actions and program resources of the General Council." At the same time he urged restraint, since it appeared to be a small minority who were doing most of the damage.

Community of Concern leaders immediately accused church officials of stifling their freedom of speech. In fact, though many claims have been made to this effect, actual martyrs are hard to find. All the ministers about whom the original inquiries were initiated are still in place and haven't changed their tune, except for those who've left the United Church of their own accord to join other denominations. In almost every case, the pattern has been to shy away from confrontation and disciplinary moves. For liberal moderates, continuing dialogue is the only way of keeping their church intact.

When dialogue fails within the church, the secular courts offer a last, painful resort. The three small congregations of Dover Centre pastoral charge seceded from the United Church in south western Ontario, but refused to vacate three churches and a manse. Presbytery offered to lease the properties to them for one dollar a year, retaining the title. The offer was rejected, and the departers wouldn't communicate further. Kent Presbytery in London Conference finally took the breakaway congregations to court. The national church believes that the Basis of Union and the enabling federal and provincial legislation assign all properties to the United Church as a whole, not to individual pastoral charges. For Dover Centre and other potential seceders it's a test case. The courts will decide.

A deep ambivalence about leadership isn't unique to the United Church. It's endemic, amounting to a crisis of faith in democracy. Ironically, while attention is diverted to the tremendous upheavals in eastern Europe, in the western democracies real freedom of choice has deteriorated practically into a question of brand loyalty. It's a downward spiral. As the marketing of candidates gets better and better, the contents get worse and worse. Voters keep handing over power to variations of the same leadership, demanding that they make everything right. When they turn out one after another to be corrupt, incompetent, or both, disillusionment mounts. Voters feel more helpless than ever, more bitter, more susceptible to demagogues and saviours with simple answers. The prospect is not encouraging.

When so many systems and institutions in which people have a huge psychological investment – democracy, free enterprise, marriage, the family – fail to deliver the security and happiness that they promise in a dangerous and unhappy world, resentment grows like a bitter weed. When, on top of that, their church isn't what people thought it was, it can be the biggest letdown of all. And if they mistake the church for God, does that mean even God has failed?

Rev Don Collett of Taber, Alberta, has a less apocalyptic way of explaining the gap between leaders and followers. "The leadership of the church wants to be prophetic, on the cutting edge of every issue. That's okay. But when the rank and file doesn't go along with that, then the leaders tend to see them as uninformed, backward, and sometimes even less faithful." Knox United in Taber is a long way from 85 St Clair in Toronto. "They say if only you'd read this report or done that study you'd be educated like we are, and you'd agree with us. That's incredibly patronizing. We have to ask how the Holy Spirit speaks in our church – through the leadership or through the congregations?"

The problem stems from a liberal assumption that, given enough educational material, people will surely change, says Hugh McCullum, for five turbulent years editor and publisher of *The United Church Observer*. "If education could solve our problems, we'd all be saints by now. Most of it's written from a reasonably educated, middle-class, urban perspective. So it's not surprising that people who don't think like that can start seeing it as manipulative. They think head office is trying to brainwash them into accepting homosexuals."

Affirm co-chair Bill Siksay also recognizes the limits to this approach. "After ten years of it, there's not a lot more educating you can do. If our church is going to be faithful to its existing policies, it has to say clearly and simply that lesbians and gay men belong to this community, and our right to belong has to be protected in some meaningful ways. It has to include sanctions against people who prevent us from belonging – that includes people who harass us, who take away our jobs or deny our call to ministry for no other reason than our sexual orientation. This wouldn't be changing church policy, it would just be putting existing policies into practice."

So who runs the United Church, the General Council? Under pressure, the executive reopened one of the most difficult and important decisions ever made by a General Council, and tacitly invited church members to react against it. And parts of the church have acted in direct contradiction to that same General Council policy. Who runs the United Church then, the executive? It seems no more able to enforce its decisions than the General Council.

As executive member Ellinor Townend sees it, an alternate leadership is trying to set up a parallel and competing church. "The issue isn't homosexuality, not any more. This is a power struggle, plain and simple, it's the General Council versus the Community of Concern. We have to be up-front about that, so the homosexuals don't have to go on being scapegoats. We have to decide whether we want to be fighting the COC, or whether we want to put our energy into reclaiming what we're about as a church."

In the meantime who runs the United Church? Catherine and Eric Mercer believe it's the "civil servants" up in Toronto. They view the national office much as they do the government in Ottawa, as a distant and arbitrary force. VIA is derailed, military bases employing thousands suddenly close in already depressed areas, regional subsidies and fish quotas are cut. These decisions may be handed down by elected representatives, but many come to believe that they're made by civil servants. "When you have people up there who work together every day, you get a kind of in-crowd," says

Catherine Mercer in Halifax. "They start talking the same language and sharing the same assumptions. And they're in a good position to influence the elected representatives who have fixed terms and who meet only a couple of times a year."

The "civil servants" are paid to put into action the decisions of the church's elected representatives. As any other employer does, the five divisions – Finance, World Outreach, Mission in Canada, Communication, and Ministry Personnel and Education – employ the best people they can find, creative individuals who know their fields and who aren't afraid to take risks. In each court of the church, committees of elected volunteers represent each division. The staff of each division is accountable to the national committees.

From the staff's perspective, a different picture emerges. Not infrequently their initiatives end up diluted by the more cautious committees to which they report. All too often the more creative and adventurous the initiative, the more likely it is to be softened, to lose the edge that made it original and worthwhile in the first place. That's especially true these days, when there's a relentless urge toward safe ground. Staff people, the civil servants, either learn to work around these restrictions, or they settle into comfortable routines and rationalize as they go. Or they give up, they quit. Or they're eased out. In times of fiscal restraint, jobs come "under review." If they become vacant they're less likely to be filled. And if these are jobs whose former occupants generated controversy, they'll probably disappear – death by attrition.

In its brave attempts to be democratic and to solve every problem that's put before it, the United Church has become a maze of task groups and volunteer committees at the local, regional, and national levels. Do these committees run the church?

Denise Davis-Taylor works on the Support Team Against Sexual Harassment and/or Sexual Misconduct for the Alberta and Northwest Conference. Like many such groups it was not initiated by the national office, but by local pressures.

Denise Davis-Taylor is a diaconal minister; she doesn't get to be called "the reverend" and gets paid less, but does most of the work of an ordained minister, sometimes more. With her partner she shares an educational ministry at St Andrew's United in Edmonton. Her faith is built on a certainty that "righteousness, or living in right relationship with God, has to include a conscious bias toward the oppressed."

She calls herself "a survivor of sexual abuse. In the last year-and-a-half I've been coming to terms with that, remembering." She sits in the living room of the small suburban townhouse she shares with her partner and their two children. "It's been an incredible journey in which I've been pushed to my limits, physically, emotionally, and spiritually, and found that I had spiritual and other resources that I've never used."

She brought these resources to the Support Team Against Sexual Harassment. "It's been overlooked, unnamed, dismissed, and excused. Most of the women who've talked to us don't want to lay charges, they just want to talk. They want someone to tell them they're not crazy and what's happened to them is not their fault." What happened to them was sexual harassment, by their ministers. "That's a terrible abuse of power and privilege," says Denise Davis-Taylor. "Someone who comes to a minister for counselling or support is particularly vulnerable." As she talks, the younger of her two sons climbs into her lap.

She believes that both sexual harassment and what she calls the scapegoating of homosexuals in the church are at least partly due to long-established Christian attitudes toward sexuality in general. "Paul has a lot to answer for, teaching us to separate love from the body, refusing to acknowledge that our bodies are an essential part of the creation." Exactly the same theology has been misused, she says, "to keep the ministry closed to women and homosexual people. Both are seen as bound to their bodies, to their sexuality – women by menstruation and childbirth, lesbians and gay men by the perception that all they're about is sex."

The Support Team Against Sexual Harassment developed kits and workshops to help people understand what sexual harassment is and to name it, the first step in preventing or stopping it. They've also helped several women to confront harassing ministers, and then to resolve the problem to everyone's benefit. But Denise Davis-Taylor admits it's a long uphill climb, with very little support from within the official church. "We get reactions like, 'Oh but ministers don't do things like that.' 'This isn't a real issue.' 'These are isolated incidents,' and one of the favourites, 'But men get harassed, too'! Of course they do, but that's a different bag of beans entirely. By their conditioning and their positions, men have a lot more power to say no and make it stick." She finds many ministers unwilling to acknowledge that their colleagues could be at fault. "They seem to be afraid that if others are challenged to change, maybe they'll have to change, too."

Do ministers run the Church?

On paper, the two thousand-plus clergypeople in the United Church certainly have more power than the 850,000-plus lay people. Half the General Council commissioners are clergy. All ordained and commissioned ministers are automatically members of presbytery, while lay members are elected by a formula according to size of congregation. General Secretary Howie Mills believes these presbyteries can end up functioning as professional associations for local clergy. "That gives the clergy considerably more vested interest than the lay people in what happens at presbytery. Recently we've seen some of the distortions this can produce, mostly by clergy who see their status and their power endangered."

What's a minister supposed to do? The traditional image is of pastor, or shepherd, to the flock. Ministers who see themselves as the shepherd and lay people as their flock tend to get along well with congregations that also accept these roles. But ordained and commissioned ministers who take seriously the church policy that encourages all believers to be ministers can find themselves lodged between a rock and a very hard place.

For Rev Gwen Symington, a retired minister in rural Alberta, The Issue only became an issue when she realized how badly some of her colleagues were abusing the power of the pulpit. "Most congregations tend to assume that their ministers know what they're talking about. They've been to theology school, they must have learned something there, and anyway that's what you pay them for. It's tempting to take advantage of that. There have been lots of times when I've realized how easily I could sway a congregation one way or the other. That's scary to me."

During many of her years in ministry, Gwen Symington and her partner also worked a farm. They've watched more and more farmland going out of production, into the hands of developers. She calls it the great land grab and wonders when people will wake up to it. "Whether or not people are to be allowed to think for themselves," she says, "that's one of the major struggles in the world today." But how does she see the power of the pulpit being abused? "In the Roman Catholic church, if the priest denies someone the sacraments, you've got them." She clamps one hand down on the other. "In our church fundamentalist clergy are trying to use this issue the same way. They want to put the screws to anyone they think is deviating from the party line."

Hugh McCullum also found evidence of clergy power at work. Over several years he noticed that *Observer* subscriptions would rise or fall as different ministers took charge of different parishes. *Observer* subscriptions tend to run parallel to the church's Mission and Service Fund donations – a little over half the congregations subscribe to both. "From the changes in both of these," he says, "you could see very clearly the amount of power that individual ordained ministers still have in determining the success or failure of church programs. This would certainly appear to contradict the ministry-of-all-believers ideal."

These days the flock is showing at least as much ambivalence about the power of the clergy as are the shepherds. Rev Ed Bentley of Belleville, Ontario, puts it bluntly. "Congregations set their ministers up on a pedestal in order to get a better shot at them. They approach the minister with this strange mixture of reverence and hypercriticism. I'd gladly give up the first of those if I could be relieved of the second."

Most ministers aren't nearly so candid. They're terrified of offending the congregations who pay their salaries, or at least of some of the more powerful members. Increasingly this is one of occupational hazards of the ministry, a job with a shockingly high incidence of heart attacks and other stress-related problems. Tensions around The Issue have made it only slightly less hazardous than being a snake-charmer. A Vancouver Island minister summed up his dual function, "All week you visit with your people, you listen very carefully to them, and then on Sunday you tell them from the pulpit exactly what they've told you they want to hear."

One of the authors of the Victoria statement, Don Collett came home from Victoria to a very angry congregation. But they didn't blame him, they blamed "the church," far away in Toronto. In return he identified more closely with his own local church than he did with the whole-church process in which he'd just been deeply involved. "I presented to the congregation a range of things we could do in protest against MMHS [*Membership, Ministry and Human Sexuality*], including secession from the church," he recalls a year later. "Finally we settled on designated giving, so that individuals could direct their givings either to the Mission and Service Fund or wherever they wanted." In Victoria Don Collett lived for a moment with the whole church. In Taber he lives every day with Knox United.

The Issue has widened the gap between the local and the national church, or at least it's made it much clearer. Most of the time many United Church people see their local church as The Church, at least until the national church does something they don't like. When a congregation splits, some members experience it with all the grim intensity of a family breakdown. Colleen Pearce is the secretary and a member at Cadboro Bay United in Victoria. Raised a Presbyterian, she feels more loyal to Cadboro Bay than she does to the United Church. She comes close to crying when she describes how her congregation fell apart. It was The Issue, she says, that did it.

"Because of what the Scriptures say, my own personal feeling is that I don't want to worship under a homosexual minister." In 1988 she decided that if General Council didn't close the door, she would quit the church. But she was torn. In a sparsely furnished, windowless meeting room at Cadboro Bay United, she outlines her dilemma. "I felt that if I believed moral standards were slipping, somehow it would be wrong just to walk away. Instead I ought to stay here and do something about it. Maybe by 1990 the General Council would realize that it's not the right time for this to happen."

As the split in her congregation deepened, people on all sides came to the church office to confide in her. She became a go-between. "I told the minister it was in his hands to keep this church together. It's like a family. Just because you've got differences, it doesn't mean you have to break up. But with the media and all the different pressures, after a while people didn't know what to think. Some left because they couldn't stand the uproar any more. You want your church to be a place of comfort, not turmoil." Her husband had made it clear that he would stay with the church. But Colleen Pearce kept her options open.

By early 1989 one group was clearly moving toward formal secession. They were busy recruiting. Working in the outer office Colleen Pearce felt she was stuck on an island. "Everything had got so secretive by then, I couldn't even talk with the ministers any more." Being sociable with people who were preparing to quit the church "was like sitting on dynamite, you didn't know when it was going to explode." At the same time she was becoming increasingly uneasy with the departing group. "They seemed to go so far in the other direction. They were very harsh and judgemental, too fundamentalist about everything. It frightened me to think of having to live in such a black-and-white world, with no grey areas." On the other hand, the senior minister's wife told her she'd have a job if she went with the departers.

One February night, without warning, the seceding group cleaned out the minister's office. They had formed a new Congregational church up the road. The minister sent his letter of resignation by courier, without a word before or since to Colleen Pearce. There's no anger in her face or her voice, only sadness. "I don't think they acted in a very Christian manner. Instead of using our church to organize this whole split, the minister should have resigned first and then gone with them." She was also surprised at the choice some people made. "To hear them talk, you'd think they would rather follow the minister than God." She chose differently. "I didn't see how I could desert the people here. My decision was based on caring for them, I felt they'd need me more than the others would. At that point I guess The Issue became secondary for me."

An interim minister worked with her to heal the congregation. Their first task was to check the membership lists to see who had left and who had stayed. After calling each person she had worked with and who had now quit the church, Colleen Pearce hung up and cried. Many of the young people were gone, most of the original leadership was gone, and 30 per cent of the financial support. Left behind was a rather elderly congregation and a lot of confusion. A new minister started in September 1989, and Cadboro Bay United began to rebuild.

At Sunday service Colleen Pearce still sees ghosts in her church. "I know who's not there. It's like going through an amputation. You know you're going to live, and you know you'll be able to do things again. But not in the same way, never in the same way."

CHAPTER 27

Church Ladies

They used to be called church ladies, and still are in some congregations. They used to wear flowered hats and white gloves. Some still do. They made the coffee, arranged the flowers, and cooked the chicken à la king or roast ham and potato salad church suppers. They baked and knit for the bazaars, mended the choir gowns, and taught Sunday school. In the church they have always done the same kind of work they've done at home: the daily, often invisible, mostly repetitive and thankless chores that sustain life. They still do.

About 53 per cent of Canadians are female. Over 60 per cent of United Church members are female. A quick scan of the pews in almost any congregation reveals that many more women than men attend church regularly. But in the same United Church, twelve of thirteen conference executive secretaries (paid staff) are men, and in 1990 ten of the incoming elected conference presidents are men. The 1988-90 moderator, a man, was elected from seven male candidates. Of the United Church's thirty-two moderators, only two have been women.

Still, though it has been led almost entirely by men, preached to primarily by men, and the loudest voices among its critics continue to be male, this is a women's church. Together, the Women's Auxiliary and the Women's Missionary Society used to handle a larger budget than the rest of the church combined. Now amalgamated into United Church Women, they still form the largest single organization in the church. It also continues to be the most formidable fund-raiser, collecting more than $17 million in 1987. Nowadays women do every kind of work that men do in the church. In a church where studying plays a crucial role, women's groups initiate most of it. Most diaconal ministers are women. Of the ministers ordained in 1989, fifty-four per cent were women.

To encounter several "church ladies" is as good a way as any to look at the spectrum of opinion and experience on The Issue, as well as what's at stake for the United Church. So widely scattered are the people of this church that none of these women know each other. All of them are grandmothers. All have done other work, paid and unpaid, inside and outside the church, much of it motivated by faith. Combined, their years of service to their church can be counted in centuries.

Ann Wynn grew up Baptist in Digby, Nova Scotia. "I learned right off that you better do right or God's going to get you!" When she moved with her husband to New Germany, farther from the coast, they joined the United Church because it was handy for the children. By then she was a nurse. In her new church she encountered another kind of God. "This was a God of love, not of wrath. I was grateful that our kids could grow up without that terrible sense of fear. You did right because you wanted to, not because you were scared stiff."

For years she taught Sunday school, to teenagers. In the sixties the controversial New Curriculum came in. "Many people hated it, but I thought it was fabulous," she recalls. "It dealt with the real problems of real life." Her husband ran the local hardware store for forty years, until he died of cancer. She tried to keep it going for a while, then sold. It's still there, Wynn's Hardware. Since he died she's had more time for church work, both in the UCW and the Division of World Outreach. "That's helped. I didn't have any time to sit around feeling sorry for myself."

She's dead set against allowing homosexual ministers to be ordained. "If we got a gay person in the pulpit, I wouldn't attend and I wouldn't give one cent." Because it's a sin? "No," she says. "It's not for me to say what's a sin and what's not. I'm not really keen on the whole idea of sin. It reminds me too much of the kind of Bible-thumping I grew up with." Why then? "I was steeped in a certain way of seeing homosexuality, it was offensive and disgusting. When you've thought that way all your life it's not easy to change."

She has three objections. The first, she says, is AIDS. "The church shouldn't be saying that homosexuality is an acceptable alternate lifestyle. We should be discouraging it to prevent disease. I'm not against pushing safer sex, but that doesn't get at the root of the problem, which is homosexual activity and promiscuity. In my day it was VD, among the heterosexuals." A nurse at the time, she recalls the epidemic of her day. "Just like AIDS today, there was no cure back then. The only thing you can do is discourage the activity."

Second, Ann Wynn sees the family threatened. Preserving the family is very important to her. "We grew up poor, but one thing we always had in our family was love." Can't homosexuals love? "Sure they can, but they can't have kids. How can you have a family without kids?" On the wall of her living room, a large framed photo displays the Wynns and their children. But what's this got to do with the church? "Sexual morality was always part of the church's basic code of ethics. Now they seem to be redefining it. As far as I'm concerned that's not progress, it's a step backwards." She believes that looser moral standards lead to divorce. "There were times in my marriage when I could have given up. Every marriage has times like that. But nowadays people hardly seem to try. One little thing goes wrong and they give up, they get divorced just like that."

Then there's the matter of role models. "How can you tell your kids 'no, you can't do that' when they know the minister is doing it right next door in the manse?" Ann Wynn has a nephew who's gay. "He's a very fine young man. He's the one who's most likely to call and see how I'm doing. He's been here with his friend," she says. Has she told him how she feels? "If he asked me, I would. But I won't bludgeon him with it. What do you gain by confrontation?" But, she says, very determined, "I wouldn't want him influencing my grandson." How could he do that? "Well," says Ann Wynn, "young fellows tend to experiment. It's like driving your car too fast or taking a few drinks. What if they find they like it?"

She joined the COC to put pressure on the church. "They ignored all those petitions telling them we didn't want homosexual ministers. They didn't listen to us." She also withdrew her contributions from the Mission and Service Fund. "The United Church approves of sanctions against South Africa, to make the government drop apartheid, so when they don't listen to us we can do a little financial prodding, too."

What has to happen for Ann Wynn to feel she's been heard? "They have to rescind the report, that's all." She stops there, and nods. Would she like to be a commissioner at the next General Council? "I don't think so. It sounds too gruelling."

As a commissioner to the Victoria General Council, Irene Wellman recalls it as gruelling indeed. She goes to Emmanuel United in eastern Ontario, a mixed congregation with some rural people, some from the outskirts of Belleville, a city of 37,000. Over the years she's been actively involved in the local Women's Institute, been president of the area United Church Women's groups, chair of presbytery, then a commissioner to General Council.

She felt no tension, she says, between representing people back home and her own conscience. "To my way of thinking homosexual practice is a personal decision. But now they want the church to say what they're doing is okay. Heterosexuals don't go to the church and say please tell us it's okay. And the Bible says it's a sin. It also says that people who aren't married should be celibate." It actually says that? "It says that sex outside of marriage is fornication." She eyes her youngest son, who's just come in after a run. "I'm sure lots of young people won't agree with me, but that's how I feel." Quite a few people at Emmanuel and in her presbytery made it clear to her that they felt the same way, more or less.

When the March report came out, the only people at Emmanuel who studied it were a few members of the UCW. That's true to form, says Irene Wellman. At an angry congregational meeting, some people declared themselves open at least to the possibility of homosexual clergy, but most said absolutely not, not now and not ever. Many of them signed the COC's Declaration of Dissent. The letters she got and the petitions she saw ran along similar lines. "Ninety per cent said get rid of that report. They didn't want to hear things like 'homosexuality is a gift of God.' Some said it was okay for homosexuals to be members, but not ministers."

She remembers five long, gruelling sessions hashing out The Issue in Victoria. A crisis point came for her late on the second day, when a majority of commissioners supported the critical phrase "regardless of sexual orientation." "I didn't know how I could live with that," she recalls. "The way it came through to me, we accepted self-declared practising homosexuals right there. Never before did we have any kind of 'regardless' in our rules. Now we were doing it for this one special segment, regardless of their sin. Who knows what other 'regardless of's might follow?"

After a flurry of desperate last-minute amendments that stressed the importance of marriage, Irene Wellman felt she could just about live with the new statement. But not quite. Even in its final form she still voted no. "If it didn't open the door," she says, "then at least it took it off the latch. But the majority passed it, so that's it for now. I'm prepared to live with it, at least until I see that it doesn't work." This is a woman who's worked for many years in groups, where things don't always come out the way she wants them to. "As far as I can tell, if a congregation does their job right it'll be harder than ever for a person with homosexual tendencies to get in as a minister."

She rejects the charge that as a commissioner she was manipulated, even brainwashed at General Council. "The groups were there, outside the auditorium – Affirm on one side, the Renewal Fellowship and the Community of Concern on the other," she recalls a year later. "But no one grabbed you by the arm. You could talk to them if you wanted to." She didn't. "I already knew what I thought." Given the way she thought, why didn't she talk at least to the COC? She makes it sound as if the answer should be obvious. "If you talked to one, then you'd have to talk to the other, wouldn't you. That would only be fair."

What does she see ahead? From her kitchen table she looks into the backyard and the woods beyond. "I suppose if I had my way, there'd be a vote on this question, right across the church, and it would say no ordination for self-declared practising homosexuals. But . . . " She stops. But what? "Well, how can you be sure it would go that way? And I know how hurtful it would be, either way. You can't just ignore that, and still call yourself a Christian. I don't know. It's all turned into a big grey mess." Irene Wellman appears to have lost steam somehow. Then suddenly her voice changes. "But I'll tell you one thing I do know. I belong to the United Church, and nobody's going to push me out."

At West Point Grey United in Vancouver, Eleanor Reid got into an argument with a man who was railing against homosexuals. "When nature made homosexuals," she told him, "maybe it just loused up somehow. Not every flower in the garden can be perfect, neither can every tree in the forest. Maybe we just have to forgive nature for its mistakes. Maybe we don't understand well enough how God works."

The Reids joined West Point Grey in 1941. She raised three kids, taught school part time as well as Sunday school, led an Explorer's group, joined the United Church Women's group and eventually was elected president. Then her husband died thirteen years ago, of an inoperable brain tumour. "The minister and some of the people in the congregation were so supportive," she recalls, "I don't know how I could have got through that without them. Since the church had given me so much, I guess I wanted to give something back." When she was asked to be vice-chair of the board, she agreed. Now she's chair.

She participated in each of the human sexuality studies that came up, from 1980 on. "We generally did our homework, and we got a lot of things out in the open. Some people got quite upset over the inclusive language," she recalls in the large, bright room where they met. "To me God is a spirit, and shouldn't be male or female. The idea of calling God 'our parent' – I think that's great." She didn't like some of what she read in the March 1988 report. "But General Council shelved that. They left things the way they've always been, the congregation can choose whomever they want for their minister. It's not like the poor Anglicans, where the Bishop dumps on them whomever *he* likes." She leans forward, as if to impart something astonishing. "We haven't even got around to calling a woman minister here. Imagine how long it'll take before we invite a known homosexual! We've had ones that no one knew about, but that's something else."

When Eleanor Reid learned that one of her daughter's best friends was a lesbian, she asked her husband what on earth they should do. Nothing, he replied. Now Eleanor Reid agrees. "No one ever asked me what my husband and I did in our bedroom. Why would I want to ask anyone else? It's no one's business."

Over the years she got to know her daughter's friend as a "decent, very low-key, hard-working person. Now she's living with a girlfriend, they're buying an apartment together." She sounds like a proud aunt, or perhaps a godmother. Eleanor Reid also knew the young woman's parents, as part of her social circle. "I could hardly believe the cruel, ignorant things that some of them would say about homosexuals, right there in front of that girl's parents. Of course none of them knew. That seemed to me less Christian and more sinful than anything to do with homosexuality. One man said to me – he was very angry – 'Eleanor, they're not even people!'" She makes a face, and shakes her head. "Well, I started to realize that if the time came when I'd have to stand up and be counted, I'd do it for that girl."

Echoes from her own past helped clarify things for her. "During the Depression when the men couldn't get jobs and some of the women could, they had to keep their husbands in the closet. Imagine that," she says. "They could never go out together. If your employer ever found out you were married, you'd lose your only source of income. When my mother was selling shoes at Woodward's, she had to pass my father off as her brother-in-law. I remember once a neighbour asked me something about my daddy. I don't have one, I said. It's always stayed with me, that moment when I denied my own father." The image hangs there, in the air. "I wonder. Is that anything like the mask that homosexual people have to wear?"

Eleanor Reid is optimistic about the future of West Point. By spring 1989 givings to the Mission and Service Fund had risen by 5 per cent over the previous quarter, and sixty-six new people had added their names to the rolls. "I happen to know that some of those people joined because they respect our church for being open and inclusive."

What about the United Church in general, is it in danger? In response she tells of a special church service she attended last spring, at Canadian Memorial United in Vancouver. "I heard that some of the people who organized it were a little nervous that people wouldn't hear about it, or they wouldn't bother to attend, and it would backfire. Some women I know in a couple of other congregations told me their ministers wouldn't even allow a notice about it to be put in the church bulletin, so they just got on the phone and called people. Well, the service was packed. We sang, we prayed, did we ever celebrate!" What were they celebrating? "Being United Church! With all the uproar and all the bad press, we were saying how proud we were to be part of a church like this. That service was one of the most wonderful experiences of my life. I just floated out of there!"

On her way to another appointment, she adds an afterthought. "The beliefs in our church have always stretched from here to there, you know. We've always managed to live together. What are people getting so het up about?" And another. "How can the Community of Concern be so self-righteous, calling themselves that? I'm every bit as concerned as they are. And I expect a few of them could afford to look in the mirror once in a while, before they go on too much about what's wrong with other people."

The Issue has unearthed many surprises. In Fredericton, Doreen Kissick was shocked to discover that "people I'd thought were level-headed have become so fixated on this one issue, they've allowed their emotions to take over. When that happens you lose the ability to think for yourself." Thinking for yourself is a cornerstone of her faith.

Doreen Kissick grew up United Church in a low-income part of Toronto, with neighbours of many national origins. Quite young she sensed that much about the world was unfair, and that one way to address these wrongs might be through the church. From her mother she learned that the United Church had been the first to ordain women, which in the eyes of that committed suffragette was an extraordinary achievement.

The young Doreen drifted away from church for a while, but then she and her husband, of Presbyterian background, chose the United Church, mainly because of its willingness to act out its faith in the real world, the world where so many things aren't fair. They moved to Fredericton twenty-nine years ago. As well as being a commissioner at several General Councils, including Victoria, she's a member of the Division of World Outreach. "I believe God speaks to us in many ways. Jesus Christ isn't just a figure in the Bible, he's alive.

I've seen his face in the marketplace in Lagos [Nigeria]. I've seen him in the barrios in Mexico. That's the Jesus I understand, who speaks for the poor, for the victims of injustice. I'm sure he was there in Peking when the students were demonstrating there."

And in The Issue, is Jesus there? "He has to be. It's a justice issue." Doreen Kissick has served three terms as president of the National Council of Women. When she went to the 1984 General Council, she had been working on the issue of inclusion versus exclusion, as it applied to women and minorities in the Canadian Charter of Rights and Freedoms, and then in the Meech Lake accord. "In doing that work we discovered that if you don't specifically include women and other minorities in legislation, then you leave it open to interpretation, and whole groups of people can be excluded arbitrarily. That's why we need 'regardless of sexual orientation' in our own statement."

Over the years she's watched large numbers of church people ignore reports such as *In God's Image . . . Male and Female.* She considered that one a good theological foundation for the other human sexuality reports that followed. "I guess church has different meanings for different people. To some it seems to be a building you go to on Sunday so you can get charged up for the week ahead. I've moved around so much, I've got used to worshipping anywhere and any time, the facilities aren't important to me. And I don't think of my church as a small local body. It's a national and international body that can speak out effectively to our country and the world."

As a commissioner from the Maritimes, Doreen Kissick was invited to a number of post-Victoria congregational meetings to explain – or defend – the new statement. At the first of these, the first question was how did she vote? As soon as she answered, "I was simply written off as 'one of them,' which ended any chance of useful discussion. That never happened to me before as a commissioner."

After that she tried another tack. She's an old hand at chairing meetings where people of widely varied backgrounds and positions are trying to form policy. "When it was obvious that people had to let off steam, I wouldn't argue with them. After they finished their tirade, then maybe we could have a real discussion." She asked people to consider, as they would with someone who was blind or maimed, what other gifts a homosexual person might have to offer. "Every minister has faults, and most of them we usually overlook. Instead we look at their particular gifts and skills."

As a member of the Division of World Outreach, Doreen Kissick knows the consequences of economic boycott. For 1990 the Division of World Outreach had to cut $800,000 from its $12 million budget, and in 1991 a further $1 million. Some Christian givings that used to fight poverty, ignorance and oppression of various kinds are now apparently being withheld to fight homosexuality.

Is the United Church in danger? It depends on how you define danger, says Doreen Kissick. "If some of us believe the church shouldn't be involved in social-justice issues and that we should be Biblical literalists, and others of us believe that the church's mission has to be in the world, then I don't think we should cling together just for the sake of numbers. Who knows, maybe through all of this we'll become a smaller church, but a better one."

Like the other women whose stories are told here, Alice Blake is a grandmother and a United Church "lady." She cares about the life of her church as much as she cares about her family. In fact she considers it an extension of her family. But there's something else. Her son is gay, and he's a United Church minister. Alice Blake is not her real name. "We're not ready yet, to come out of the closet," she says. "One of these days we will, we surely will. But not yet."

She grew up attending a small rural United Church in northern Saskatchewan. Then she and her husband Carl moved; his work took them east. Now they're both well integrated into a large congregation there, and both play active roles on a variety of its committees. The Blake children grew up in this church, in its Sunday school, its junior choir, and its youth group. Alice Blake's eldest son, "Terry," was invited to join the governing board, as its first youth member. A few years later when he heard, or felt, a deep call to be active full time in the church, this congregation sponsored him proudly as a candidate for the ministry.

By that time he knew he was gay. Alice Blake didn't. Terry prayed, studied and agonized through three years of theology school. Was his sexuality right or wrong for a Christian? Finally he decided that if he entrusted his life fully into the hands of God, he would be healed one way or another. If his sexuality was wrong he'd be healed in one way, if it was right then he'd be healed in another way. In 1985 he was commissioned as a diaconal minister. The next year he told his parents that he was gay, and they met his lover, "Paul."

"It's been hard for us," says Alice Blake. "I guess more so for my husband than for myself. Other people have told me the same thing, it seems to be harder for a man than for a woman." Like everyone else they started from scratch. "The way we were brought up, we never even thought about homosexuality before. You just don't think there's any way it's going to affect you. It was something you never talked about, but somehow you knew it wasn't acceptable. But once you start looking into it and educating yourself, you get more comfortable with it."

Is she comfortable with it? "I'm getting there. With all the conditioning and the pressure against it, I started to wonder if maybe I was just rationalizing that it was all right. But I prayed, I prayed a lot and I read a lot. And we trust our son." As she says this she's speaking to a stranger, trusting that she'll be understood.

At a noisy congregational meeting in spring 1988, a large majority of those present condemned the March report.

"Some very hurtful things were said at that meeting," Alice Blake recalls. "But we were still struggling with our own feelings, so we couldn't respond. We just listened." After the Victoria General Council produced its new statement, with the minister's blessing another meeting voted support for the Community of Concern. "I guess they felt the United Church of Canada wasn't leading us in the right direction, and the Community of Concern could do better." Her voice strains with the effort to be fair.

Alice Blake spoke out against the motion to join the COC. Ten of fifty-seven people at the meeting voted no, in a congregation of about two hundred. "There are some who just go along with the minister because they like him and they don't want to rock the boat. But there's a small number of us who are for the United Church of Canada and for the decision that was made at Victoria." Some people have left the congregation for a more tolerant one elsewhere in the city. Others have left the United Church entirely, saying that the national church is too radical by far. Why do the Blakes stay, when they're at odds with both the minister and the majority of members? "As long as there's that small group, we feel there's still hope. And it's our church, too, we belong there as much as anyone else."

Now Alice Blake finds herself in hiding like Terry. Very few people know that she and Carl have a gay son. "It makes me realize for the first time," she says, "the kind of hurt we in the church have been putting on gay people." Terry's sister was supportive from the beginning, but his brother was quite upset for a while. Only one of Carl's sisters knows. She's a minister herself, and more open than the others to variety among God's children. None of Alice's relatives know. And the Blakes haven't told anyone in their second family, their friends in the local church. "We share everything else with them, but we can't tell them about this particular aspect of our lives." Why not? "Terry's not out. With the way things are in the church, he doesn't feel he can risk that yet. And we can't risk it for him."

Is safety for Terry the only reason they're in hiding? "No," she says slowly. Her voice is shaky. "Those people are our friends. But then there's the feeling that if we lose them because of this, they're not really friends, are they? But they're the only friends we have." Her voice breaks, then she recovers. "Maybe when we're feeling stronger in ourselves. . . ."

Alice Blake's isolation is painful, but it's not total. With several others she's forming a support group in the regional church for parents of lesbians and gay men. "Just to meet with those other people has been a great relief for us, to know that they exist and that they care."

What does she think will become of The Issue, and her church? "As far as I'm concerned there's a place for everyone in our church. Jesus loves all. But from what I read, the Community of Concern is determined to drag this thing out until they can get it squashed once and for all. It's hard to tell what our church is doing to stop that from happening. I just hope and pray the Community of Concern isn't as powerful as we've been led to believe, and that they can be stopped."

CHAPTER 28

Amen

In the past few years many United Church people have discovered that their church is not the church they thought it was. The loss of that comforting assumption has caused some to quit. Of the many who remain, a fair number have been moved to clarify what their church actually means to them and what might become of it. Given the history of this church, what becomes of it could have a significant impact in the life of Canada.

Many in the church are anxious to resolve The Issue, to get back to "the real work of the church." But how each person sees the real work of their church tends to define how they see The Issue. Some believe the real work of the church *is* to resolve The Issue, no matter what it takes, as a model for other issues just as thorny that lie ahead. Others believe the church's real work is to be "fishers of men," as the Bible reports Jesus said, reeling in one lost soul after another. Some believe it should be a safe haven from the storms of life, others that it should be out there in the full fury of the storm getting as wet and cold as the rest of the world.

There may be as many visions as people in the United Church of Canada. Some of these visions can coexist. But as time passes, it becomes increasingly clear that some cannot. Listen:

Jacqueline Istvanffy, Calgary: "There has to be a change in both the leadership and the direction of the church to take it back to what it was meant to be – people committed to Jesus Christ and his way of life. I don't want the church to take a stand on every contentious issue that confronts Canadians. We as a church cannot afford to hire the highly paid expertise that we need to make these pronouncements, and nor should we. We should go back to moral and spiritual leadership of the people."

Rev Don Gillies, Toronto: "If the leadership of the church keeps backing away from its responsibilities, and from General Council decisions, there's a real danger we could lose all our creative edges. If we rescind the Victoria statement, what's next? Are we going to rescind the ordination of women that was passed in 1936? With all of our best initiatives dropped or whittled down to nothing, most of the best people would leave in disgust. The United Church could end up completely irrelevant – in which case who'd care whether or not it survived? That's what I fear. If that happens I'd rather spend my time working in a refugee centre somewhere. That way at least I could feel I was doing something worthwhile."

Pearl Griffin, former UCW president, Vancouver: "We mustn't get caught up in the numbers game – how many people have we lost, how many have we got, what percentage are for, what percentage against – that's not what we're about. If being faithful to the Gospels means we can't be the biggest denomination any more, so be it. We have to do what we've always done, root ourselves in the Scriptures, in prayer and in the life of our community."

Rev Leander Mills, Saint John: "If we're going to continue to be a united church, we have to agree on the basics – faithfulness in marriage and celibacy in singleness. In any family you've got to have that basis of agreement or you're bound to end up in divorce. Also the congregations have to be given more say in policy-making. Any issue that affects the life of the whole church has to be submitted to a plebiscite."

Corinne Toews, Regina: "Our church is threatened by people who don't want to ask questions, people who want a straight and narrow road with no curves in it. How can we say we believe if we never question what we believe or why? Why do we read the Bible? What is the Bible? Why do we believe in God? What does that really mean to us? But with some people, when you ask them to question, it threatens their security and they get defensive. That's what happened after General Council, and it's the biggest threat to our church."

Rev Don Ross, Portage la Prairie: "I think as the COC takeover proceeds, more people will see it and resist. A year ago many ministers were saying, 'If we don't talk about it, it'll go away.' Now I'm talking a lot more with my congregation about how decisions are made in the United Church, and they aren't turning off. We have to know our church very well. We have to know which of our values are important to hold onto and which aren't. That way if we lose the church, at least we'll know what to save and what to mourn."

Erin Shoemaker, Saskatoon: "I'm more committed to a spiritual journey than to the United Church as an institution. But even at its worst the church is at least as good as any other institution in our society. It offers us at least as much support and room for growth. And through all our struggles with the church, it's been church people who've sustained us – gay and heterosexual people in the church. That feels a lot like family to me. And that's why I stay, why I keep fighting."

Rev Ralph Garbe, London: "There are two incompatible visions within the United Church. One is that Jesus Christ is our sovereign Lord, and the Bible is the authority for our beliefs and our lives. The other is that there is new truth to be discovered and pursued, even if it leads away from what we have been given by the apostles and prophets and Jesus

Christ himself. It's no longer a question of Christians agreeing with each other or working toward an agreement. Now it's a real question of the Christian way of thinking versus a non-Christian way of thinking."

Barbara Rumscheidt, Halifax: "At stake is whether this is to be an inclusive or an exclusive church. If it turns out that we can't keep it inclusive, we couldn't just exit and forget it. We'd have to stay in and join with others to discredit such a church. The parallels are there – South Africa, Nazi Germany – where theology has been perverted to justify discrimination. We'd have to do everything we could to unmask that."

Very Rev Clarke MacDonald, Toronto: "I signed a resolution asking the Israeli prime minister and the PLO to enter into peace negotiations. If we can expect those two parties to talk, surely we have an obligation to do the same in The United Church of Canada. If anyone says that nothing is negotiable, then that's what we should be talking about. The refusal to lose face is a refusal to be penitent. If need be we should lock the different parties up in a room together with a skilled negotiator – it's that serious. We claim to believe that with God all things are possible. Do we really believe that?"

Joe Brinton, Halifax: "Some people would like to straddle the fence on this issue, to try and please both sides. The United Church has tried to be all things to all people. It can't be, otherwise it'll have nothing left to stand on. There's a belief in this church that any issue can be resolved if you just have enough discussion and dialogue on it. Not on this issue. Either you believe that the particular behaviour is sinful or you don't. All the discussion in the world won't change the way people think. On this one there's no room for compromise."

Marion Best, Naramata: "No matter what the next General Council does, within a year we're going to have to make some tough decisions about what kind of church we can afford to be. We can't just keep nibbling away, cutting back a little bit here and a little bit there, because we're crippling everything. Can we afford to maintain such a highly democratic four-court system when fewer and fewer people are contributing to it? Can we afford to fund these little rural congregations that can't support themselves? We're the primary funder of the Canadian Council of Churches, and the biggest Canadian giver to the World Council of Churches – will those ecumenical coalitions have to get along without us? It's sad that we have to make these kind of decisions, but the way things are going we don't have any choice."

Rev Eilert Frerichs, Toronto: "For some time now in the family and in our culture, men have been losing status bit by bit. And for some time in our church, ministers have also been losing their traditional status bit by bit. Many of them are absolutely, mortally terrified. They're taking that out on lesbians and gays, and they're taking it out on the church. Do we have enough courage in the United Church to address those very deep fears? A way has to be found that's challenging but not life-threatening to men. Until it is, one way or another this struggle will continue, in the United Church and in the world."

Rev Graham Scott, Burlington: "The church has always been tempted by apostasy, right from the beginning. Though some of my best friends have left – to the Presbyterian, the Greek Orthodox and the Anglican churches – I can't imagine the conditions that would force me to leave. Perhaps if they came right out and said that Jesus Christ was a fraud – but they wouldn't do that, they're too smart. In any case all the churches are so problematic now, what's the point of leaving this one and going to another? If God weren't in the church somewhere, it would have fallen apart a long time ago."

Pat Krug, Duff: "If the United Church changed in such a way that we [she and her husband, Murray] had to work against it, we'd probably leave and form a small congregation that would take faith and action very seriously. People say they want their church to be a bulwark against society, they want to feel safe. They're so afraid of ambiguity that they'll hand over all their power to authority just to avoid it! But when was life ever safe? We don't know whether we'll still be alive ten minutes from now. We don't know what the church is, we don't know who Jesus is, not really, and we don't know what God's intention for us is. The only thing that's absolutely secure to me is that we live in God's love and nothing can separate us from that."

Rev Brenda Ferguson, Binscarth: "I can't believe that God wants us all to be alike. We've been living with our differences for a long time now, but we can only continue doing that if somehow we can find ways to be more moderate in how we express them. As a woman I feel there has to be a better way than a continual win-lose tug of war. There has to be."

Rev Alf Dumont, Winnipeg: "Western thinking is built around one universe and one system of thought. Native thinking says there are many universes and many systems of thought, which all work in parallel. For the church this time can be used for a power struggle that just keeps getting worse, or we can try to reach consensus on how to receive into our circle all the people who walk in different ways. Obviously that can't happen by the next General Council, but isn't it worth taking the time?"

Bill Fulford, Morris: "I'm really proud of my church. We've come an awful long way on this issue. And five years from now we'll have moved on again. But that's only one issue we're talking about. What's going to happen when all our people over fifty have passed on? To me that's the biggest question of all. Someone was telling us we're doing pretty well in Morris, we're keeping our young people in the church. He was talking about forty-year-olds! Young people are the future. What are we going to do about that?"

Rev Glenna Beauchamp, Shoal Lake: "If I had my way, I'd much rather just be ministering to my congregation. But how can you avoid getting involved? Some people are trying to take our church back to the fifties, when the minister was still boss. I don't want to be the kind of minister that people pay to be Christian for them. And as a woman I've learned to fear and resent barriers. When I see people setting up barriers in our church, I can't help wondering: Am I next?"

David Moors, Dartmouth: "We could do with a lot more joy in the United Church, and a lot less talk about sin and sinners. As far as I'm concerned, sin is doing something that God doesn't like. And whatever the Bible says, I couldn't tell you what's a sin and what isn't. Only God can do that. He has his ways of letting us know. Right now the earth is telling us that we're destroying it. Can we hear that before it's too late?"

Denise Davis-Taylor, Edmonton: "The church is challenged to be what it says it is – a body of Christians whose goal is to nurture the spirit, to act out Christ's teachings. If we really do that of course we're going to suffer. The United Church has been very sheltered, it's never had to face crucifixion before. But resurrection involves letting go, it involves pain. Some people in the church are clinging so desperately to old power structures that they'll never have the chance to experience new life."

Rev Bill Fritz, Barrie: "With the institution of marriage and family life in such turbulence, I don't know why our church simply cannot say no to homosexuality, the same way it does to alcoholism. Why do we continue to obfuscate and circumlocute and bring down reports that are confusing, convoluted, and unedifying? Why can't we just say no to something which is unnatural and unhelpful to the family of humankind, namely homosexuality. If we don't do that, we will continue to fight among ourselves and to do irreparable harm to our church. Though I'd rather it had been able to fade into the woodwork, the Community of Concern is here to stay."

Dorothy MacNeill, Halifax: "The church – the community of people who are committed to following Jesus Christ – will survive. It's survived much worse crises than this. Of course it won't be the same. Ministers may have to think a little more deeply about what they preach. And we lay people may have to learn more about the way our church works and what it stands for, to make sure that church isn't just a habit. The church has to be inclusive and accepting; we can't put conditions and ranks in membership. And we certainly can't designate in advance whole categories of people who we set apart for ministry. That's God's work, not ours."

Rt Rev Sang Chul Lee, Toronto: "As soon as we draw lines we make our God smaller and more narrow. At this time we see the whole secular world moving toward greater sharing, we see ideologies mixing – I don't think you can find pure communism or pure capitalism anywhere today. I believe that pluralism will be the philosophy of the next century. How can the church go in the opposite direction, especially this church? I hope we can be mature enough to recognize the strength in each other's approaches."

Genevieve Carder, Scarborough: "This isn't a theology debate, it's a power struggle. If the Community of Concern gets its way, they could destroy what the United Church has always been – a uniquely Canadian church, which is not accountable to any other body, which has always celebrated diversity, and which acts out its faith by standing by any of God's people who are threatened or oppressed. I think that we've been an important voice in the life of Canada, as a church that cares and doesn't mind saying so. We haven't always been popular for that. But we hear that challenge all through the Bible, it's a biblical stance we're taking. If we lose that, we lose our reason for being a church."

Rev Duncan White, Port Hope: "The United Church has always had a process by which people could enter the church, but it's never had a process by which they could leave. We need to change the constitution of our church to include provisions by which congregations can withdraw, with dignity and with their property, from the fellowship of the United Church. If the majority decide to withdraw, or perhaps a two-thirds majority, then they have a moral right to the property."

Reverend "Kim," a Prairie city: "Even though it drives me crazy sometimes, the diversity of our church is very important to me. It wouldn't feel like true community without that mix. In a wonderful Jewish lesbian seder [a ceremonial dinner on the first night of Passover], a grandmother retells the story of the exodus from slavery, the crossing of the Red Sea. As men tell it, it was a triumphant moment when the sea crashed in and drowned the Egyptian oppressors. But this old woman tells it differently. 'When we looked back and saw the faces of those drowned boys, we recognized them, every one of them – this one carried straw for me, that one I sold bread to in the market, that one was the youngest son of so-and-so.' Sometimes I have the same kind of vision for our church. These people who've declared themselves my enemy, they're also – despite everything – my beloved. I don't want to walk away from them, and I don't want them to drown. I want them over there on the other side with me. The question is, how the hell are we going to get them there?"

Rev Allen Churchill, Ottawa: "The only way we can avoid a major split in the church is by calling a moratorium on all debate around any of the really divisive issues that face the church, for at least ten years – and even that may not be long enough. In the meantime the thirty-third General Council has to make *Membership, Ministry and Human Sexuality* an historical document, it has to reject it in toto. In any case it would be pointless to ordain lesbian or gay ministers. There isn't a single congregation in this church that would accept a self-declared practising homosexual as their minister. There'd be no home for them, which could only be terribly frustrating for them. Why don't they form their own congregations, even their own denomination like the Metropolitan Community Church? Surely they'd be more comfortable that way, and so would everyone else."

Katherine Hatfield, Calgary: "If the church were to exclude lesbian and gay people, and if I felt there was no hope of reversing that, then I'd have to leave and find a worshipping community that didn't think like that. I can't imagine leaving. But we have to move on, we can't get stuck. Over the years I've had to question God's exclusive maleness. If as the Bible tells me I'm made in God's image, and I know I'm not male, then I have to adjust my sense of God, don't I? We live in such an awesome universe. Surely asking a few questions isn't going to hurt God."

A journey through the United Church leaves far too many impressions to record. But two images recur. One of them is a white church, plain but handsome. It has a small spire, modest stained-glass windows, and a church house attached. It's Sunday morning, a warm sunny day. The doors are open. A silver-haired gentleman in a black robe stands on the steps, he greets the flock as they depart for home. The ladies wear white gloves, the men suits and ties. The children are bright and clean. Everyone is smiling. It's a moment in time, frozen. Like a Norman Rockwell painting, this image is not easy to find any more. But for many it represents church as it ought to be, for now and forever.

The other image is harder to make out, it's blurred as if the subject had moved. It has the feel of a church, that much is clear. But the outlines aren't. The walls – if they are walls – seem to fade into the surroundings, there's no telling where it begins and ends. The people are moving, purposefully out beyond the borders of the place. It's impossible to tell whether these are the same people as in the other image. The whole effect is one of movement. It's both exhilarating and disturbing.

Whatever happens at the thirty-third General Council, it certainly won't settle The Issue. But even if the church marks time in a place it's already reached, it will have moved. And whichever way it moves, it will change. The change will hasten the departure of some, and give hope to others. But it won't end the agony of the church. That's just beginning.

What will become of The United Church of Canada?
God only knows.